TWENTIETH CENTURY VIEWS

The aim of this series is to present the best
in contemporary critical opinion on major
authors, providing a twentieth century perspective on their changing status in an era
of profound revaluation.

Maynard Mack, *Series Editor*
Yale University

PIRANDELLO

A COLLECTION OF CRITICAL ESSAYS

Edited by

Glauco Cambon

Prentice-Hall, Inc. *Englewood Cliffs, N.J.*

A SPECTRUM BOOK

For my children

Acknowledgments

Quotations from the works of Luigi Pirandello (essays, poetry, drama, and fiction) are reproduced in the studies which make up this anthology by kind permission of his Italian publishers, Arnoldo Mondadori of Milan, and of the copyright holders, Stefano, Fausto, and Lietta Pirandello (in whose names, as children and heirs of the author, the copyrights were renewed in the years 1950 and 1951). Quotations from the following late plays of Pirandello, in my translation, are reprinted by kind permission of their copyright holder, Marta Abba: *Diana e la Tuda* (*Diana and Tuda*), copyright 1950 by Marta Abba Millikin; *Questa sera si recita a soggetto* (*Tonight We Improvise*), copyright 1932 by E. P. Dutton and Co., Inc., copyright 1959 in renewal by Marta Abba Millikin, copyright 1960 (revised and rewritten) by Marta Abba; and *I Giganti della Montagna* (*The Mountain Giants*), copyright 1958 by Marta Abba.

As editor of this book I wish to express my gratitude to the following persons and/or organizations for their kind help: Professor Mario Vinciguerra, President of the *Società Italiana Autori ed Editori;* the *Amministrazione dei Figli di Luigi Pirandello* through its representative, Attorney Enzo Scipioni of Rome; Professor S. B. Chandler of The University of Toronto; Mrs. Helene Leo of Neuhaus i. Sollingen, Germany; Dr. Alfredo Barbina of the *Istitute Pirandello* in Rome; and the Research Council of Rutgers University which enabled me to attend to this and other projects in Italy itself. Special thanks are due to my wife, Marlis Zeller Cambon, for reading my manuscript and making useful suggestions, and even more for being a constant inspiration.

Contents

Introduction

by Glauco Cambon

The privilege of making his own name broadly synonymous with some poignant aspect of the times in which he lived was shared by Pirandello with very few among the important modern writers: Kafka, Proust, Gide . . . . A dubious privilege indeed, if it misleads us into reducing the significance of each writer to a convenient formula, especially in the case of Pirandello who, having spent a lifetime of literary effort in undermining the stereotypes that pass for reality with so many people, could not bear, even posthumously, the irony of being in turn identified with a stereotype of his own making. Perhaps for this reason Pirandello insured his work against such hazard by incorporating in some of his pivotal plays, like *Ciascuno a suo modo* (*Each in His Own Way*), the very critical quarrels he had unleashed from the stage; and fierce they were almost beyond belief, if we remember what happened at the first performance of *Sei personaggi in cerca d'autore* (*Six Characters in Search of an Author*) inside and outside the Teatro Valle in Rome.

That, along with many other episodes in Pirandello's career, makes instructive reading in Federico Nardelli's lively biography of the enigmatic Sicilian playwright. One emerges from such reading with the realization that Pirandello's idea of humor, critically formulated in his essay *L'umorismo* (1908), was a prime force in his work and certainly in his life. The angry crowds of fighting spectators who were on the verge of attacking that "shocking" author of *Six Characters* at the theater exit in 1921, thereby compelling him and his family to make a quick getaway, did not know that they were going to become characters in his plays to come—a humorist's revenge! And they hardly realized how well they fitted the spirit of Pirandello's drama which aimed at involving the audience's reaction in its protean dialectic.

Anger certainly pleased him better than apathy or mild applause, for he thought of himself as an arouser of consciousness and not as

1

a mere entertainer. The stage would be the focus, but never the absolute limit, for his fictional action; and this (apart from its emphasis on intellect) was a conception of theater sharply opposed to that of Brecht, who expressly wanted to "estrange" (*verfremden*) his audience from the action onstage instead of involving them empathically. But both the German and the Italian playwright expected thought in response, no matter how sharply the former's doctrinaire ideology might clash with the latter's problematic approach.

The astonishing thing is that a man so passionately committed to the hazards of the theater should have led (unlike his famous contemporary D'Annunzio) a very untheatrical private life, marked though it was by more than its share of dramatic ordeals. A family man of unswerving loyalty, Pirandello chose to keep his mentally deranged wife at home for as long as he could, thus facing untold discomfort and even personal danger, rather than having her immediately committed to an asylum and securing domestic peace for his ceaseless work as a teacher and writer—the work on which his family depended for support after his once rich father's financial collapse. Even though fame brought money in the '20s, he preferred to follow his plays' vicissitudes from hotel rooms, when he could have had a comfortable home and a villa on the Riviera; and he ended his days in a room of Spartan austerity, in the Rome apartment (now housing the Pirandello Institute) from where the hearse, according to his will, left for the crematorium without escort or pomp. A humorist's protest against the theatrical bombast of the period? It was in any case the gesture of a character who did not have to search for his author.

Still more astonishing is the fact that this revolutionist of world theater came to drama rather late in the course of his writing career, after decades of endeavor in verse, essay, and fiction. A freak mishap at the last moment had prevented his first play from being performed and the stubborn islander vowed to keep away from the theater forever. He almost managed to do so. Chance (in the shape of the Sicilian dialect actor Angelo Musco) made him reconsider during the years of World War I. His good luck continued when he met the actress Marta Abba, who was to prove the ideal interpreter of the plays he had already written and the inspirer of many to come. The eventual benevolence of chance, needless to say, had been earned by lifelong devotion to his own art in the face of recurrent hardships, but the hard-won success never lulled Pirandello into complacency, as his late play *Quando si è qualcuno* (*When Someone Is Somebody*) shows by its merciless exposure of official glory as spiritual death.

In tristitia hilaris, in hilaritate tristis, Giordano Bruno's self-descriptive saying, could very well provide a motto for the withdrawn dramatist of humor who made a point of viewing the trials of existence as something tragic and comical at the same time. This is indeed what enabled him to survive. Humor in his definition was the feeling of contrast, determined by the perennial clash of experience and thought. Humor was the ability to laugh in sadness, to realize and accept the contradictoriness of the human condition—to transcend its absurdity even while recognizing it as our unavoidable lot. Thus reduced to relativity, no blow of fate, no grief could retain its paralyzing force, and no joy could abolish wisdom. Humor, therefore, as the awareness of immanent paradox in human reality, was the best way to exorcize horror. No facile remedy, to be sure, but a way to heightened consciousness: it is the priestly initiation of so many Pirandellian characters, from Mattia Pascal to Cosmo Laurentano and Mrs. Ponza, from Laudisi to "Henry IV" and Baldovino and the wizard Cotrone. Clown-like Ciampa, the cuckolded wearer of "cap and bells" in *Il berretto a sonagli,* can hold grief and shame at bay, and turns the tables against the world. *In tristitia hilaris, in hilaritate tristis.*

Yes, Pirandello was the main character of Pirandello, and this point is worth making to remind ourselves—when confronted by the less felicitous variations upon the basic themes in his abundant production—that his philosophy sprang from deep personal experience. It was certainly not borrowed from abstract sources, even though he was conversant with German thought as a result of his academic experience in Germany. It is a pity that the philosophy at times did tend to harden into a preconceived thesis for the theatrical manipulation of a play, as his authoritative critic Adriano Tilgher saw in 1923. But there can be no doubt that he put all of himself unsparingly into his writings, and that the lapses are incidental to the demanding venture. He is at times a hasty writer, marred by unevenness, and perhaps none of his masterpieces by itself gives an adequate idea of his range. Only a survey of his whole endeavor, from the early verse volumes of the 1880s and 1890s to the unfinished play *I Giganti della Montagna (The Mountain Giants)* of the mid-'30s, can do justice to his unrelenting engagement and to the richness of the results. In a sense, Pirandello as the overall persona of his work is greater than any one fictional embodiment, hard though it may be to follow the entire gamut of these incarnations.

The self that Pirandello put into his work was first and foremost his irreducible Sicilian self. For a native writer, Sicily (like Ireland) is what one could not help being born to and trying to escape from, with the consequence that, just as the seminal work in modern English literature has come from dissident Ireland, self-involved Sicily has been the cradle of much of the keenest Italian writing for the last hundred years. (This parallelism, fleetingly glimpsed by Walter Starkie, is worth exploring.) Sicily is, emphatically, an island— turned inward upon itself. So much history burdens it that it has become skeptical and superstitious. Sicilians tend to be, unlike most continental Italians, rather taciturn and introverted, with a fierce pride as their addiction. A separatism of the soul has grown from the very soil there, with occasional political manifestations. It was an Irish writer, Joyce, who had his own persona say "History is a nightmare from which I am trying to awake," but it could have been a Sicilian just as well.

Pirandello knew the burden of history, and what it meant to carry his ancestors on his shoulders. We see it in his big novel of post-*risorgimento* Sicily, *I vecchi e i giovani* (*The Old and the Young*), a veiled story of his own Garibaldian family in the context of the new Italy's ordeals and failures. Garibaldi had come in 1860 to stir the island from its immemorial self-absorption; many young heroes answered his call, but in unified Italy, after the leader's disappearance from the political scene, they aged into stale reverie, finding no scope for their awakened energy. Workaday life killed them physically or morally; they got involved in financial scandals or died in clashes between the disaster-stricken sulphur miners and the Italian troops called in to restore order. At best, they kept dreaming of their flamboyant past. History broods over the Greek temples of Girgenti, Pirandello's birthplace, where a large part of the action occurs. Time is frozen, and the brief stirring of Garibaldian epic has subsided into a new paralysis. Consciousness withdraws into the anachronism of dream, and we have, in *The Old and the Young*, the Laurentano brothers, or that dauntless Quixote, Mauro Mortara, the hero who cannot quite retire from history.

In Pirandello's Sicily every man is an island—an island besieged by history and compelled to acknowledge the incommensurability between one's own inner reality and public reality. Who is to say what truth is? Anachronism may breed philosophical detachment, as in Don Cosmo Laurentano, or the idiosyncrasy of his brother, who tries to "preserve" history in a willed delirium. And the novel itself—a monument to historical despair—is an anachronism, because it saw the light in 1913, long after the demise of the Naturalist style in which it was couched, and which Pirandello himself had decidedly left behind in 1904 with the far more successful *Il fu Mattia Pascal* (*The Late Mattia Pascal*). For all that, it is a moving work, leavened by genius and rich in clues to all the motifs to come. No one can really understand Pirandello without having read it. It lays bare his roots as no other book does—roots gnarled and deep like those of his island's olive trees.

Separatism and anachronism may be two attributes of the insular mind, but they alone do not suffice to account for Pirandello's imaginative growth beyond those potentially paralyzing limits. To become a great "Sicilian" writer he had to leave Sicily, just as Joyce had to abandon Dublin for the Continent in order to become a great "Irish" writer. Pirandello's heritage was given him as something to fight against, the better to work with it. He knew this when he left for Bonn in the 1880s—to graduate there with a dissertation on his native dialect of Girgenti. And he knew it when he went to live in Rome and wherever else his artistic career brought him. Significantly, in the book that dramatizes history as a destiny of paralysis (*I vecchi e i giovani*) the tragic note prevails, and the book which portrays the birth of the artist in man as a deliverance from paralysis (*Il fu Mattia Pascal*) rings with the note of gentle humor, swaying between comedy and elegy. *The Late Mattia Pascal* is in some respects the Italian equivalent of Joyce's *Portrait of the Artist as a Young Man,* and even more of Mann's *Tonio Kroeger* and *Felix Krull*. It may even have had an impact on the latter novel, if we think of the remarkable similarity between the train-ride scenes in which each picaresque hero muses on the weird freedom his metamorphic impersonation is bestowing on him.

Mattia Pascal conquers his freedom by turning away from his village background and officially dying to it, with the help of chance, so he may wander from place to place as an unattached observer of life. He has to die twice: once to his original public self and once to his invented self, thereby renouncing the boundless liberty that has come to taste bitter in his mouth because it is really an alienation. He will not reenter the initial identity, but will withdraw to a library and write his life's story. The only deliverance from life is in art and not in life itself; art is a kind of dying (to common life) and rebirth (at one remove). Thus the islander's alienation has sublimated itself into heightened consciousness, and Pirandello shares the problematic themes of Gide, Joyce, and Mann.

The Late Mattia Pascal had been a success, to the point of wresting favorable comments even from Benedetto Croce, who was to reject everything else of Pirandello's after that (their polemical ex-

changes are notorious). But neither *I vecchi e i giovani* (1913) nor
*I quaderni di Serafino Gubbio operatore (The Notebooks of Serafino
Gubbio, Cameraman,* 1915), one of the most original among Pirandello's works, won the response they deserved. *Serafino Gubbio,
Cameraman* was a striking experiment in fiction, anticipating (as
A. L. de Castris has seen) the latter-day techniques of the *roman
nouveau.* The experiment is perfectly consistent with Pirandello's
themes. Mattia Pascal's alienation has reached a climactic degree
here in the plight of the cameraman who becomes so attuned to his
mechanical device that eventually he cannot help clinging to it,
paralyzed by horror, to film the unforeseen slaughtering of an actor
by a real tiger in a make-believe jungle. The incident is told by the
cameraman in first-person narrative, with a nervous style worthy of
the best Faulkner, but the whole book has this objective quality of
dramatic reportage, and it is noteworthy that the style should have
shown such a resourceful flexibility to suit the changes of the rest-
less Pirandellian persona from novel to novel (or short story).

The novel to follow, *Uno, nessuno e centomila (One, No One and
A Hundred Thousand,* publ. 1925), like many of the short stories
Pirandello had been publishing, deals with the predicament of root-
less anonymity in the modern city and the tortuous adjustments one
can make to it if one is a Pirandellian persona. Meanwhile the problem of identity and communication has come to the fore in his dramatic production, which, since the Rome scandal and Paris triumph
of *Six Characters,* absorbs all our author's energies and overshadows
his accomplishment in fiction. The stage is the ideal arena for enact-
ing the age-old drama of appearance versus reality to shock the modern crowd into realizing how they are self-duped into believing they
know what they are. At his experimental peak, Pirandello reverses
—and intensifies—Shakespeare's dictum that "the world's a stage"
by making the theater dramatize itself, since stage fiction can have
a higher degree of reality than ordinary existence. *Six Characters in
Search of an Author* functions on several levels (hence Wylie Sypher
suggestively calls it "cubist"), but it focuses on the play in the making, just as Gide's novel *The Counterfeiters* focuses on the novel in
the making, and Mallarmé's, Valéry's, or Stevens' poetry turns on
the poem as process. Beyond this metaphysical threshold, especially
as regards formal experiment, Pirandello could not go, and we see
him revert to more conventional dramatic structures. Toward the
end, however, he abandons the casuistical realism from which such
plays as the uniquely serene *Liolà* or the grotesque *L'uomo, la bestia
e la virtù (Man, Beast and Virtue)* and *Il berretto a sonagli (Cap*

and Bells) had germinated, for an allegorical type of staged fairy tale. The unfinished *I Giganti della Montagna* (*The Mountain Giants*) places a roving company of quixotic actors, who must perform their play at all costs, under the power of a brutal audience they cannot reach. It was better for them to follow the advice of the wizard Cotrone and stay within the spellbound domain of his mansion. Cotrone is Pirandello's Prospero (as "Henry IV" is his Hamlet), but the "tempest" is not of the wizard's making and has catastrophic results. The artist seems to have no choice between the ivory tower of socially powerless imagination and the aggressive crassness of a mob unresponsive to his message.

The occasionally exasperating tortuousness of his casuistry, and the occasional reliance on melodramatic stage effects, cannot obscure the authenticity of experience at the roots of Pirandello's conceptions. Every man tends to be an island, his own prison, and communication can only make sense if the real selves speak instead of the masks. But what are the real selves, and can they be known? Conversely, do not the fictive selves (or personal masks) at times acquire greater validity than the so-called "real" ones? We are not sure of knowing ourselves. Socrates' exhortation to self-knowledge is hard to fulfill (to the point where it reverses itself into Gorgias' denial that anything can be known at all or even communicated), yet it remains the constant goal of the dramatist and thinker. Idiosyncrasy verges on madness, but madness can be an extreme, if perilous, form of lucidity, as "Henry IV" knows. What themes could be more pertinent to a world that keeps swaying between facelessness and collective derangement? Existentialist French theater, as Thomas Bishop documents, acknowledged in Pirandello its founding father.

Critical response to Pirandello's work has been itself something of a Pirandellian drama, and no limited selection like the present one can give a fair idea of its spectrum. One indispensable landmark for orientation in the bewildering scene is Adriano Tilgher's comprehensive essay, which affected Pirandello himself. Too long to be included in its entirety, it will suffice as here excerpted to point the way toward a reading of the later spirited contributions of Luigi Baccolo, Robert Brustein, Auréliu Weiss, and William Herman in historical perspective. A vitalist philosopher deeply interested in contemporary theater, Tilgher saw all of Pirandello's work as a convulsion of (Bergsonian and Schopenhauerian) ideas, turning on the dynamic polarity of Life and Form; and his irrationalist approach established the main tradition of Pirandello criticism, variously challenged but still recognizable behind the recent existentialist interpretations. Another philosopher, Croce, dismissed Pirandello because he did not think such a thing as poetry of ideas was possible, and his position, with considerable modifications in favor of our disputed author, has been restated by Ulrich Leo.

Tilgher's irrationalism came to be neatly reversed by another Italian critic, Puglisi, who defined Pirandello as "the poet of reason" in view of the capital role dialectic plays in his work. While I have been unable to sample from this sensitive contribution or from that of Arminio Janner, another Italian interpreter who did his part for the postwar revaluation of Pirandello in his native country, I have included A. L. de Castris. He is well equipped with aesthetic flair and historical awareness to vindicate Pirandello's social relevance, which critics of Antonio Gramsci's Marxist persuasion had flatly denied. It is true that a more recent Marxist, Carlo Salinari, ideologically rescued Pirandello from that condemnation by acknowledging in the author of *L'umorismo* an exemplary embodiment of the "consciousness of crisis" (in the Italian bourgeoisie). Robert Brustein in turn places Pirandello among the rebels who subverted classical conceptions, yet, in the wake of Francis Fergusson's broad-minded Aristotelianism, he points out that some of the devices applied to this subversion are of Greek ancestry. I would say that Pirandello's main revolution was aimed at the late Naturalist conventions from which he himself grew, and by exploding them he reasserted the rights of the imagination in a Shakespearian way, as Stark Young was the first to see long ago. Thus Sinicropi can trace the unfolding of "life" and "art" as Pirandello's central theme down to the late mythical phase, which utters a hope beyond despair. De Castris has thrown overdue light on Pirandello's performance as a novelist, while claiming that his fiction intrinsically tended to the dramatic form, but Ulrich Leo probes the work stylistically to conclude that the transition from fiction to drama was a false step, for Pirandello's real talent lay in the former genre. The theater, Leo claims, can hardly do justice to the contemplative vein, to the poetry of "silence"; on the other hand, Tilgher, Bentley and others emphasize the articulateness of Pirandello's stage characters as a decisive poetical factor.

Must we then make a choice between Pirandello's theater and his fiction? There need not be so drastic a choice, but one thing is sure: too many critics, especially outside Italy, have ignored Pirandello's novels and short stories as if he were exclusively a playwright, or exclusively significant as such. The time has come to take his fiction into account. Regarded in fuller perspective, his work will provoke more focal questions and supply richer clues to the answers. Thus, for instance, when we ask ourselves whether we should interpret his attitude as a withdrawal from history or as a deeper awareness of it, precious evidence may come from a novel like *The Old and the Young*. Those who are vexed by the presence of aesthetic (and ethical) iconoclasm in Pirandello are likely to discover, if they pursue their inquiry with due thoroughness, that he destroyed to innovate, and that in some respects the innovation amounted to a renewal of Shakespeare's, Calderón's, and Cervantes' tradition in the broken, prosier idiom of our bewildered age.

If Pirandello does explode the notion of a fixed personal identity, this by no means implies the moral annihilation of the individual self; on the contrary, the effect may be to dissuade human beings from taking themselves and one another for granted. In Pirandello's fictional world, the elusive reality of personal existence impinges on our awareness precisely because it is felt to be inaccessible to ready-made definitions. The capital question of whether his work is poetry or just abstract speculation will have to be settled case by case, and more attention to the physiognomy of his style than has generally been applied so far should prove very helpful here. As a result, instead of labeling him a dramatist or novelist of ideas, we can more aptly speak of his whole work as an exploration of consciousness. It is as a drama of consciousness that it retains relevance, to the extent that the ideas operate functionally in each formal embodiment. Once this focus is established, many critical problems will become clearer; but whatever solutions may have emerged from the welter of formulated opinions, I shall leave the reader to argue the issues with the critics and, in the last resort, with the author himself. Pirandello deserves no less.

The Pirandello Play

by Stark Young

The Living Mask (Henry IV) by Luigi Pirandello, translated
by Arthur Livingston. Forty-fourth Street Theatre. January 21,
1924.

The Pirandello play at the Forty-fourth Street Theatre is important not by reason of any display or novelty or foreign importa-
tion but through the mere occurrence on our stage of a real intellectual impact, a high and violent world of concepts and living. So
far as the practical end of it goes Pirandello's *Henry IV* is difficult
for our theatre. Its range and complexity of ideas are made more
difficult by the presentation that it gets now and that it would be almost sure to get one way or another from any of our producers.

Mr. Livingston's rendering is always speakable on the stage, even
when it is inexact and is often padded out far beyond Pirandello's
economy.

Mr. Robert Edmond Jones' two settings—save for the two portraits in the first scene, which obviously should be modern realistic
in the midst of the antique apartment—are ahead of anything
Pirandello would be apt to get in Italy, more precisely in the mood
and more beautifully and austerely designed. Otherwise the trouble
begins with the acting. Bad Italian actors would, congenitally, if in
no other way, be closer to this Italian play and its necessities than
many actors of our own would be. The actors in the opening moments at the Forty-fourth Street Theatre could not even cope with
the necessary delivery of the words. They not only could not whack
out the stresses needed for the mere sense of the lines, but had no
instinct for taking the cues in such a manner as would keep the
scene intact. All that first part of the scene Pirandello means to keep

flowing as if it were taking place in one mind; and the actors should establish that unity, speed, and continuity by taking fluidly their lines as if from one mouth. Miss Lascelles' portrayal of Donna Mathilde is not definite or elegant enough; it is muffled and it is not full enough of a kind of voluptuous incisiveness. Mr. Louden's Doctor is wrong, too flat and narrow; the part is rough and tumble—out of the old *commedia dell'arte* very nearly—and a satire on specious scientific optimism and incessant explanation. And Mr. Korff's troubles with the language make his lines, which are hard enough already to grasp, confused and elusive.

Much of the meaning of *Henry IV* will depend of course on the actor who does the central character. Mr. Korff is a very good actor indeed in a certain style. He has a fine voice and a good mask in the manner of the Flemish or German schools of painting. But his portrayal of Henry IV lacks most of all distinction and bite. It is too full of sentiment and too short of mental agitation; it has too much nerves and heart and too little brains. The average audience must get the impression from Mr. Korff that we see a man whose life has been fantastically spoiled by the treachery of an enemy, that the fall from his horse began his disaster, which was completed by the infidelity and loose living of the woman he loved. But this weakens the whole drama; the root of the tragic idea was in the man's mind long before the accident; Pirandello makes that clear enough. The playing of this character which is one of the great roles in modern drama, needs first of all a dark cerebral distinction and gravity; the tragedy, the irony, the dramatic and philosophical theme depend on that. Mr. Korff has theatrical power and intensity, but too much waggling of his head; he is too grotesque and undignified vocally; he has too little precision and style for the part; and not enough intellectual excitement and ideal poignancy. And the very last moment of the play he loses entirely by the rise that he uses in his voice and by the kind of crying tumult that he creates. Pirandello's idea cannot appear in such terms as Mr. Korff's. Pirandello is concerned first and last with a condition of life, an idea, embodied in a magnificent personage, not with personal ills and Gothic pities.

A man dressed as Henry IV of Canossa fame rides beside the woman he loves, who goes as Mathilde of Tuscany. His horse is pricked from the rear and lunges; the man when he comes out of his stupor believes himself to be the real Henry IV. For years the river of time flows past him; his beloved marries and has a daughter, she becomes the *amante* of his rival. He chooses, when his reason returns, to remain in the masquerade of the character that for an evening's pleasure he has put on. Life has cheated him, made a jest of him; he gets even with life by remaining permanent in the midst of everlasting change. All men play a part in life; he plays his knowingly. And the people who come out of life to him must mask themselves before they are admitted; he makes fools of them. The woman he has loved comes with his nephew and the doctor to see him, bringing also her *amante*—well played by Mr. Gamble—with her and her daughter, who is the image of what she herself was in her youth. They are the changing Life brought now against the fixed Form in which the supposed madman lives. Driven by the sense that years have passed and are recorded on these visitors from his past and that he has not lived, he tells his attendants of his sanity and his masquerade. They betray his secret. In the end he sees that in the young daughter alone can he recognize his renewal and return to life. There is a struggle when he tries to take her, and he kills the *amante*. Necessarily now, after this crime, he remains shut up in the mask under which he has masqueraded.

With this the Pirandello theme appears—the dualism between Life on one hand and Form on the other; on the one hand Life pouring in a stream, unknowable, obscure, unceasing; on the other hand forms, ideas, crystallizations, in which we try to embody and express this ceaseless stream of Life. Upon everything lies the burden of its form, which alone separates it from dust, but which also interferes with the unceasing flood of Life in it. In *Henry IV* this man who has taken on a Form, a fixed mask in the midst of flooding, changing Life, remains in it until the moment when his passion and despair and violent impulse send him back into Life. But only for a moment: the impetuous violence of the Life in him expels him into his masquerade again: in the struggle between Life and Form, Life is defeated, Form remains.

Nothing in town is to compare to Pirandello's *Henry IV*—well or badly done—as worth seeing. If there is a tendency in many of his plays to think, talk, analyze, without embodying these processes in dramatic molds that carry and give them living substance—and I think that is one of Pirandello's dangers, his plays too often when all is said and done boil down too much to single ideas—this fault cannot be laid on his *Henry IV*. In this play Pirandello has discovered a story, a visual image, and a character that completely embody and reveal the underlying idea. This drama has a fantastic and high-spirited range in the spirit of the Italian comedy tradition; it has also a kind of Shakespearean complexity and variety; and in the second act, at least, something like a poetry of intellectual beauty.

Pirandello's Commedia

by Stark Young

Right You Are If You Think You Are (It's True if It Seems So
to You), by Luigi Pirandello, translated by Arthur Livingston.
Guild Theatre. February 21, 1927.

The production of Pirandello's famous *Così è (se vi pare)* by
the Theatre Guild players is at least passable, with some muffing
and not too much precision or distinction, and with two admirable
performances. Mr. Edward G. Robinson plays Ponza, the tortured
employee, with fine concentration and unity; Miss Beryl Mercer's
Signora Frola is one of the most expert and stirring performances
of the year. The whole interpretation of the play, however, is greatly
thwarted by Mr. Reginald Mason, to whom is allotted the all-im-
portant role in which the dramatist himself speaks.

This Lamberto Laudisi is the protagonist, or perhaps the chorus,
of the drama. The Pirandello theme—that relation of fiction and
reality and the nature of truth that is the hero of most of his plays—
supplies the dramatic continuity of *Così è (se vi pare)* and is completely entrusted to this ironical and smiling philosopher who sits
on the edge of the events and human emotions that we see taking
place in the Agazzi drawing room. The role should be played directly, with clear stresses, direct reason, urbanity and sequence. Mr.
Mason seems to have the impression that Pirandello was writing to
give archness a chance. The most pointed remarks, remarks most
necessary to the play's idea and progress, he delivers as if he were
the whimsical uncle of an English country house. His hesitancies,
sly humors and coquetries, of theory and whim, as when, for example, he speaks Laudisi's lines to his own image or self in the mirror, appear to make some of the audience laugh, but they blur the

"Pirandello's Commedia" by Stark Young. From *Immortal Shadows* (New
York: Charles Scribner's Sons, 1948). © 1948 by Charles Scribner's Sons. Reprinted
by permission of the publisher.

sting of the thought, shift the intellectual basis of the play, and help
to turn into a smiling moment what is not so much comic or personal as it is exhilarating or ideal. Such a performance as Mr. Mason's is a deplorable intrusion into the clarity and precision of
Pirandello.

Pirandello's theatre and ideas have been so long famous now and
this particular play so long available, either in companies abroad or
as a book here, in Mr. Arthur Livingston's translations, that we are
free to leave accounts of *Così è (se vi pare)* and turn to points almost
academic.

First, then, we may speak of the element of characterization in
this Latin play. The acting at the Guild Theatre might wisely aim
at less relation between many of the speeches and the particular
character that speaks them, and more relation to the play's general
scheme. This rather undue degree of individualization might be
said to appear even in the translation of the title, for *Così è* does not
mention you but it, and does not say that you are right but that it
is so, if it seems so to you. That, however, is of no importance, obviously. I mention it only for whatever suggestive comment may be
involved. In many cases a speech in *Così è (se vi pare)* might be said
by any one of half a dozen of the people in the story. It does not
proceed from the depths of any particular person, but serves rather
to keep the argument up, the analysis alive, the structure building.
Indeed, the people in this play are hardly people at all; they are
figures in the game that Pirandello is playing. They are human
traits, situations, mental aspects. If on the stage it so happens that
they are made too personal, too actual, the play becomes more cruel
and arch; taken on that ground what could be more cruel than the
use it makes of such grief, despair, and confusion as possess the three
people about whom the town's inquiry and our excitement center?
With less individualization and reality in the characters, less comedy
and laughter would be necessary to make the play palatable.

This ought to be a good lesson for us Northern races with our obsession about character in drama. Is Pirandello's play poor because
the characters in it are but perfunctorily related to its story and idea,
are in themselves as characters not profound creations? Not at all.
It would doubtless be a greater play if the character element were
deeply creative and deeply related to the plot and the theme. But
that does not prevent its being an excellent piece of drama through
the excellence of its idea and plot. This play exists most in its outline, to which everything else contributes. In this case we are to
judge not too much by the degree of character creation; and it is

well to remember that to Pirandello a character often appears to be as definite an entity almost as a figure on a chessboard—*ma non,* he says, *si dà vita invano a un personaggio*—but not idly does one give life to a character.

This outline quality, this exhilarating game of motives and ideas, is one of the traits in *Così è (se vi pare)* that tie it to the *commedia dell'arte.* This piece, as much as any that Carlo Gozzi admired in the public squares of Italy, is made up not of people but of stock characters, which are here not Harlequin, Punchinello, Brighella, Colombina, Dottore, and the rest, but Mental Habits, Characteristic Human Emotions, Thematic Ideas. This is no less a comedy of intrigue, though the game played and the victory plotted for concern not some hero but ideas: the nature of truth is the hero whose fortunes underlie the story. And over this whole play, as in the *commedia dell'arte,* lies the air of improvisation. However bitter its living material, however tragic the human matter that it engages, it is gay with its own ingenuity and speed, it delights in its invention and ruthless vivacity. At the very end we see Ponza maintaining that his wife is dead and, to comfort the mother-in-law, keeping up the fiction that his second wife is still alive; and the mother-in-law insisting that her daughter is not dead but that her son-in-law's delusion has made it necessary to go through a second wedding ceremony and pretend that there is now a second wife; we see then the woman in question when she is brought in to settle the matter. Which is she, they ask, the daughter who is still alive or the dead woman's successor? She is, she says, whatever you think she is. With such an arbitrary end the plot intrigue resolves itself, and at that we are slapped in the face with the unreality and the pure theatricality of the piece, which thus kicks up its heels with its own high spirits and dark joyous game.

New as he seems, Pirandello through the profound sources behind his origin is old. He was born in Sicily, in Girgenti in the south, the Acragas that Pindar called "the most beautiful city of mortals." It was a part of that Magna Graecia that composed a great section of the Greek world and mind; it was later under the domination of Carthage, then of Rome, and in the ninth century was taken by the Saracens and became a part of that Arabic world that was anything but lacking in violence, philosophy and mathematics. Across the strait this same Southern world was that of Thomas Aquinas and Vico—Hegel's source, we may remember—and today of Volterra, Croce, and other great names. His use of subtlety and passion are thus by no means new with Pirandello. He knows that, speaking generally, the passions have their own logic; fiercely and darkly they work, sorting their elements together, squaring them at last in that final conclusion in violence. Only vague, soft, and fuddled emotions are without this inner and final logic of their own. The stronger the passion is, the more logical, taken alone in itself, since the more completely it will come to a resolution according to its own nature.

Not only do these type characters—these lively abstractions, traditional, though of a new content, more or less—denote the Latin and classic family of *Così è (se vi pare)*; there are, also, speeches long enough to have come from the Attic dramatists, from Seneca and Plautus, and on down through the course of drama in modern Latin countries. Here again, are these *longueurs,* these tirades, speeches longer in wind than the Homeric Nestor boasted, that we of the North have been taught to dread and fear. It is amusing to sit listening to Miss Mercer's fine reading of those pages and pages that Signora Frola speaks, and to observe how this classic form may carry life as well as any other, when there is really any life to carry, and how the tense life in it now, as Pirandello is using it, covers up the traditional form. Technically, too, we may observe that the point is not so much that the speech is long. The point is that the very length itself of a speech should become dramatic, that there should be also a dramatic progression in the thought, and that, when it is delivered, the stress should fall accurately and with a just degree of that resistant flexibility by which the spoken language becomes expressive and exciting. The length of a speech can be made as dramatic and exciting as anything about it.

Life Versus Form

by Adriano Tilgher

(1) Nature: living without feeling oneself live.

(2) Man: living and feeling oneself live.

(3) Dualism of Life and Form.

(4) Detachment of Thought from Forms: humor and cerebralism.

(5) Antithesis as the law of Pirandello's art.

(6) Modern relevance of Pirandello's art.

(7) The ineluctability of Forms: *Il fu Mattia Pascal* (*The Late Mattia Pascal*).

(8) Practical wisdom of Life: Corrado Selmi of *I vecchi e i giovani* (*The Old and the Young*).

(9) Assertion of Life in its absolute nakedness: Vitangelo Moscarda of *Uno, nessuno e centomila* (*One, No One and a Hundred Thousand*).

(10) Renunciation of Life: Don Cosmo Laurentano of *I vecchi e i giovani*; Mrs. Ponza of *Così è (se vi pare)* (*It Is So if You Think So*).

(11) Fear, tedium, compassion of life.

(12) Seeing oneself live: the paralyzing *mirror*.

(13) Destruction of *character:* the individual, a chaos of warring forces.

(14) *Uno, nessuno e centomila*: the incommunicability of individuals.

(15) To be is to seem: *Così è (se vi pare)* (*It Is So, if You Think So*).

"Life Versus Form" by Adriano Tilgher. From *Studi sul teatro contemporaneo* (Rome: Libreria di Scienze e Lettere, 1923, 1928). © 1923, 1928 by Adriano Tilgher. © 1941 by Livia de Paoli Tilgher. Translated by Glauco Cambon. Reprinted by permission of Livia de Paolis Tilgher. The pages used here are a part of Ch. VII ("Il teatro di Luigi Pirandello"), pp. 186-95, 230-48.

(16) The chasm between past and present: *Ma non è una cosa seria (It Can't Be Serious)*.

(17) The present feeling itself as past: *Lumíe di Sicilia (Sicilian Limes)*; *Il fu Mattia Pascal*; *Enrico IV (Henry IV)*, the tragedy of unlived life.

(18) Pirandellian drama: a clash of Life and Mask.

(19) Opposition between the individual and his image as construed by others: *Sei personaggi in cerca d'autore (Six Characters in Search of an Author)*; *Tutto per bene (All for the Best)*; *Come prima, meglio di prima (As Well as Before, Better than Before)*; *Cappiddazzu paga tuttu (Cappiddazzu Pays for All)*.

(20) Destruction of the individual's self-built mask: *Il berretto a sonagli (Cap and Bells)*; *Enrico IV*; *Vestire gli ignudi (Naked)*; *La Vita che ti diedi (The Life I Gave You)*.

(21) Acceptance of a forcefully imposed mask: *La patente (The License)*.

(22) A mask voluntarily put on by the individual: *Il gioco delle parti (Each in his Role)*.

(23) Revolt of life against the mask: *L'uomo, la bestia e la virtù (Man, Beast and Virtue)*; *Il piacere dell'onestà (The Pleasure of Honesty)*; *Come prima, meglio di prima*; *Ma non è una cosa seria (It Can't Be Serious)*.

(24) The triumph of the irrational: *L'innesto (The Grafting)*; *Pensaci, Giacomino! (Think It Over, Giacomino!)*.

(25) Immanent morality of the Pirandellian world. Pirandellian women.

(26) Thinking thought, the center of Pirandellian drama.

(27) Pirandello's anti-intellectualism: the levels of reality.

(28) The dramas of dialectic: *La ragione degli altri (Other People's Point of View)*.

(29) *Sei personaggi in cerca d'autore (Six Characters in Search of an Author)*.

(30) Flaws of Pirandello's theater. His style.

(31) The progress of Pirandello's art. Conclusion.

(1) What, in Pirandello's view, distinguishes man from the other beings of nature? This, and only this: that man lives and feels him-

self live, while the other beings of nature just live, live purely and simply. The tree, for instance, lives completely immersed in its own vital sense; its existence equals the slow and dark succession of vital vicissitudes in it; sun, moon, wind and earth surround it, but it sees and knows nothing of them: it senses them, of course, but only insofar as they become states of its own being, from which it fails to distinguish itself. Since it knows nothing of anything else, the tree knows nothing of itself as different from anything else.

(2) But in man, no matter how uncouth, life splits in two: even to the most uncouth of men it is essential to be and to know that he is, to live and to know that he lives. In man, life has projected and detached from itself as its own opposite something that Pirandello calls the feeling of life and that I would call, in philosophically stricter terms, consciousness, reflection, thought. In such detachment, with the attendant delusion of assuming as objectively and externally existing reality this mutable inner feeling of life, there lies the first cause of human misery. For once it has detached itself from life, the feeling of life (or consciousness as we may call it) by filtering through the brain tends to cool off, to clarify and idealize itself; from the particular, changeable, ephemeral state it was, it will eventually crystallize into a general, abstract idea (see Pirandello's essay "L'umorismo" [in the book of the same name], second edition, pp. 168ff.).

(3) Having risen through logical abstraction to its own second power, having become reflective thought, the feeling of life tends to confine life within fixed boundaries, to channel it between chosen banks, to pour it into stiff, definitive molds: the concepts and ideals of our spirit, the conventions, mores, traditions, and laws of society. That causes a basic dualism. On the one hand, blind, dumb Life will keep darkly flowing in eternal restlessness through each moment's renewals. On the other hand, a world of crystallized Forms, a system of constructions, will strive to dam up and compress that everflowing turmoil. "Everything, every object, every life carries with it the penalty of its form, the pain of being so and never otherwise, until it crumbles into ashes" (see the short story "Candelora" ["Candlemas"]). "Every form is death. We are all beings caught in a trap, detached from the unceasing flux, and fixed to death" (see the short story "La trappola" ["The Trap"]).

(4) Most men live within those frozen forms, without even so much as surmising that a dark, furious ocean may stir under them. But in some men, thought, that very activity which, lightning-like in its mystery, has split life asunder, separates from the forms into

which life's hot flux has clotted and perceives them for what they really are: merely ephemeral constructions, under which the tide of life roars unconstrained by any human illusion. In the man who has achieved this deliverance from the forms of life, any human construction arouses a sense of contrast which topples it under his very eyes. There is something comical and grievous at the same time in that crash. The crash is comical because it lays bare the intrinsic unreality of human constructions, but grievous too, because, however flimsy, the demolished structure did afford man a shelter from the mad storm of life.

In such intimate mixture of laughter and tears, of comedy and sadness, is humor as Pirandello feels it to be and defines it. "I see something like a labyrinth, where through so many crisscrossing paths our soul rambles without ever finding a way out. And in this labyrinth I see a double herma which laughs from one face and weeps from the other, laughs indeed from one face at the weeping of the twin, opposite one" (see *Erma bifronte* [*Two-faced Herma*], preface). Since humor is the attitude of the man whose thought, having attained self-consciousness, has broken through the screens of conceptual constructions to look out on life's abysmal tide of tumultuous incoherence, it has to be an essentially cerebral state of mind. Humor and cerebralism: all of Pirandello's art is summarized in these two words.

(5) Therefore, antithesis is the basic law of his art. The customary relationships of human existence are triumphantly subverted. Among the comedies, *Pensaci, Giacomino!* (*Think It Over, Giacomino!*) features a husband intentionally forcing the (to him only too well known) young lover of his wife to come back to her, while *L'uomo, la bestia e la virtù* (*Man, Beast and Virtue*) shows a lover dragging the betrayed husband back to the marriage bed. *Ma non è una cosa seria* (*It Can't Be Serious*) deals with marriage as an antidote against the danger of marriage. Of the short stories, "Da sé" ("By Himself") presents the supposedly dead man who traipses to the graveyard thereby enjoying many things which are lost on quick and dead alike. "Nené e Niní" ("Nené and Niní") acquaints us with two little orphans who bring ruin to a whole series of stepfathers and stepmothers. "Canta l'epistola" ("Sing the Epistle") develops the motif of a mortal duel caused by the plucking of a leaf of grass. "Il dovere del medico" ("The Physician's Duty") tells the story of a doctor who, from sheer sense of duty, lets his patient bleed to death, then in "Prima notte" ("First Wedding Night") we see two newlyweds spend their first wedding night weeping respectively on the

grave of her fiancé and of his first wife; finally, "L'illustre estinto" ("The Illustrious Deceased") (to put an end to our practically inexhaustible examples) is the tale of an illustrious deceased who gets a hidden burial by night, like a dog, while a perfect nobody receives honors and gifts in his place.

(6) Dualism of Life and Form (or Construction); the necessity for Life to sink into a Form without possibly ever being exhausted by it: here is the fundamental motif underlying all of Pirandello's work in such a way as to organize it into a strict unity of vision. That suffices to show the remarkable modern relevance of this writer of ours. All of modern philosophy, from Kant on, rises from this deep insight into the dualism between absolutely spontaneous Life, which in its perennial upsurge of freedom keeps creating the new, and the constructed Forms or molds which tend to imprison that upsurge, with the result that Life every time shatters those molds to dissolve them and go beyond in its tireless creativity. The whole history of modern philosophy is the progressive deepening of this basic intuition into self-possessed clarity. To the eyes of an artist like Pirandello, who lives on just such an intuition, reality will appear dramatic at its very roots, the essence of drama lying in the struggle between Life's primal nakedness and the garments or masks with which men must by all means insist on clothing it. *La vita nuda* (*Naked Life*), *Maschere nude* (*Naked Masks*). The very titles of his works are telling.

(7) To enjoy Life in its infinite nakedness and freedom, outside all constructed forms into which society, history, and the events of each individual existence have channeled its course, is impossible. Mattia Pascal tried that, who, palming himself off as dead and changing name and aspect, believed he could start a new life, in the enthusiasm of a boundless liberty. He learned at his own expense that, having cut himself off from all social forms and conventions, he was only allowed to witness other people's life as a foreign spectator, without any further possibility to mingle with it and enjoy its fullness. Since he had estranged himself from the forms of Life, it now no longer conceded itself to him except superficially, externally. And when, surrendering to its call, he deluded himself that he could plunge again into the river of Life to be enveloped by its waves, that river rejected him, and again at his own expense he learned that it is not possible to act as living and dead at the same time. Thus in despair he resolved to stage a resurrection—too late to sit down again at the banquet of existence, in time only to see others partake of it (see the novel *Il fu Mattia Pascal* [*The Late Mattia Pascal*]).

Of course it is possible to estrange oneself from the forms of Life, but only on condition that one gives up living.

(8) To accept the Forms or constructions into which Life has been forced; to participate in them with heartfelt belief and yet avoid crystallizing oneself in one of them or in one of their systems, but to retain so much spiritual fusion or fluidity that one's soul may go on from form to form without finally coagulating in any, without fearing the impurities it inevitably carries along in its ceaseless flow, since that very flowing will purify it: here is the practical wisdom of life. It is a wisdom of precarious value, far from insuring perfect happiness, since some form may always emerge to obstruct so firmly the soul streaming at white heat that the latter fails to melt the obstacle and finally subsides into it, stifled.

That is the case of Corrado Selmi of *I vecchi e i giovani (The Old and the Young)*, in whom Pirandello has embodied this refreshing ideal of wisdom. Corrado has to commit suicide one day when certain past actions of his come to light, because these actions, for all the redeeming freshness of life he had put in them and the good he thus managed to spread around by their means or in their spite, do appear vile and dishonorable to society that looks at them from the outside.

(9) But Selmi's idea of practical wisdom can only be achieved by a soul endowed with the strength to pass on from form to form without either being imprisoned in any one of them or losing in the passage the sustenance of its vital illusion. That means a soul capable of attaining in itself a balance between Life and Form and of dwelling there contentedly. But whoever radically lives by the Pirandellian insight that any Form must always be a limiting determination and therefore a denial of Life (*omnis determinatio est negatio*) will have only two choices left. Either (like the Vitangelo Moscarda of *Uno, nessuno e centomila [One, No One and A Hundred Thousand]*) he can try and live Life in its absolute primeval nakedness, beyond all forms and constructions, focusing on a vibrantly fleeting present, experiencing time moment by moment, without even thinking of time in the process for that would mean to construe it, to give it a form and thus limit and stifle it (This is an enactment of Bergson's intuitionalism, with a timeless *pure present* substituted for *pure duration*. Such an ideal of life is, however, attainable at the limit, i.e., practically unattainable.);

(10) or else, having discovered the provisional nature of Forms along with the impossibility to do without them, the ineluctable

penalty one will eventually have to pay for the Form that Life donned or let itself be dressed in, one can renounce life: and that is the case of Don Cosmo Laurentano of *I vecchi e i giovani (The Old and the Young)*. "One thing only is sad, my friends: to have seen through the game! I mean the game of this mocking devil who hides within each of us and has his fun projecting for us as external reality what, shortly after, he himself will expose as our own delusion, laughing at the pains we took for it and laughing also . . . at our failure to delude ourselves, since outside these delusions there is no reality left. . . . And so don't complain! Do trouble yourselves with your endeavors, without thinking that it all will lead to no conclusion. If it does not conclude, it means that it should not conclude, and that it is therefore useless to seek a conclusion. We must live, that is, we must delude ourselves; leave free play to the mocking devil within us. . . ."

*　　　　*　　　　*

(25) Just because the Pirandellian Weltanschauung does not admit of one reason, of one logic, and of one law, but of as many as there are individuals, and indeed as many for the same individual as feeling creates in its endless variations, each character from his own viewpoint is right, and no such thing exists as one higher point of view from which to judge all others. Thus in the end Pirandello does not judge, absolve, or condemn any of his characters; rather, his judgment is implied in the portrayal he gives of them and of their actions' consequences. That makes for a firmly immanent morality, to the absolute exclusion of any reference to transcendent norms. For each one, the judgment is implicitly given by the results of his actions.

Thus, for instance, not one word of condemnation is ever uttered by Pirandello on his many fictive women, even though, personifying blind instinct unrestrained by reason and thought, they seem to be crazy, amoral, conscienceless creatures, addicted to orgies of sensual cerebralism as well as to hangover nausea and horror of it, with sudden yearnings for purity and motherhood. Such are Silia of *Il gioco delle parti (Each in His Role)*, Beatrice of *Il berretto a sonagli (Cap and Bells)*, Fulvia of *Come prima, meglio di prima (As Well as Before, Better than Before)*, the Stepdaughter of *Sei personaggi in cerca d'autore (Six Characters in Search of an Author)*, the Murdered Woman of the "lay mystery" *All'uscita (At the Exit)*, Ersilia of *Vestire gli ignudi (Naked)*, all of them full of hatred against the man each confronts (respectively Leone, Ciampa, Silvio, the Father, the Fat Man) since he embodies what is directly contrary to them: order, reason, pondering calm, and prudence.

(26) In the Pirandellian view of things, Life must needs give itself a Form and withal not exhaust itself therein. Also, in the human world the creator of Form is thought. Thus, while with other artists conscious thought only accompanies the unfolding of inner events from the outside, and throws on them a cold superficial light, so that drama is generated and consummated exclusively in the emotive sphere, the possible intervention of thought never being crucial, with Pirandello thought finds its way into every moment of psychological becoming.

His characters justify, condemn, criticize themselves in the very act of living through their torments; they don't just feel, they reason rightly or absurdly on their feelings, and in so doing transfer them from the level of mere emotionality to a level of higher, more truly human complexity. Man after all is not just feeling, but also and especially thought, and he reasons, whether rightly or absurdly, especially when he suffers. Feelings, passions, affections are always thrown into perspective by thought which colors and imbues them with itself, yet by the same token it, in turn, is colored by them and warmed by their flame. Thought here is life and drama, and takes shape gradually through ceaseless lacerations and contrasts. We thus have cerebralism, of course, but one and the same with the torment and passion of drama. Thinking thought, which is activity unfolding through continuous struggles and wounds, places itself at the center of art's world: with Pirandello, dialectic becomes poetry.

(27) Pirandello's art, chronologically as well as ideally contemporary to the great idealist revolution that took place in Italy and Europe at the beginning of this century, carries over into art the anti-rationalism which fills modern philosophy and is now culminating into Relativism. Pirandello's art is anti-rationalist not because it denies or ignores thought to the total benefit of feeling, passion, and affections, but rather because it installs thought at the very center of the world as a live power fighting with the rebellious powers of Life. Anti-rationalist (or anti-intellectualist) do I call it, because it denies that a complete, self-contained and wholly determined order of truth preexists thought, as if the only thing left for thought itself to do were humbly to take notice of preordained truth and bow to it; yet it is a thought-affirming art, instinct with the drama of thinking thought. . . .

Thought actually leavens Life. Therefore, while for other writers reality is massively compact and monolithically rigid, given once for all, with Pirandello it flakes off into several levels which in turn then endlessly complicate one another. Not only what is commonly called real is such, but also, and with the same right, whatever appears to be real in the warmth of a feeling. A deeply dreamed dream (as in the short story "La realtà del sogno" ["The Reality of Dream"]), a memory (as in the short story "Piuma" ["Feather"]), or a fantasy (as in the short stories, "Se . . . ," ["If"], "Rimedio: La geografia" ["The Remedy: Geography"], "Il treno ha fischiato" ["The Train Whistled"]) are as real to him who intensely lives them as this thick world of things and people to which alone we usually ascribe the name of reality. As a consequence, what is real to one person may not be to another, or may be real to still another in a different way, and what was reality to the same man fades off in his eyes once the engendering sentiment has failed. Jocularly, the short story "Il pipistrello" ("The Bat") tells of one such clash between different levels of reality, and of the attendant troubles.

(28) Two plays by Pirandello above all show this living dialectic of Spirit in action: *La ragione degli altri* (*Other People's Point of View*) and *Sei personaggi in cerca d'autore* (*Six Characters in Search of an Author*). In *La ragione degli altri* a situation has arisen whose inner logic by its own unfolding determines the action's development and leads the characters to the only admissible end. The central character, Livia (who is fully aware of the situation's logic), has broken off with her husband Leonardo upon learning of a mistress, Elena, who has borne him a daughter. The weary mistress would like to send her husband back to her, and she is willing to forgive him, on one condition, however: that Elena surrenders to her the child to be raised as Livia's own daughter, in the comforts destitute Elena cannot give her. Elena took Leonardo away from her as a husband, and she is returning him as a father; well then, let the father either stay with his child's mother, or come back to his lawful wife, but with the child. To have him back only by half, a husband with herself and a father with the other woman, will never do. "Where the children are, there is the home!" and Leonardo had no children from Livia. "Two homes, that is out! I here and your daughter there, that is out!" (Act II).

Such is the situation, of which Livia represents and interprets the inner logic, for her feeling has risen to the highest degree of rationality. Around her the other characters move on different levels, all of them lower than Livia's: in all of them passion to some extent dominates reason. Each of them defends a particular right of his:

Elena, as the mother she is, wants to send Leonardo back to Livia, but to keep the child; Guglielmo, as the father-in-law, regardless of the child, wants Leonardo to be reconciled to his daughter Livia, or else Livia to return to her parental home; Leonardo claims his right as a husband in love with his wife again and as a father who won't ever give up the child. The action is a continuous dialectic, through which all these one-sided rights and reasons gradually become aware of their one-sidedness to yield finally to the right and reason of Livia, which contains them all and is therefore superior to all, for it interprets the good of the child, the strongest right and need. Livia is of course taking her mother away from the little girl, but she is giving her another, equally affectionate one, along with the father, and wealth and a name for good measure.

(29) In *La ragione degli altri* (*Other People's Point of View*) we see a dialectic operate whereby a higher truth or reason conquers the lower ones. In *Sei personaggi in cerca d'autore* (*Six Characters in Search of an Author*) we see the very dialectic of truth or illusion taking shape. In this admirable play, which takes its cue from a motif outlined in the short story, "La tragedia di un personaggio" ("The Tragedy of a Character"),[1] Pirandello wants to portray scenically the laboring process whereby the riot of phantoms born by the artist's imagination, throbbing with life as they no doubt are yet at first still confused, dark and chaotically unaccomplished, aspires to a final composure in whose encompassing harmony what had initially flashed in the artist's mind as faintly distinguishable splotches of color may find the proper balance in an ample, luminous, well organized picture.

One is born a fictional character as one is born stone, plant, or animal, and if the reality of the character is an illusion, any reality will likewise turn out to be an illusion once the animating feeling has changed. Who was born a character, then, has even more life than the so-called really existing men, for they change in every way from day to day, and pass and die, while the fictional character, instead, has his own incorruptible life, eternally fixed in his nature's unchangeable essential traits. "Nature uses the instrument of imagination to pursue its own creative work on a higher level" (Act I). And once he is created, the character detaches himself from his author, lives by himself and imposes his will on the creator, who must follow and let him do as he pleases. One day six characters, whom

[1] There occurs an analogous motif in Miguel de Unamuno's novel, *Fog* (Chapter XXXI), anterior to *Six Characters* but posterior to the short story "La tragedia di un personaggio" ("The Tragedy of a Character").

their author had sketched and provisionally composed in an undeveloped, unfinished scenic plot, turn to a *stage manager* to propose that he allow them to act out onstage the drama irrepressibly stirring within them.

Not all of these characters are equally achieved. Two, the main ones (*Father* and *Stepdaughter*), are very close to accomplished artistic achievement, some other instead is little more than brute nature, blind impression of life (the *Mother*), still another (the *Son*) is lyrically achieved and rebels against a dramatic enactment. These six characters in search of an author do not, then, share the same level of consciousness: they are the scenic realization of the several levels of consciousness on which an artist's imagination has dwelt. Pirandello's play would realize in scenic terms the process of coalescence leading to the work of art, the transition from life to art, from impression to intuition and finally expression. The turmoil of scarcely sketched phantoms who, full of an incoercible life the author gave them and cannot withdraw, play at overpowering one another, at securing each the center of the whole work and drawing to themselves all the interest of the *stage manager,* is very well rendered through a broken, panting dialogue. Pirandello has deeply seen that right here, in this *eccentricity* (literally meant), in this blind rushing to develop to the bitter end each separate seminal motif lies the whole essence of Nature or Life, what distinguishes it from Spirit, Art, which instead is coordination, synthesis, discipline, and thus choice and conscious sacrifice.

But this, which should be the play's central motif and indeed dominates it throughout Act I, finds no adequate development in Acts II and III, where we do not see, in scenic terms, the passage of characters from a lower to a higher level, for they fail to proceed from confusion to order, from chaos to artistic cosmos. Who was nature remains nature, who was realized only lyrically remains so. The play cannot come to light. Why? Because the *son* rebels against acting his role in the play, he is not cut out for scenes. The play fails, because instead of a coordinating spirit the characters meet a mediocre manager who tries to improvise it, and no work of art is to be improvised; it cannot be a mediocre manager, with no artistic experience or depth, a manager who sees only the so-called requirements of theater, to set up in a few hours a play needing no less than a painstaking elaboration. Yet this seems to me a particular reason, devoid of universal value and incapable of demonstrating anything. What universal meaning can be inferred from the fact that a tradesman of theater is unable to bring to fruition a theme left in its inchoate phase? To lead to complete expression of characters in whom whatever life was infused has not yet expressed itself?

In Acts II and III the dominant motif of the play interweaves with the one of the distortion actual life undergoes when passing into the mirror of art (a motif which reappears in Act I of *Vestire gli ignudi* [*Naked*]). In Act II there operates again the evil mirror which sends back to the individual his own unrecognizable image. For when they see the actors, exclusively preoccupied with the scenic truth to be achieved, repeat their own gestures and those words they had uttered in the urgency of unstilled passion, the characters no longer recognize themselves, and in their bewilderment, they burst into laughter or despair. The mirror is in this case the art of the stage (though whatever is said of it can be said of art in general), and when it is reflected in it, actual life in the common sense of the word, the life of interest and passion, appears to itself distorted and false. But by dwelling at length on this theme, Pirandello unknowingly transforms his characters (who should be more or less achieved artistic phantoms) into real beings, and by thus transferring them from the level of imagination onto the level of actual life he splits the play at the seams.

But there is still a third motif which interferes with the others to the play's detriment. Of the six characters in search of an author, each one already knows what will happen to himself and to the others: they have the total vision of their destiny. For instance, whenever the *father* and the *stepdaughter* place themselves at a certain point of the story and try to pick its thread up from there, there is present to the scene the *mother* who already knows how it will end, and in her foreknowledge she is induced not to witness the action passively, but to implore that she be spared the horrible spectacle about to take place. Thus sentimental considerations may emerge to trouble, tentatively, the necessary architecture of a work of art, which has its own inner logic not to be disturbed by any regard for the spectators' tender hearts. But this motif should have been developed much more deeply and with greater emphasis. Besides, Act III after all only treads in the footsteps of Act II, and the end of the play is quite absurd; it's any old epilogue, stuck there just to wind things up and let the curtain fall.

Yet despite these structural faults the play does remain the strongest attempt in Europe so far to realize scenically a process of pure states of mind, by analyzing and projecting onto the stage the various levels and phases of one stream of consciousness. The attempt had already been made by others in Italy, but never with such violence and daring ambition. The drama the six characters carry inside without yet managing to express it (as we saw in 19) is typically Pirandellian. The hints we get of it, broken, uncorrelated and confused as they must needs be, since they constitute a sketch and not an accomplished work of art, still have as much tragic power as one can imagine.[2]

(30) The dangers such a theater incurs are intrinsic to its very nature, and the word *cerebralism* may sum them up (meaning, this time, arid intellectualistic contrivance). Of course it cannot be denied that Pirandello's characters look too much alike; rather than various characters, they seem one and the same character placed in ever different yet identical situations. Of course the progress of Pirandellian art moves not toward enrichment but toward the greater deepening of one and the same Weltanschauung. As all of Pirandello's work tends to the theater, so all his theater tends to one perfect work totally expressing the Pirandellian intuition of life, like a pyramid tending to one point into which everything underneath may converge and be resolved.

Often the play is the belabored and gray scenic dressing of an abstract reflection or of a situational device which preceded and replaced dramatic vision. Figures then become skeletal, frozen in a grimace, stuck in a mania which is the wooden covering of a set theme. Artistic value in those cases finds refuge entirely in the details of some scene. Words, circumscribed in their common meaning, are pale and deprived of imaginative radiance. The pattern will usually consist of a weird picturesque preparation serving to introduce abstract cogitations on a psychological or metaphysical truth.

But there are the plays born of a lively and powerful dramatic vision, to which abstract meditation is coeval and not preconceived: first of all, *Enrico IV (Henry IV)*; then *Sei personaggi in cerca d'au*

---

[2] The real drama of the six characters is not the drama they carry in themselves as protagonists of a theatrical action, but the far more original and modern drama of six creatures who, having remained at the stage of a confused sketch, of merely subjective virtuality in the author's mind, yearn to pull away from him, to live as accomplished characters, endowed with autonomous existence, though merely ideal, in an autonomous world, though merely imaginary. The drama is given by the conflict between the desperate will to be (as accomplished characters) of the six characters and the resistance of several obstacles (inability of the characters to compose into a coherent art system; the manager's ignorance; distortion imposed on the character by scenic interpretation, etc.). That resistance dooms their efforts to failure and them in turn to grope forever between being and non-being, like will-o'-the-wisps on a dark chasm. The six characters are the drama of possibility vainly aspiring to the actuality of being, of virtuality vainly longing for the finality of form *(Addition to the Third Edition)*.

tore (*Six Characters in Search of an Author*); *Il berretto a sonagli* (*Cap and Bells*); *Così è* (*se vi pare*) (*It Is So, if You Think So*); *Il piacere dell'onestà* (*The Pleasure of Honesty*); and, some notches down, *Pensaci, Giacomino!* (*Think It Over, Giacomino!*); *L'innesto* (*The Grafting*); *Come prima, meglio di prima* (*As Well as Before, Better than Before*); *Vestire gli ignudi* (*Naked*). Here whatever may be wooden or skeletal is a function of the peculiar dramatic insight, but under that deathly cold one senses the deep subterranean throb of life which finally breaks through; the frozen spasm will then melt into tears. Remaining always very simple (in fact the most sober and bare, the farthest from literary artifice, the most truly spoken idiom ever heard on our stages), the language of these plays is nimble, witty, juicy, bursting with vitality; dialogue is concise, detailed, unornate, and its fresh, relevant imagery admirably helps it to match the sinuosities of psychological becoming.

(31) And all the art of this great writer seems to be caught in a magnificent ascending movement. It seems to me that he is gradually liberating himself from the biggest flaw of his first theatrical works: what I once called, in *Voci del tempo* (*Voices of Our Time*), the imbalance between the smallness of results, all steeped in the particular, and the metaphysical grandiosity of Pirandello's preliminary intentions. It's an imbalance between the grandeur of such intentions and the story which should have expressed them scenically, usually a story of hopelessly pathetic petty bourgeois creatures living in backwoods small towns, of little boardinghouse tenants, of people catering to village clubs, in a bleak, depressing atmosphere.

How on earth, for instance, can we recognize the universal drama of self-knowledge as death (*As Well as Before, Better Than Before*) in the story of courtesan Fulvia who, after many years spent in shameful abjection away from her husband's home, returns there to contemplate herself in the image her daughter Livia has conceived of her through blessed ignorance of her real identity as a person or as a mother? Or, again, in the story of State Councillor Martino Lori, who after six years of unbelievable gullibility wakes up to the fact that neither wife nor daughter were ever his own? The sorrow of the wretched man in Act III of *Tutto per bene* (*All for the Best*) is doubtless heartbreaking, but to share it we must postulate on his part an absolutely incredible, or at least unique blindness, which removes him from our compassion into a kind of estrangement.

Surely, even in these first plays, when the meaning Pirandello wants to squeeze from the story and the story itself succeed in finding their harmony we get actual masterpieces like *Il berretto a sonagli*

(*Cap and Bells*). Where this harmony is not reached, beauty takes refuge in the details of some scene or character, mostly in the final scenes, when the mask drops and lays bare a sorrowing visage. But in *Six Characters* and in *Henry IV* the metaphysical urge shatters the puny frames which once throttled it, and it gets free play in ampler vicissitudes. The drama throbs with stronger life, its underlying metaphysical torment conquers an apter expression. The motifs are still the same, but tragedy unfolds in a higher, purer atmosphere. And Pirandello has not yet said his last word. He seems now to become increasingly aware of his original dramatic potential.

The first progress of the Sicilian artist took place when, having gone beyond the phase of the peasant short story in Verga's regional-naturalist mood, and beyond the subsequent phase of the ironic, skeptical short story based on manipulation of incident, and having passed from small- and large-scale fiction to the theater, he managed to integrate dramatically those motifs which in his earlier works of fiction lay side-to-side without substantial correlation, like gunpowder lacking a spark to fire it. In the production antedating *The Late Mattia Pascal* the synthesis of Pirandello's special humor is not yet really achieved. Pirandello endeavors to attain the artistic effect through a pessimistic narrative form in Verga's dramatic style, but intellectual negation prevents him from sharing wholeheartedly the anguish of his creatures. He would have us experience as drama what in his mind has been already overcome in a kind of philosophically resigned humor. In this phase of his art feeling and thought are juxtaposed rather than fused, and disturb each other.

This state of mind finds its most felicitous expression in *The Late Mattia Pascal*, where sorrow is overcome in the resigned acceptance of its absolute uselessness. After this novel, the art of Pirandello develops in such a way as to make ever more intimate the synthesis of its two basic elements, so that thought will be born along with feeling as its accompanying shadow. Live anguish gradually sheds any ironic felicity, any expressive indifference and intermediate nuance, to embody itself in ever leaner and more convulsed forms. That is when Pirandellian drama rises, from an intimate need. A second progress is now being made by the artist, who tends to clench the expression of his authentic dramatic center in all its purity and metaphysical universality. The progress made to date is the sure promise of the inevitably forthcoming masterpiece, in which Pirandello's vision of life will fully possess and express itself.

So far, one thing is sure: that with Pirandello for the first time Italian literature discovers how the spirit, far from being the simple, two-dimensional entity it once believed, is a chasm unfathomable by the eye, an unexplored region sounding with strange voices, streaked by phantasmagorias, peopled with monsters, where truth and error, reality and make-believe, wakefulness and dream, good and evil struggle forever tangling in the shadow of mystery.

Action as Theatrical:

Six Characters in Search of an Author

by Francis Fergusson

There is a kinship between what I have called the Shavian theatricality, especially as it emerges in the later plays, and the much
deeper, more consistent and more objective theatrical forms of Pirandello. Shaw as theater artist seems to have been feeling for something which Pirandello achieved: the restoration of the ancient
magic of "two boards and a passion," frankly placed in the glare of
the stage lights and the eye of the audience. In both theaters, the
human is caught rationalizing there in the bright void. But Pirandello, having the seriousness of the artist, presents this farcical-terri-
ble vision with finality and in an integral theatrical form; while in
Shaw's complex case the artist is always being thwarted by the draw-
ing-room entertainer or dismissed as romantic by the Fabian optimist
or the morally fit man of good will. It is therefore Pirandello that
one must study in order to see how the contemporary idea of a theater (as held by its most accomplished masters) emerged from nineteenth century Realism and Romanticism, including and transcending those genres as well as Shaw's solitary farce-of-rationalizing.

Six Characters is a convenient example of Pirandello's art: his
most famous work, and his first unqualified success. I here remind
the reader of the main outlines of its plot.

When the play begins, the curtain is up, the set is stacked against
the stage-wall, and a troupe of actors with their director is rehearsing
a new play by Pirandello. The rehearsal is interrupted by the arrival
of a family in deep mourning: Father, Mother, grown Daughter, and
Son, and two younger children. These are the "characters"—fictions

of the imagination of an author who has refused to write their story —and they have come to get their story or their drama somehow realized. They ask the actors to perform it instead of the play by Pirandello which they had started to rehearse. From this point, the play develops on several levels of make-believe. There is the struggle of the "characters" against the actors and their director, who find the story confusing, or boring, or not good box-office. There is the more savage struggle between the various characters, who cannot agree about the shape, the meaning, or even the facts of their story, for each has rationalized, or mythicized it, in his own way. A few sordid facts emerge: the Father had sent the Mother away to live with another man, whom, he thought, she would love better, and the three younger children are hers by this other man. Hovering near the family, watching its life at a little distance, the Father had met his wife's Daughter at a house of assignation, Madame Pace's dress shop. Complicated jealousies had developed among the four children of the double brood, culminating in the suicide of the little boy. The crucial episodes are reenacted by the tormented and disputing characters in order to show the actors what the story is. When the suicide of the little boy comes up again, by a sort of hellish eternal recurrence, all breaks up in confusion—the fictive characters more real, in their conscious suffering, than the flesh-and-blood acting company.

The story of the six characters, as we gradually make it out, is melodramatic and sensational. The disputes which break out from time to time about "idea and reality," "life and art," and the like, are based on paradoxes in the Shavian manner: romantically unresolved ambiguities. The whole work may seem, at first sight, to be shop-worn in its ideas and, in its dramaturgy, hardly more than a complex piece of theatrical trickery. When it first appeared, in 1921, some critics were disposed to dismiss it in this way. But the fine productions which it received all over the world gradually revealed its true power and interest, which is not in the literal story of the characters, nor in the bright, paradoxical play of ideas, but in the original sense of action underlying the whole play. Pirandello has explained all this with great clarity in the preface he wrote in 1930 for the ninth edition. This preface is almost as important as the play. It deserves to rank with Cocteau's *Call to Order* and Eliot's *Dialogue on Dramatic Poetry,* as one of the works which endeavor to lay the basis for a contemporary theory of drama.

The action of the play is "to take the stage"—with all that this suggestive phrase implies. The real actors and the director want to take it for the realistic purposes—vain or (with the box-office in mind) venal—of their rehearsal. Each of the characters wants to take it for the rationalized myth which is, or would be, his very being. Pirandello sees human life itself as theatrical: as aiming at, and only to be realized in, the tragic epiphany. He inverts the convention of modern realism; instead of pretending that the stage is not the stage at all, but the familiar parlor, he pretends that the familiar parlor is not real, but a stage, containing many "realities." This is, of course, a narrow and violently idealist view of human life and action; but if held with Pirandello's strict consistency, it cuts deep—very much as the narrow idea of the Baroque theater, to which it is so closely akin, cuts deep, enabling a Racine to search and reveal the heart. Certainly it is a version of action which enables Pirandello to bring the stage itself alive at levels of awareness far beyond those of modern realism.

By the time Pirandello wrote the preface to his play, he had had time to read criticisms of it from all over the world, and to discover how its audiences had interpreted it. These audiences were trained in the modes of understanding of modern realism, and they almost automatically assumed that the point of the play was in the literal story of the characters, and that Pirandello's new idea therefore was simply a new way to present the sordid tale. If so, then the play would be only another melodrama on the edge of psychopathology. It is this interpretation which Pirandello is at pains to reject first of all. "Now it must be understood that for me it is not enough to represent the figure of a man or a woman, however special or strongly marked, for the mere pleasure of representing it," he writes; "to tell a story (gay or sad) for the mere pleasure of telling it; to describe a landscape for the mere pleasure of describing it." When the story of the characters first occurred to him, it was in this realistic form; and as such it did not seem to him to be, as yet, the material of art, which must be "more philosophical than history." He was, in fact, through with modern realism: the literal scene, the actual individuals, and the sensational events of individual lives, no longer seemed to have any form or meaning. But when he sensed the analogy between his problem as an artist and the problems of his tormented characters who were also seeking form and meaning, he had the clue to his new theatrical form, and to the peculiar sense of human action (as itself theatrical) which this form was to realize. His inspiration was to stop the film of his characters' lives; to play over and over again some crucial episode in this sequence; to dispute its form and meaning on the public stage. By this means he found a mode of action which he, and the actors, and the characters, and the audience could all share by analogy, and which could thus be the clue to formal relationships and a temporal order. And he lifted the action, as it were, from the realm of fact and sensation, of eavesdropping and the curious intrigue, to the more disinterested realm of contemplation. "Always on opening the book we shall find the living Francesca confessing her sweet sin to Dante," Pirandello explains; "and if we return a hundred thousand times in succession to reread that passage, a hundred thousand times in succession Francesca will utter words, never repeating them mechanically, but speaking them every time for the first time with such a living and unforeseen passion that Dante, each time, will swoon when he hears them. Everything that lives, by the very fact that it lives, has form, and by that same fact must die; except the work of art, which precisely lives forever, in so far as it is form." Francesca's life, as developing potentiality, is stopped at the moment when her peculiar destiny is realized. And it is the crucial moments in the tangled lives of his characters—the moment in Pace's dress shop, the pistol-shot in the garden—which must be played over with the vitality of improvisation, "as though for the first time," yet because they are played *over*, lifted to the realm of contemplation— it is these moments which the characters must interrogate in the light of the stage, as we all must mull over (though in secret) the moments when our nature and destiny are defined.

I have explained that Chekhov, in his way, also to some degree transcended the limits of modern realism: by selecting only those moments of his characters' lives, to show onstage, when they are most detached from the literal facts and the stultifying rationalizations of the daily struggle. But in Chekhov these moments are suffered in abstraction from thought and purpose, and so his image of human action may seem too pathetic. He lacks both Ibsen's powerful moral-intellectual will and Shaw's fitness-in-the-void. But Pirandello, by means of his fiction of unwritten characters, can show the human creature both as suffering and as willfully endeavoring to impose his rationalization. This fiction-of-fictive-characters enables him to play over his catastrophes; and it was this resource which the realistic stage denied to Ibsen. When his Mrs. Alving, in *Ghosts*, suddenly sees Oswald's infatuation with Regina as a return of her husband's infatuation with Regina's mother, she gets the passionate but disinterested intuition which is the material of art, and is rewarded with the poetic vision that "we are *all* ghosts." But her final catastrophe —Oswald's collapse—strikes her for the first time only, and so remains, when the curtain falls, undigested and sensational. Pirandello's inspiration is to stop the action with Mrs. Alving's scream, and to play it over, in the actual light of the stage, the imagined lamp- and dawn-light of Mrs. Alving's parlor, and the metaphysical light of her, and our, need for some form and meaning.

Pirandello is at pains to explain, in his preface, that his play transcends not only modern realism, but also the various romantic genres with which some critics had confused it. The characters may be romantic, he says, but the play is not. The Daughter, for instance, when she takes the stage with her song, her deep feeling, and her abandoned charm, would like to seduce us into her own world of passion, as "the old magician Wagner" does in *Tristan*. But the scene is the stage itself, not her inner world; and her action meets perforce the actions of other characters who also claim the stage. Pirandello might also have said, with equal correctness, that his play transcends the Shavian irony, and at the same time realizes the farce of rationalizing with a depth and a consistency beyond that of Shaw. The Father, for instance, has a taste for the paradoxical platform, the unresolved ambiguity, and the logical consistency on the irrational premise, which reminds one strongly of Shaw. But he is present as a "real Character" first, and a rationalized platform second; hence we can believe in his sufferings as well as in his conceptualizing—and see both in a scene wider than either. The basis in reality of the Shavian farce appears, at last, to be in Shaw's own "gift" of abstract fitness and verbal agility; but Pirandello, in the stage itself and in our need not only to rationalize but to mythicize, has found a wider basis, on which many versions of human action may be shown together to the eye of contemplation.

There would be much to say of the extraordinary theatrical fertility of Pirandello's plot. The basic situation—the characters claiming the stage for their incommensurable tragic epiphanies, the actors claiming it for the marketable entertainment they are trying to make—has both comic and tragic aspects, and Pirandello exploits both, shifting from one to the other with perfect mastery. The situation, fictive though it admittedly is, has the firmness and clarity, once we have accepted it, of Racinian tragedy or Molièresque comedy. And just because it is so firm and unmistakable there is great freedom within it: it may be explored and developed with the apparent spontaneity of circus-clowning, the alertness and endless surprises of the *Commedia dell'Arte,* where the actors improvised a performance on the broad clear basis of the plots of Latin comedy. The scenes may break into confusion—into philosophical arias and disputes; into laughter; into violence—but we are never lost. The stage, and the need to take the stage, frame the action as a mirror might, which no amount of grimacing can destroy—or like the *ampulla* in which the sibyl hangs, wishing to die, in the epigraph to *The Wasteland*. It is the static quality of this basic situation which is both its triumph and its limitation; and in order to understand it more fully, one must also think of some of its limitations.

I have remarked that the play is always breaking down in disputes about the idea and the reality or, more generally, art and life. It is in these issueless disputes that the Pirandellesque brilliance most closely resembles the Shavian brilliance; and indeed the unresolvable paradox on which they are based is like the basis of the "free" Shavian irony. But Pirandello, unlike Shaw, transcends his paradoxes by accepting them as final—or rather (since he does not, like Shaw, see human action as rationalizing only, and the world as merely conceptualized) he accepts his paradoxes as various versions of a final split in human nature and destiny itself. In the same way Racine, accepting the split between reason and passion as final, thereby transcends it: i.e., transforms it into an object of contemplation. Pirandello's version of this tragic contradiction (after the endless explorations of modern realism and romanticism) is more general than Racine's, and his concept of art is (after modern idealism) deeper and wider than Racine's *raison,* which corresponds to it. Pirandello's utter darkness of unformed Life (or *élan vital,* or *Wille,* or libido) is perhaps even more savage and less human than Racine's passion. Pirandello is not limited, like Racine, to the rigid scene of the enlightened moral will; he can present characters of various degrees of heroism and enlightenment; and, as I have remarked, he can accept and exploit the comic as well as the tragic aspects of his basic contradiction. Nevertheless, his tragedy is a limited, an invented, an artificial tragedy, on the same principle as Racine's; and in the same way it offers to the eye of the mind the eternity of the perfect, and perfectly tragic artifact—the human damned in his realization—instead of the transcendence of the tragic rhythm, which eschews the final clarity and leaves the human both real and mysterious.

One may also understand the limitations of Pirandello's theater by thinking again of its relation to modern realism. I have said that he "inverts" the scene of modern realism, and thus vastly increases the suggestiveness and the possible scope of the stage itself. But of course he does not, by this device, provide the chaotic modern world with a "theater" of action in the ancient sense. One might justly say that his attitude is more "realistic"—more disillusioned and disbelieving—than simple-minded positivism itself, for he does not have to believe in the photograph of the parlor, and he can accept the actual stage for the two boards it is. But he is left, like Ibsen and Chekhov, with neither an artistic convention like the Baroque, nor a stable scene of human life like the Greek or Elizabethan cosmos; and, like Ibsen and Chekhov, he has only the plot as a means of defining his action. The inspiration of *Six Characters* is thus not only the view of action as theatrical but the plot-device whereby this vision may be realized: the brilliant notion of making his protagonists unwritten "characters" and setting them to invade a stage. This plot is so right, so perfect, that it almost exhausts, and certainly obscures, the deeper insights into life and the theater which it realizes. Hence the natural though unjustified tendency to think of the play as a brilliant plot idea, a piece of theatrical trickery only, and so miss its deep and serious content. The complete dependence of the play upon its plot-idea constitutes a limitation; but it points to the fundamental problem of the modern theater, which no individual can solve alone.

Pirandello was quite right to think of his characters as being like Dante's Francesca. They too are caught and confined in the timeless moment of realizing their individual nature and destiny, and so imprisoned, damned, as she is. This vision has great authority. It develops naturally out of several diverse versions of the modern theater which I have mentioned, those of Ibsen, Wagner, and Shaw. At the same time it is deeply rooted in the Italian temperament and natural theatricality; and it revives crucial elements in the great theater of the Baroque. It is close to the author's place and to his times, which we share; yet one must remember that it takes as all-inclusive, as the whole story of human nature and destiny, a mode of action and understanding which Dante thought of as maimed, and which he presented in the realm of those who have lost, not the intellect, but the good of the intellect; *il ben dello intelletto.*

The most fertile property of Pirandello's dramaturgy is his use of the stage itself. By so boldly accepting it for what it is, he freed it from the demand which modern realism had made of it, that it be a literal copy of scenes off-stage; and also from the exorbitant Wagnerian demand, that it be an absolutely obedient instrument of hypnosis in the power of the artist. Thus he brought to light once more the wonderful property which the stage does have: of defining the primitive and subtle medium of the dramatic art. "After Pirandello"—to take him symbolically rather than chronologically—the way was open for Yeats and Lorca, Cocteau and Eliot. The search could start once more for a modern poetry of the theater, and even perhaps for an idea of the theater comparable to that of the Greeks yet tenable in the modern world. . . .

Pirandello's Influence on French Drama

by Thomas Bishop

It is, perhaps, no mere coincidence that the man who is considered France's leading playwright today is also the playwright who reflects most clearly the influence of Pirandello. In its themes, its treatment, and its general atmosphere, the theater of Jean Anouilh is the most Pirandellian in France.

. . . Anouilh's characters, like Pirandello's, are engaged in the search for escape from life's sordidness, and they too usually choose irreality as the solution to their problems. Whereas Pirandello's plays resemble one another to the extent that they are sometimes thought of as variations on a theme, Anouilh's do not follow a master pattern. We therefore find Pirandello's influence on the French writer diffused and uneven, more pronounced in some plays and less in others. The division into *pièces noires, roses, brillantes,* and *grinçantes* underlines the varying moods in which they are written. Actually, the categories themselves are rather loose, and each one includes plays that differ radically from one another. Pirandello's influence transcends the four groups, but one must seek it in individual plays rather than in entire groups, for it is not present everywhere.

One of the Sicilian's themes recurring most markedly in the Frenchman's theater is multiplicity of personality. In the pattern of *Enrico IV, Siegfried,* and *Le Pêcheur d'ombres, Le Voyageur sans bagage* (1937) is the story of a man without a present, reaching the point of no return between his past and his future.

Amnesia is the convenient vehicle for creating this unusual situation wherein the multiplicity of a man's personality can be ideally studied, for, in his recovery, the hero, Gaston, reaches precisely that moment in his life when his past unfolds in direct opposition to his new self, revealing the painful dichotomy between the two aspects of his mind. Gaston is as different from the young Jacques who disappeared in the war as it is possible for two people to be—and yet they are the same person. By admitting that he is Jacques, Gaston would have to accept the horrid past that his former self had left behind—a past that is unbelievable in view of his gentle nature as a grown man. Therefore he reaches the difficult decision of renouncing his family and a part of himself in order to be true to himself as he now is.

Like Enrico IV, Gaston-Jacques has two totally distinct personalities, and in both cases the split occurred as a result of amnesia. Anouilh's basic conception of his hero is wholly Pirandellian. Yet Enrico becomes a tragic figure who is defeated, whereas Gaston sheds his past in a fairly satisfactory resolution of his conflict by accepting his new role as the little English boy's nephew. The character of Enrico brings up the question of insanity, and his difficulty lies in accepting the outside world. For Gaston, neither madness nor the outside world are problems. It is himself he cannot accept. "I had become used to myself," says Gaston, "I knew myself well, and suddenly here I am having to leave myself, to find another me, and to put him on like an old vest." He is, to use the Pirandellian frame of reference, a character in search of himself, a man longing for a past, yet having the most unusual liberty of being able to choose it. Anouilh expresses it with his characteristic irony:

> *Gaston.* It obviously frightened people that a man can live without a past. People are even wary of foundlings. . . . But a man, a fully grown man, who hardly had a country, no home town, no traditions, no name. . . . Blazes! What a scandal!

This liberty is precious to Gaston, and he is not willing to surrender it for the past of a man who had cheated, stolen, lied, crippled his best friend, and stolen his brother's wife. Valentine, like an Existentialist, tells him: "Listen, Jacques, after all, you must accept yourself. When you get right down to it, our whole life with our fine morality and our fine liberty consists of accepting ourselves as we are."

Valentine does not understand that liberty does not mean accepting what one was but what one is. For Gaston to accept what he is, he must, perforce, deny Jacques. He goes into the future without the burdensome baggage of his past in a supreme affirmation of his freedom, whereas Enrico's act of violence—it too a free act—shackles him forever in his world of fiction.

. . . In *Signora Morli, una e due,* Pirandello has confused a double personality with multiple facets of a single personality. *Colombe* (1951) is the treatment of a basically similar situation. Anouilh does not, however, commit the Italian's error; instead he leaves it to his hero, Julien, to think that there are two separate people called Colombe—the innocent, childlike girl he had married, and the worldly wise actress she becomes. "I forbid you . . ." he tells Colombe, referring to the wife he knew before his army service, "I forbid you to besmirch that one." He can explain the drastic change only by imagining a dual Colombe, when in fact, her life in Paris was merely the catalyst that enabled the carefree facet of her personality to emerge dominant.

Another phase of the personality puzzle is given in *La Sauvage* (1934) and *Antigone* (1942). Here reappears the mask motif—people (women, as is usual in Pirandello also) who appear to the world in two contradictory manners. For Thérèse, a mediocre violinist with a shady past and a sordid background, marriage to the kind and wealthy Florent offers the unique opportunity of escape from the baseness of life. Yet, despite her longing for respectability, she deliberately plunges back into the mire of her former existence. The mask will not adhere to the face that hides behind it, and when it is torn away, Thérèse's personality conflict is resolved through the victory of her baser self.

Antigone is similarly torn in two opposing directions—her instinctive love of life is contrasted with her unrelenting drive for justice, even though the latter necessarily involves her death and the destruction of her city. Like Ersilia Drei and like Thérèse, Antigone is bent on self-destruction, and in her case also, the mask of participation in life is not solid enough to ward off her basic nihilism. She epitomizes what Anouilh has succeeded in capturing so well in the heroines of his *pièces noires*—the tragic flaw. But the flaw is not a personality trait exploited by an impassionate fatality; it is inherent in the personality structure itself.

Pauvre Bitos (1956) presents an interesting variant of the multiplicity-of-personality theme. In it, a man is forced to assume a personality not his own, but one which is similar enough so that he glides easily from one to the other. André Bitos is a young public prosecutor with many enemies. His former schoolmates dislike him for the excellent grades he had received—Bitos, the poor, scholar-ship-supported student, who had spent all his time studying. Others hate him for his methodical, ruthless prosecution of collaborators after the liberation. To get revenge, Maxime arranges a *dîner de têtes*, a gathering at which the participants disguise their heads as those of historical characters.

Bitos is asked to portray Robespierre; others come as Danton, Mirabeau, and sundry figures of the Reign of Terror. The accusations leveled at Robespierre are all too obviously double-edged, and Bitos is forced to defend both himself and his historic counterpart. The climax of the evening is the reliving of the shooting of Robespierre by the policeman Merda. The gun used is not loaded, but Bitos faints and then dreams of himself as Robespierre. The remainder of the play is taken up with the efforts of the guests to placate Bitos, and with the latter's inability to differentiate between those who are hostile to him and those who have genuine sympathy for him.

Pauvre Bitos is perhaps Anouilh's most bitter play. Its cynicism is unrelenting and unrelieved. As a result, one is too overwhelmed by so much vitriol and the spectator cannot help but breathe more easily when the final curtain rings down. The multiple personality theme is, however, very cleverly used by Anouilh. Bitos' personality blends with Robespierre's until the two become one. Robespierre's faults and qualities are Bitos', their backgrounds the same, their careers similar; and when Bitos indulges in a fantasy in which he is Robespierre, it seems perfectly natural. The whole conception of Bitos is well within the Pirandellian picture of personality.

A considerable number of Anouilh's plays involve, in some way, the problem of the relativity of truth. Most often, this relativity is brought into play in a situation which concerns the preservation of people's private worlds—an idea with which Pirandello, like Ibsen before him, was preoccupied. But while the Norwegian's attitude showed social protest and the Italian's somber pessimism and outrage at man's stupidity, the Frenchman's work is permeated by sadness and by an irony, sometimes savage, that accompanies the conviction that happiness is, at best, very difficult to attain and that most human beings move in mutually exclusive spheres.

Both *Ardèle ou la Marguerite* (1949) and *La Valse des toréadors* (1952) deal with generals' households living in sham, and in both cases a private fiction is allowed to dominate outsiders, with damaging effects. Pirandello maintained in *Il Giuoco delle parti*, in *Liolà*, and in other plays, that a person is entitled to his private idea of himself as long as it does not hurt someone else. Anouilh provides us here with two cases in point.

The marriages in Ardèle's family are pretenses. Husbands and wives, lacking the courage to admit that they no longer love each other and concerned only with their mistresses and lovers, would rather pretend to the outside world that they are happily married couples. This, by itself, would not bring harm to anyone else, but they try to impose these artifices on Ardèle, the hunchbacked sister, who falls in love with the equally hunchbacked tutor. Confused and morally twisted itself, the family does not even recognize the importance of a true love, and, aware only that the tutor's social position makes a liaison with Ardèle unacceptable, it proceeds to break up the romance and drive the deformed couple to suicide.

The children in this play also suffer because of the examples of conjugal relationships set for them. When they play at being adults, they only fight and scream and beat each other. "You know perfectly well," the countess tells her husband, "that it is only a matter of respecting appearances, of not presenting a scandal for the world to see." But she does not realize that, in building a fence of fiction around the family group, unwilling members are included who, unable to escape, perish.

General Léon Saint-Pé of *La Valse des toréadors* is guilty of the same crime. The fiction of his marriage, enduring through his wife's illness and his seduction of countless girls, is preserved not so much for appearances as out of cowardice. Without realizing that he is destroying himself and those around him, Léon refuses to end his marriage because he wants to spare his wife. As a result, the patient Ghislaine, his true love, wastes seventeen years of her life, and *la Générale* has to endure his constant infidelities. Clearly, the proper solution would have been to cut cleanly and swiftly, to avoid ensnaring innocent people in the general's fiction.

La Répétition ou l'Amour puni (1950) is one further variation of the sham marriage motif. Into the heart of an aristocratic *ménage à quatre* comes Tigre's love for Lucile, the teacher he has hired for his orphanage. This is an intolerable situation for both his wife and his mistress, not because it involves their love but because it involves their dignity: Lucile is from a much lower station in life. Their solution, to destroy the couple, succeeds with the help of the villain, Héro—a villain of very unlikely motivation.

All these are people attempting to protect, at the expense of other people, the world they have created. Their moral position is untena-

ble, and they either fail completely or destroy themselves along
with the outsiders who become entangled in their web. *L'Amour
puni* is the subtitle of the last play, and it might well serve for all
three, for it emphasizes the stalemate which love suffers.

Structurally, *La Répétition* differs from the other two plays in a
way that is strongly reminiscent of Pirandello. Tigre and his friends
are rehearsing Marivaux's *La Double Inconstance,* and the dialogue
of the play-in-rehearsal blends in and becomes a part of the words
spoken by the characters themselves, just as the situation in the
eighteenth century play is an echo of what is transpiring at the
chateau. (The interplay is heightened by the *marivaudage* with
which Anouilh endows his dialogue.) This intimate relation between
a play being enacted and another, included in the first, being re-
hearsed, makes one think inevitably of *Sei personaggi.* Hortensia
says to Tigre, as the actors might tell the Father, "If it's a game you
are playing, it is not funny! You have just told us that we were not
ourselves. . . ."

Moreover, the characters are aware that their lives as people and
as actors overlap. "I have to disgust a little," Héro explains. "It's
part of my role. Not the one in Marivaux's play, but in the other
one—the one I really play." And later, Hortensia tells Villebosse,
who is anxious for rehearsal to start: "We're already acting. Hadn't
you noticed?" Life, these characters feel, as does Pirandello, is composed of roles that its participants play.

A little Pirandellian touch, too, is the dropping of the curtain at
the conclusion of Act II, as the group rehearses its curtain calls,
bringing to mind the accidental curtain in *Sei personaggi.* Of further
interest are Tigre's ideas as director for the presentation of the
Marivaux comedy. He conceives the play as a direct outgrowth of
life, which becomes animated in front of spectators, an idea very
reminiscent of *Questa sera si recita a soggetto.* "A character gets up
from the table and he calls on another, they begin to talk, people
listen to them and believe they actually have something to say to
each other. . . ." To prepare for this, an eighteenth century turn is
to be given to the conversation, and the transition is complete: *La
Double Inconstance* will emerge slowly, as a perfected illusion, out
of a twentieth century dinner party.

Y'avait un prisonnier came early in Anouilh's career (1935), but
it already anticipated the later themes. Ludovic, returning from fifteen years in prison, resists his family's attempt to ensnare him in
their world of business deceit, although they threaten to commit
him to an insane asylum unless he espouses it. His desperate dive

into the ocean to seek freedom is the symbol of every man's struggle for his own privacy and man's desperate rebellion against having to share others' secret illusions.

Illusions are needed, but they must remain personal. In prison, Ludovic was alone, craving companionship. He would think of a person and "I concentrated on the memory of him until, in some way, I created his invisible presence around me." Ludovic's wife tries to foster his illusions by becoming what he wants her to be:

> Finished, the ardent, strong, magnificent woman you know; perhaps he wants a frightened woman in love, coupled with a good little house-wife . . . ? From that point it was only a simple step to transform myself completely with my feminine flexibility. I took that step. Overnight . . . I became a different woman; . . . since it was not this personality which suited him, I wanted to try another one.

The concept of the changing personality is here, but not on the involuntary inner level, as in Pirandello or as displayed in *Maya*. Rather it is a deliberate and basically false desire to distort oneself willfully to conform to what others would like to see.

Weakness in plot and characterization reduce the effectiveness of this play, and the general impression is one of artifice not too skillfully contrived, but *Y'avait un prisonnier* contains the germs of the later Anouilh.

In *L'Invitation au château* (1947), we find the marked contrast between the profound reality of the person of Isabelle, who is actually a sham, and the falsity of the very real characters of the play. Truth, as it concerns the validity of their existences, is again proven to be relative.

Lastly, two Anouilh plays, both *pièces roses*—*Le Rendezvous de Senlis* (1937) and *Léocadia* (1939)—clearly illustrate the Pirandellian antithesis. Georges, the hero of the first-named play, belongs to the line of characters who create around themselves intricate fictions to compensate for unpleasant facts. To make up for the baseness of his parents and of his best friend, Robert, he creates new parents and a new Robert. This process takes place in his imagination at first. It is then extended to Isabelle, the girl with whom he has arranged the rendezvous in Senlis. Finally, it assumes reality through the physical presence of the "parents"—enacted by hired actors. That this use of players is only the last stage of the creative process is borne out by Georges' advice to the actors. "You must understand however that I did not send for you to have you imagine theatrical fathers or mothers at will. These characters exist. These characters are already half alive. Someone believes in them. . . ." These parents, in other words, came into existence when Georges conjured them up in his imagination, and they became alive when they were impersonated in Senlis. Even Robert recognizes this in saying "appearances are more than enough to create a world."

In this play, Anouilh also strays into another of Pirandello's themes—the art-life opposition. As the hired father and mother rehearse their roles with Georges, they are all carried away by their inventions until they believe that they are participating in reality. They are acting, but the play they are performing is more convincing than the life that gave rise to it. Thus does it happen that, unwittingly, Georges addresses the actors as if they were truly his parents and they in turn regard him as their son. Here too, in a small way, art has imposed itself upon life.

The final Anouilh work to be considered here is *Léocadia*. It is not one of the author's most effective plays, but it is worthy of attention because of its affinity to *Enrico IV*. As in the Italian drama, a man's mind becomes unbalanced by unhappiness in love—in this case, the death of his beloved—and a wealthy relative attempts to create for him a surrounding in which he can maintain the illusion that the past is not yet over. To foster the Prince's illusion that Léocadia is still alive, the Duchess re-creates on her grounds the places to which the young man had been with his love in the three days they knew each other before her death. But the Duchess then contrives a scheme to bring her nephew back to reality. She hires Amanda, a seamstress who bears a remarkable resemblance to Léocadia, to impersonate the dead beauty, hoping to shock him into the realization that Léocadia is no longer alive. The method used is exactly the same as in *Enrico IV*. The result, however, is different, for the Prince is not defeated. He comes to love Amanda and thereby succeeds in transcending the impasse of his passion for the deceased Léocadia.

If Anouilh's theater is thus found to be thoroughly imbued with Pirandello, it must not be assumed that his plays are copies of the latter's. Henri Clouard says that Anouilh "frenchifies Pirandello," but he adds, as many other critics have, the names of Gérard de Nerval, Giraudoux, and especially Musset as those whose influence is seen in Anouilh. Above all stands out his own creative genius. Anouilh is no imitator. His theater is original, but, of course, no playwright writes in a vacuum. If, first, Pirandello and, second, Musset are the two strongest influences on him, it is proof of Anouilh's originality that he has been able to weld such different antecedents into a new entity bearing his own individual stamp. Anouilh's great debt to Pirandello resides in the themes that he has adapted and in the Pirandellian flavor of much of his dialogue and atmosphere. His is "a sort of Pirandellian drama of a single character in search of himself, and it reiterates the familiar theme of escape from the ugliness of life."

The distinctive contribution of Anouilh is the light touch of the *pièces roses* and *pièces brillantes,* woven with strands of his peculiar irony, the more mordant humor of the *pièces grinçantes,* the characters so unreal yet alive because of their passions and their foibles. Out of these qualities is created the complex of the theater of Jean Anouilh, whose eminence among French dramatists has been achieved by a long series of thought-provoking, technically brilliant, and very actable plays.

*   *   *

As acknowledged leader of the Existentialist school, as editor of the influential *Les Temps modernes,* as a dramatist whose plays have stirred widespread discussion, Jean-Paul Sartre is the foremost theatrical figure of the postwar era. His skill in creating a theater out of philosophical attitudes was largely responsible for the vogue of Existentialism—a remarkable achievement, for it is indeed rare when a philosophic movement enjoys real popularity, and it marks the first time that the theater was the instrument of this popularity.

Sartre's merit lies in his ability to adapt his esoteric ideas to the requirements of the stage. This transfer necessitates simplification and a choice of theatrical illustrations: Sartre the philosopher has never hesitated to do the former and Sartre the playwright possesses the artistry required for the latter. As a result, his plays can be enjoyed by the uninitiated and by those opposed to his ideas. A pioneer in a virgin field, Sartre has set high standards for those in the future who would wish to propagandize a philosophy in the theater.

Sartre has left no doubt about what he considers to be Pirandello's influence in France. Recently asked who was the most timely modern dramatist, the author of *Le Diable et le Bon Dieu* answered "It is most certainly Pirandello." And, indeed, that Pirandello is very much up to date is borne out in Sartre's own theater.

For example, underlying his plays is an attack on all pretense in human behavior that tends to turn men away from the full acceptance of their responsibilities. This may be equated to Pirandello's concern with pretense as a danger when it harms others. The climaxes in Sartre's dramas occur as the main characters, breaking through the fictitious armor in which they have been clothed, face themselves and their acts in the stark glare of their liberty. In similar situations, the Sicilian's characters suffer the human anguish of self-confrontation; the Frenchman's feel the Existentialist anguish of full responsibility. In the mirror in which the former see their souls, the latter see the absurdity of life.

In *Les Mouches* (1943), the illusion of guilt is fostered on Argos by Aegisthus and Clytemnestra, with Jupiter the instrument of their deception. The God explains that he creates this enslavement-through-make-believe by hypnotism: "I have been dancing in front of men for a hundred thousand years. A slow and somber dance. They must look at me: as long as they have their eyes fixed on me, they forget to look within themselves. If I forgot myself for a single moment, if I let them turn away their eyes. . . ." It is Orestes' role to stop the dance and thereby shatter the illusion of culpability that has enthralled the citizens. By killing the royal couple, the hero takes upon his shoulders all the guilt and all the responsibility for past events. He lifts the collective mask of the populace and forces existence on them.

Inès performs the same function in *Huis clos* (1944). The only one of the play's unholy trio of characters to see clearly her own reality, she taunts the other two until all their illusions are unmasked. "Here we are stark naked," she says, referring to that same nakedness that is Ersilia Drei's and that of other Pirandellian characters agonizing in self-revelation. Inès possesses the keen insight and the sharp tongue required to make Gracin and Estelle see precisely what they are, what they have done, and how they have concealed their truths behind the pretense of respectability. "Hell is Other People," only because they are each other's conscience, the constant reminder of their sordid reality.

Inès, too, tears down the illusion that life is still possible in the infernal Second Empire drawing room. She makes clear that their visions of the earth are fading, that they have to stay together forever, and that the absurdity of their coexistence is complete because, being dead, they cannot even kill one another. The three have no choice but to accept the consequences of their lives, as Enrico IV had no choice but to accept his.

The illusions must be replaced by reality because they have hurt other people. This is the same criterion for behavior that Pirandello expressed consistently. "Certainly the characters in *No Exit* 'half lucid and half overcast' strip themselves naked and wallow in their anguish much as Pirandello's six characters." Garcin and the Father of *Sei personaggi* express the same objection to being judged on the basis of one isolated act. The Father feels that the Step-Daughter had caught him in a brief, unrepresentative moment of his existence and was trying to attach his entire reality to that moment. Garcin, for his part, asks "Can one judge a life on a single act?" and Inès replies tersely "Why not." Likewise, in *Morts sans sépulture*, Canoris states: "It is on our whole life that each one of your acts will be judged." In Garcin's case, however, that one act is not truly isolated; Inès proves it to be part of his general pattern. Cowardice is his reality and heroism merely the illusion he had created for himself. Because his wife had suffered from this illusion, Garcin is guilty and is relegated to the hell of Inès' probings.

"The anguished situation, the climate of torment in *Six Characters* is common to all of Sartre's plays and within it Sartre's heroes attempt to realize themselves like Pirandello's partially constructed characters. . . ." *Morts sans sépulture* (1946) points this out also. The Resistance fighters of the play are placed by Sartre in a situation of extreme stress and torture, wherein they see clearly into their own selves. It is a terrible moment of truth for them. Some come face to face with the image of their cowardice for the first time; others discover that their heroism is tainted by dubious motives. Even those whose valor remains unchallenged find themselves drained of true human emotions, their bond to mankind severed by their singular bravery, which sets them above all others. They represent the epitome of suffering as conceived by Pirandello.

The mirror and the face behind the mask shift to the domain of politics in the masterful denunciation of the degrading sophistry of Communist ideology—*Les Mains sales* (1948). The reality that is revealed to Hugo does not concern his self; it concerns the truth about the Party. Hoederer's death is the catalyst. Upon his release from prison, Hugo learns that the man he had killed at the Party's orders has been "rehabilitated" posthumously. His act of murdering a man he respected emerges futile and absurd and the Party a ruthless tyrant with no use for idealism. Nurtured on the illusions of Communist justice, Hugo suffers as much in his disenchantment as Pirandello's most moving characters. His *raison d'être* has been destroyed and he goes willingly to his death.

Le Diable et le Bon Dieu (1951) is the example of the shattering of metaphysical illusion. What Goetz attempts to do in this epic of atheism is to rid the world of its illusion of God and force men to behold themselves in all their liberty. It is still basically the same theme of Existential man emerging from behind pretense to assume his responsibility and freedom.

By 1955, *Nekrassov* proved that Sartre had lived to regret *Les Mains sales*. His change of allegiance to the totalitarianism he had condemned and his recent public repudiation of the Soviet Union would indicate that the author frequently shares his characters' inability to differentiate between fact and fiction. Perhaps his by now frequent reversals would not prove so embarrassing if he did not mark each stage of his vacillation with a play that lasts longer than his latest attitude.

While *Les Mains sales* was a serious, dramatically effective demonstration of the bankruptcy of Communist methods, *Nekrassov* is a farcical attack on anti-Communists, naïve in its conception and puerile in its argument. Again the device of illusion is used—a newspaperman's scheme to boost circulation by "creating" a Soviet minister who has escaped and is selling his memoirs. It is a gigantic hoax that he tries to impose on his readers for the sake of his job, notwithstanding the international discord that can arise out of the deception.

Sartre shares two elements with Pirandello: the absurdity both men discern in life and the frequent repetition of the illusion-reality theme. The French writer has, however, penetrated to attitudes underlying the dichotomy and charged it with the implications of Existential thought. Sartre's high opinion of Pirandello, placing him at the head of modern authors, is explained by the similarities in their works—similarities which are actually far greater than a superficial glance would suggest.

In the last few years Albert Camus has replaced Sartre as the most discussed and most highly regarded French author. If his theater remains too abstract and lacks Sartre's dramatic flair, his novels, or *récits* as he prefers to call them, and his long essay, *L'Homme révolté*, have demonstrated his remarkable gifts. After a period of adhering to Existentialist thought of a more or less orthodox nature, Camus veered away from it somewhat toward a broader humanism. Always aware of the utter absurdity of man's existence in this world, he is not content to accept this absurdity—his answer is revolt. This revolt is the solidifying bond of mankind, the simple "no" that expresses the refusal to accept the unreasoning tyranny of fate. The positive values that emerge out of unblinking recognition of man's situation are Camus' specific contribution to contemporary literature.

The absurd is the bond between Pirandello and Camus. As is the case with Sartre, Camus understands the absurd in clearer and more conceptual terms than does Pirandello. Human values are implicit in Camus' theater, and perhaps because these values are never explicit, it remains too impersonal, too systematic, and too abstract. These factors certainly have been responsible for denying his theater the unqualified success of his other works.

Caligula (1945) is probably Camus' best endeavor in the dramatic medium. The Roman Emperor, who concludes that only arbitrary action can overcome the absurdity of existence, is a pathetic figure of defeat as he realizes finally that his liberty of peremptory terror was delusion because it was gained at other people's expense. Francis Jeanson compares this play to *Enrico IV* because both heroes are alike in their isolation despite their omnipotence in their own realms.

One will agree that from *Henry IV* (1922) to *Caligula* (1945), the essential preoccupations and themes did not become basically different. It is very much the same denunciation of this world which is not what it ought to be; the same disdain for those who get along with it; the same feeling of solidity; the same pessimism; the same recourse to the choice of the absurd against the very absurdity of existence; the same frenzy of denying and destroying, of pulling the world out from under the feet of those who have them firmly planted on it.

This statement points out very correctly the similarities between these plays. One must add, however, that the problem of responsibility, which is basic to *Caligula,* does not figure in *Enrico IV*.

One conversation between Caligula and his friend, Chéréa, is notable for its Pirandellian character:

> *Caligula.* Chéréa, do you think that two men whose souls and whose pride are equally great can, at least once in their lives, speak to each other absolutely frankly—as if they were naked, face to face, stripped of the prejudices, of the personal interests, of the lies by which they live?
>
> *Chéréa.* I think that it is possible, Caïus. But I believe you are incapable of it.
>
> *Caligula.* You are right. I only wanted to know if you thought as I do. Let us cover our faces with masks, therefore. Let us use our lies. Let us speak to each other the way people fight, covered up to the hilt. Chéréa, why don't you like me?
>
> *Chéréa.* Because I understand you too well and because one cannot like that face which one tries to mask in oneself.

The references to masks concealing the reality of a person, to
Chéréa's several faces, to the pretense in the relations between people, are very reminiscent of the Italian dramatist. Whether they
stem from Camus' knowledge of Pirandello cannot be determined,
but they are certainly attributable to him indirectly, for these ideas
had, by 1945, become thoroughly naturalized in the French theater.

If, as we have attempted to show in the preceding pages, there is
a bond between the absurdity that Pirandello portrays in personal
terms and the one that the Existentialists visualize as an impersonal
metaphysical reality, there is definitely a bond between the former
and Samuel Beckett's *Weltanschauung.* The depiction of absurdity
as the dominant aspect of life in *En Attendant Godot* is so devastating and heart-rending because it is seen, as Pirandello saw it, in a
profoundly human light, tempered with compassion for the victims
caught in its web.

Vladimir and Estragon symbolize mankind. Their pathetic efforts
to distract each other in their never-ending wait for salvation are an
attempt to create the illusion that they really exist, while actually
they are merely dangling helplessly at the end of the perfidious rope
of life. The great merits of the play are the ultimate *reductio ad
absurdum* of the human condition and, despite the prevalent non-
sensical atmosphere, its deeply moving quality on the individual
level. In this respect, Beckett has contributed something new to the
stage. *Fin de partie* (1957) continues in the same vein, but it is even
blacker in mood, less humorous, less humanistic in conception.

Pirandello had elicited compassion in his plays, but he did not
aim at a generalized philosophy of absurdity; the Existentialists
dramatized the absurdity of man's existence in this world without
ever feeling pity for that trapped humanity; Beckett achieves the
synthesis of both. His universal truth prevents him neither from
sympathizing with mankind nor from participating in its fate. This
reverting to the humanistic tradition is of primary importance in
this postwar French theater, which tends too much to the abstract.
It may explain Jean Anouilh's great enthusiasm at the opening of
En Attendant Godot: "I think that the evening at the Babylone
[Theater] is as important as the first Pirandello produced by Pitoëff
in Paris in 1923."

Arthur Adamov, whose reputation has been made in experimental
theaters since 1950, reduces absurdity to the everyday life of or-

dinary people. His universe is often akin to the world of George Or-
well's *1984*—a world in which the citizen is helpless against forces
which victimize him for no purpose and in a haphazard way. Adamov depicts the anguish and the senseless terror of the police-state
age. His pessimism is so overwhelming that he envisages life for the
individual as only an illusion of reason until total absurdity an-
nihilates it.

This horror of the modern totalitarian state is dramatized in
Tous contre tous (1952) and *La grande et la petite manœuvre* (1950).
Le Mutilé, the principal character—for one cannot speak of "heroes"
in Adamov's works—of the latter play, is deprived of all his limbs,
one by one, in a senseless persecution by the authorities. Still he
maintains the illusion that life holds happiness for him because a
woman, Erna, loves him. The reality of the chaos of existence becomes clear for him only at the end as Erna, in an act fully as gratu-
itous as the quadruple amputation, vilifies him and pushes him out
onto the street on his caster—a pathetic stump of flesh facing certain
death. He brings to mind Kafka's Joseph K., who was also destroyed
by an impassive fate without ever understanding why.

Although he does not use devices that tend to bring the audience "into" the play, Adamov attempts to make the play transcend
the limitations of the stage in order to confront the spectators directly. He achieves this effect by means of what one might call an
ultrarealistic technique—that is, not the faithful reproduction of
realism, nor the emphasis on sordidness of modern neo-realism, nor
again the suggestion of a superior reality of surrealism, but a fusion
of all three, in which the complete naturalness of the dialogue (to
the exclusion of all theatricality), together with the sharp, brutal
outline of authority, infers the ultimate absurdity.

Because the language seems spontaneous and because both the
situations and the terror are products of a society that is no longer
fictitious but is already developing, the audience can identify with
the action without an undue effort of the imagination. As a result,
the stage itself becomes more than the traditional boards, curtain,
scenery, etc.; it becomes the willing accomplice of the dramatist, in-
asmuch as the play is projected *by means of* the stage rather than
on the stage and is thus given life. Insofar as this is possible in a
medium which, despite all efforts, is still artificial, Adamov succeeds,
obtaining an additional, convincing dimension out of his stage. "The
precursors whom Adamov admits besides [Antonin] Artaud . . . are
all playwrights who grasped and gave material expression to the

idea of the theater as an autonomous art inseparable from the physical space of the stage: Kleist, . . . Büchner, Strindberg, and Pirandello."

In two plays mentioned above, Pirandello's influence is restricted
to the concept that the life we live is mere illusion and to the heritage of absurdity. It is more widespread in other works. *L'Invasion*
(1950) stresses the relative nature of truth in a world wherein absolute truth is impossible to attain. The title refers to an unfinished
manuscript which intrudes into the life of the family and friends of
its deceased author. The laborious struggle of these people to de-
cipher the handwriting and clarify the work ends in a dismal stalemate, for, in addition to disagreeing among themselves, they indi-
vidually find different interpretations for each word until no one is
certain of the real meaning. The chief would-be editor finally tears
up the manuscript and dies, an apparent suicide. The symbol of the
enigmatic opus, whose meaning is impervious to comprehension, is
akin to Signora Frola's veil, emphasizing the impossibility of deter-
mining the truth.

La Parodie (1952) suggests again that life is lived in an illusion,
with reality hidden and far removed. The motions of the characters
in the play are, like our own motions, only a parody of existence
itself. Lastly, *Le Professeur Taranne* (1953), concerns a Pirandellian
type of self-confrontation. The university scholar of the title is incapable of living up to his reputation, and as he grows aware of the
gap between his true self and the person he is thought to be, he resorts to plagiarizing the ideas of his colleague Ménard. But Taranne
cannot endure his own deception any more than he could endure
mediocrity. Subconsciously craving to be exposed, he carries to an
extreme the act of stripping himself of all deceit; he is caught walk-
ing the streets stark naked. He thus shows his true self without the
illusions imposed by the plagiary. Ironically, people mistake Taranne for Ménard when he tries to identify himself. The illusion has
even conquered others.

It is evident that Pirandello's ideas infiltrate these five plays in
varying degrees. While Adamov added his personal qualities, he remained very true to the Italian's concepts. His theater is compelling
and almost frighteningly modern in its emphasis on the suppression
of the individual and on the impossibility of communication between people. The absurdity of contemporary life, seen in abstract
terms in Beckett's plays, is very concretely pictured in the theater
of Arthur Adamov.

Eugène Ionesco represents, together with Adamov and Beckett, the successful new voice in the French theater.[1] His plays place him with the writers of the absurd, but the world of Ionesco lacks the brutality of Adamov or the total despair of Beckett. He does share with the latter one quality, rare indeed among innovators today— humor. Much of his work is filled with jokes, puns, amusing nonsense, and apparently meaningless sentences that are often uproarious.

His first play, *La Cantatrice chauve* (1950), seems to have the same basic goal as Adamov's *La Parodie*. Like his elder colleague, Ionesco calls attention to the mechanical ritual of living, which creates the illusion of life but which, in fact, is only a parody of it. His subject is that often satirized English society of proverbial reserve, lack of humor, vapid social banter, and sentimentality. Despite the absurdity of the dialogue and the situations, *La Cantatrice chauve* is really a hilarious play, proving that social criticism can be amusing.

In *Les Chaises* (1952) and *Amédée ou Comment s'en débarasser* (1952), Ionesco deals with the married couple. Of these two, the first play moves on a real and on an illusory level. Amédée and his wife Madeleine find a dead man in their apartment. While this corpse, symbolic of the love that they have killed in each other, grows constantly, taking up more and more room in their apartment, until it becomes gigantic, the couple continues to behave in an entirely normal way as if the situation were completely natural. In other words, the illusion of the enlarging body becomes a part of their everyday reality.

Les Chaises projects the interior existence of a very old couple onto a semicircular stage, which soon fills with chairs. These chairs are occupied by imaginary guests, including the Emperor, entertained by the old man and woman. Whereas the illusion in *Amédée* is materialized as a corpse, in *Les Chaises* it is left an illusion: the increasing number of imaginary people are reflected only by the ever larger number of chairs that clutter the stage. Besides this Pirandellian illusion theme, Ionesco suggests also the multiplicity of the old woman's personality. Suddenly, she becomes grotesque and vulgar, and the stage direction demands "a style of acting completely different from the one she has used up to now and from the one she is to use afterwards, and which is meant to reveal a hidden personality in the old woman." This is her erotic self coming to the fore.

[1] It is interesting to note that all three men stem from countries other than France. Ionesco was born in Rumania, Beckett in Ireland, Adamov in Russia.

Ionesco, like Beckett and Adamov, attempts to use the theater for new, essentially dramatic expression. These three authors and other *avant-garde* playwrights like Neveux, Genet, and Vauthier approach the play primarily as a function of the theater. Therefore, they investigate every avenue of theatricality and invention that might extend the limits of the stage. In Pirandello they found a logical precursor who had tried the same thing. Ionesco explains that "Luigi Pirandello's theater does, in fact, meet the ideal exigencies of the structure, of the dynamic architecture of the drama. He is the manifestation of the inalterable archetype of the idea of the theater which we have in us. . . ." [2]

Brief mention should be made of *L'Autre Alexandre* (1957), a play essentially in the experimental tradition, by Marguerite Libéraki, who has not yet reached prominence as a playwright. She, too, delves into personality structure and does so by the novel process of creating a set of illegitimate brothers and sisters to match, down to the very names, a set of legitimate half-siblings. The effect is like a mirror placed in front of this family: the reflections are at once so similar and so different that they appear to be reality and the reflections of a single set of characters.

Although his theater is best classified as *avant-garde,* Georges Neveux is neither a young nor a recently discovered author. His *Juliette ou la Clé des songes* was written in 1927 and won him considerable renown at the time of its production in 1930. *Ma Chance et ma chanson,* his next play, did not follow until 1940, and since then he has written regularly for the stage.

The experimental element of Neveux's works is the technique: the dramatization of a heavily symbolic dream; the encounter with the dead, the living, and the unborn; the face-to-face meeting of a man and his self; the experiencing of an action before it takes place. The content of his theater is, however, surprisingly traditional. His subjects are fate and the human experiences of life and death. Neveux is not a philosophical playwright, and one need not seek a system of thought or a portrayal of the absurd in his dramas. Germaine Brée points out that the "bitter existential revolt against man's 'absurd' condition is completely alien to him. In *Plainte contre inconnu* [1946] he reverses the basic existentialist theme, pointing to the 'ab-

---

[2] Eugène Ionesco, quoted in "Pirandello vous a-t-il influencé?" *Arts,* No. 602 (Jan. 16-22, 1957), 2.

surd' human refusal to accept life, all of life, as it is given." [3] This emphasis on life's positive values is in welcome opposition to the gloom of most of Neveux's fellow *avant-gardistes.*

. . . Neveux assigned to *Sei personaggi* an enormous influence in the history of the modern French theater. Recently, on the occasion of the twentieth anniversary of Pirandello's death, a French periodical asked several French playwrights if they had been influenced by Pirandello. Georges Neveux's answer explains not only what he himself, but also what an entire generation of French dramatists, found in Pirandello:

> Pirandello is, first of all, the greatest prestidigitator of the Twentieth Century, the Houdini of interior life. In his most important play, *Six Characters,* he took the very center of the real world and turned it inside out right in front of us, as the fisherman turns inside out the skin of an octopus to lay bare its viscera.
>
> But what Pirandello laid bare before us is not only the work of the actors, nor that of the author, not only the other side of the scenery, but something much more universal: *the other side of ourselves.*
>
> It is our inner life which is suddenly found projected on the stage and decomposed there as if by a prism.
>
> What are these fantoms, condemned to relive endlessly the same scene (all of a sudden one thinks of *Huis clos*) if not the most obscure part of ourselves? These six characters are not only the unfinished creatures of an author at a creative impasse, but also, and more important still, those impulses which each of us keeps within him and does not manage to live out.[4]

This sudden confrontation with one's inner self and these hidden desires are the Pirandellian elements in Neveux's theater. His Pirandellism is always on the human level; he is not concerned with the artist's dilemma.

In *Le Voyage de Thésée* (1943), the Minotaur that Theseus finds in the labyrinth of Cnossus looks like Theseus himself; it is, in fact, an aspect—the happy side—of the young Athenian's personality which suddenly confronts him. The secret of the Minotaur's deadly power over the many youths sent yearly to slay it was its ability to appear as the hidden self of each of its victims, which paralyzed them

[3] Germaine Brée, "Georges Neveux: A Theatre of Adventure," *Yale French Studies,* XIV (Winter 1954-55), 67.

[4] Statement by Georges Neveux in "Pirandello vous a-t-il influencé?" *Arts,* No. 602, *loc. cit.*

in the agony of this encounter. Theseus alone has the strength to
look at himself honestly, to reject, by tearing the thread linking him
to his bride, that Theseus who longs for happiness, and to accept his
fate by recognizing it in the labyrinth of this existence. The Pirandellian mirror in *Le Voyage de Thésée* is the Minotaur.

Self-confrontation is achieved in a more conventional manner in
Plainte contre inconnu (1946). The six plaintiffs against God or the
Unknown—who appear in the prosecutor's office as gratuitously as
do Pirandello's six characters on the stage, and who, like them, demand to register their protest against the injustices done to them—
are dissuaded from their planned suicide by being afforded a long
look at themselves. This is made possible indirectly by the prosecutor. Having attempted and failed to change the determination of the
sextet bent on self-destruction with the customary reasons in favor
of life, the public servant unwittingly offers them hope. He points
out what a perfectly happy man he is, shielded from any conceivable
annoyance or misfortune. In so doing, he lays bare the empty existence of a man whose impervious armor shelters nothing within him.
Upon seeing what a "happy" man looks like, the six reconsider their
decision. Each of them searches deeply within himself and realizes
that life is worth being lived: they all choose to resume their lives.
The image of his own hollowness is not lost on the poor prosecutor
either, and it is he who finally shoots himself.

Additional Pirandellian elements can be observed in Neveux's
other plays. Although the employee of the dream bureau in *Juliette
ou la Clé des songes* makes it clear that dreams and reality must remain in mutually exclusive worlds for a sane man, Neveux nevertheless punctuates the attraction existing between them. For Michel, the
illusory realm of Juliette has far greater appeal than the life in which
Juliette escaped him. He is reluctant to abandon his travels through
the symbolist maze for the less enchanting, if truer, light of the everyday world.

In *Ma Chance et ma chanson,* the dead materialize on the scene
when they are needed with the same sort of improvised magic that
brings forth Madama Pace in *Sei personaggi*. Lastly, one element of
Zamore (1953) also evokes the Italian play. With the help of *la fièvre
de tout à l'heure* ("the in-a-little-while-fever"), a condition that enables one to see the near future, the Police Commissioner tells Zamore that he will be killed by Charles Auguste, his wife's lover.
From that point on, try as they will to escape their fate, the curious
ménage à trois plunge relentlessly forward in their destined roles
with as little real hope of avoiding the culminating shot as there is

for the six characters. The three are, in fact, like characters falling in spite of themselves into the trap an author has set for them.

Neveux's use of Pirandellian techniques and motifs is a good example of how modern playwrights—even of the *avant-garde*—benefited from Pirandello. He is certainly not an imitator, and none of his plays is overwhelmingly in the Italian's tradition; but Neveux's theater as a whole incorporates much of what is best in Pirandello.

Jean Genet's *Les Bonnes* (1946) dramatizes a double transfer of personality. The sisters Claire and Solange, Madame's maids, engage in frequent excursions into other personalities, with one "playing" their employer, the other taking her sister's role. On the day of the action, it is Claire who, as Madame, heaps abuse on Solange, whom she calls Claire. What had started as a game for the sisters has become starkly real. With the "imitation Madame" wearing the clothes and assuming the manner of speaking of the actual Madame, the two lash one another with their tongues and verbalize their resentment against their mistress. Their occasional lapses, when they call each other by their true rather than their assumed names, stress only more strongly how fully immersed they are in their adopted identities. Having prepared a poisoned tea for the real Madame without succeeding in getting her to drink it, Claire, completely consumed by her impersonation, drinks the fatal brew.

By accepting Madame's death, Claire fuses into Madame's personality. This alter ego—only an illusion at first—is complete reality at the end. Genet's view of disintegrating personality is directly in the Pirandellian line, with the emphasis on the imagined aspect of multiplicity rather than on the innate one.

*   *   *

Pirandello has been applauded enthusiastically in France since the initial performances of *La Volupté de l'honneur* and *Six Personnages en quête d'auteur*, and his techniques and propositions have been mirrored with equal enthusiasm by many French playwrights. French plays depicting the relativity of truth, the multiplicity of personality, the art-life opposition, and the overwhelming absurdity of life have become familiar on the Parisian stage during the past three and one half decades. The striking modernity of his approach appealed to many French dramatists, and the lessons Pirandello taught them were taken seriously. His influence reached a considerable segment of dramatic authors both great and secondary. It was with only slight exaggeration that Georges Neveux said:

Without Pirandello and without the Pitoëffs (because one can no
longer separate them, the genius of the Pitoëffs having given its form
to Pirandello's) we would have had neither Salacrou, nor Anouilh, nor
today Ionesco, nor . . . [sic] but I shall stop, this enumeration would
be endless. The entire theatre of an era came out of the womb of that
play, *Six Characters.*[5]

A great part of the French theater of our era was, in fact, influenced in one way or another by Pirandello, or showed certain similarities to his. Some playwrights, like Anouilh, are Pirandellian in a
major group of their plays; others, like Cocteau, only in one or two
plays. While many were directly influenced, others found that their
ideas were in accord with his, and still others—especially some of
today's younger dramatists—have felt the impact indirectly through
their seniors, who had already made Pirandellism a part of the
French theater. Pirandello is "French" now not only because his
plays have been produced regularly in Paris for the past thirty-seven
years, but also because his ideas and methods were made essential
elements of French dramatic expression during this period. The Sicilian is still a potent force in the contemporary scene. Until, and
unless, the French theater revolts completely and rejects all that has
been done in the past thirty-seven years, Pirandello will remain one
of its leading figures.

It is rare for a dramatist to wield a truly extensive international
influence. Besides Pirandello, only Shakespeare and Ibsen have left
such a legacy, and it is unlikely that either has affected the theater
of a single country of any one era more than the author of *Sei personaggi*. Of all the various forces that combined to mold the theatrical imagination of the French writers of our age, none was more
widespread, none more penetrating, and none more productive than
his.

The essence of Pirandello's theater is the marrow of contemporary
ideas, of modern anxieties and pessimism. This is what the French
writers admired in him. Elements of Pirandellism can be detected in
the works of other European playwrights: László Krakatos, Kurt
Goetz, Miguel de Unamuno—in whose case similarities are seen
rather than influence. In this country, Pirandellian concepts might
be found illustrated in the plays of Thornton Wilder, Elmer Rice,
and Arthur Miller. But these are all isolated cases and indicate no
concentrated influence by Pirandello on a country's theater. Even in
Italy, where one might expect to find an important school of drama-

---

[5] *Arts,* No. 602, *loc. cit.*

tists influenced by the master, only a relatively few well-known authors reflect Pirandello's contribution. One might mention Gherardo Gherardi, Ugo Betti, Eduardo de Filippo, Diego Fabbri, and Cesare Viola, but they are in no way disciples.

It was France which was most receptive to Pirandello and which adopted him as its own. The Italian, who had been most responsible for liberating his country's drama from simple imitations of French models, turned the tables by giving France bold new ideas and daring techniques. Pirandello's great role in France is an outstanding example of international theater, a challenging study in comparative literature.

Cubist Drama

by *Wylie Sypher*

When Luigi Pirandello wrote *Six Characters in Search of an Author* in 1921, he called it a "comedy in the making." It is a very highbrow study of oscillation of appearances in the theatre. Just as the cubist broke up the object into various planes, or as photomontage gave its own sort of polyphonic vision by means of combined shorts, so Pirandello offers a compound image in drama. He surrenders the literary subject while the cubist is surrending the anecdote, and treats this theatre as a plane intersecting art and life, explaining in his prefatory note that "the whole complex of theatrical elements, characters and actors, author and actor-manager or director, dramatic critics and spectators (external or involved) present every possible conflict." He is concerned with the collision between art and actuality, the theatrical crisis where the imitation of life and life itself appear as a passage between events on the stage and events in our existence. His play is a research into the plural aspects of identity, and he concludes that there are many possible levels of reality at which things can happen. He has penetrated the old theatrical plot by thought, much as the cubist penetrated objects, and having conceived his problem as an encounter of art with life, he has discovered a "way to resolve it by means of a new perspective"—a perspective like a flat-pattern cubist illusion.

In *Six Characters* the action (which is not a "play" at all) improvises upon certain dramatic situations as being reality and upon certain events in life as being art. While a company of actors is rehearsing a play—by Pirandello himself, for the planes of reality begin to shift at once—six members of a family (father, mother, legitimate *and* illegitimate children) enter the bare stage and ask to be allowed to act out (or "realize") the drama of their lives; for an author has conceived them but not written them into any script. Theirs is a history of a broken home caused by the mother's infidelity. Against the manager's inclination, against the inclination of the actors, the six characters try to represent their sad lives in acted form, which at once brings the difficulty that they cannot interpret for the professionals the meaning of the plot they have lived and are attempting to realize. "The drama," explains the Father, "is in us, and we are the drama." In other words, theatre breaks down. The effort of the characters to represent themselves on the stage is finally blocked when one of the six, the unhappy Boy, in a fit of despair, shoots himself. Some of the professional actors take this to be an artistic climax; but it is a genuine suicide. The Father shouts "Pretence? Reality, sir, reality!" By this time the director does not care: "Pretence? Reality? To hell with it all. . . . I've lost a whole day over these people, a whole day!" The ambiguity of the illusion is emphasized when at the close of the second "act" a stage hand drops the curtain by mistake, leaving the Father and the director in front of it, before the footlights, isolated from both audience and the "characters" and other actors. The end of the first act comes when the director, to gather his wits, calls off rehearsal—which is not rehearsal at all, but an equivocal passage from life that is being translated into art by characters who wish to express their life in dramatic form.

By refusing the momentum of plot Pirandello is left with the formal art-problem of writing a drama about the writing of a drama, a final purification of the nineteenth century problem of treating life as art, or taking the art-view of life. Like the cubist painting about the painting of a painting, Pirandello's play is a sort of *tableau-tableau* showing the relation between actuality and its representation. The cubists used the textures of actuality in the form of collage to bring their art-structure into proper focus; and they used it impromptu. Sometimes they quoted a few legible details of objects in a frankly photographic way so that the clichés of painting could be better contrasted with the fictions of flat-pattern perspective. In thus avoiding the tyranny of the literary subject they discovered what Piet Mondrian a little later emphasized, that "the expression of reality cannot be the same as reality." Into his formal study of the writing of a drama Pirandello has deliberately inserted a good many theatrical clichés as a sort of collage: the professional actors, whose vocation is like that of the traditional model or lay figure used by painters, rely on all the customary mechanisms of the stage; and the director takes the attitude of the commercial theatre toward doing a play. He fails entirely to mediate between the professional troupe who are rehearsing a Pirandello script and the six displaced characters who have blundered into the commercial theatre from reality.

These six belong to life yet at the same time they do not belong to it; they are like the things Picasso "assassinated" in the interest of total representation. Their impromptu appearance on the "legitimate" stage is a double exposure of reality and illusion. There is also the bona fide audience (which may or may not represent actual life). All these levels of representation are held together in a simultaneous perspective of transparent dramatic planes to be read in many directions at the same time. The final test, of course, is whether the events of life are susceptible of being interpreted by drama anyhow, or whether the experience of the six characters can be realized until they appear in some artistic composition. The Boy's suicide is a shocking collage. We cannot say that these persons exist off the stage; and we cannot say they live on the stage. Above all, what is the stage? Hamlet had already raised Pirandello's questions about drama's being a mere dream of passion. The six characters, the director, the actors rehearsing Pirandello come into every sort of encounter. If the six exist at all, they do so in some state of emergence. When they enter, "a tenuous light surrounds them, almost as if irradiated by them—the faint breath of their fantastic reality." This is their cubist iridescence of form.

The instant the six appear, the planes of representation are displaced. The Father tries to state their situation: "The drama consists finally in this: when that mother re-enters my house, her family born outside of it, and shall we say *superimposed* on the original, ends with the death of the little girl, the tragedy of the boy, and the flight of the elder daughter. It cannot go on, because it is foreign to its surroundings. So after much torment, we three remain: I, the mother, that son." But the Son stands in the background refusing to be identified with the rest of the six, commenting upon the whole enterprise as being merely "Literature." In vain the Father protests, "Literature indeed! This is life, this is passion." Yet the Son will not take his part in any theatrical representation; nor does he belong to life either. "Mr. Manager," he insists, "I am an 'unrealized' character, dramatically speaking; and I find myself not at all at ease in their company. Leave me out of it, I beg you." There he is, a figure to be fitted into the composition against his will, adding a further difficult dimension as if he had broken loose from the terms of the problem as Pirandello posed it. We cannot even place him as collage.

For the Father the drama lies in taking a point of view on events —a prehension, Whitehead would call it. He argues, "For the drama lies all in this—in the conscience that I have, that each one of us has. We believe this conscience to be a single thing, but it is many-sided. There is one for this person, and another for that. Diverse consciences. So we have this illusion of being one person for all, of having a personality that is unique in all our acts. But it isn't true. We see this when, tragically perhaps, in something we do we are, as it were, suspended, caught up in the air on a kind of hook." This is the cubist suspension of the object. When the Father sees the professional actors trying to play his "role," speaking his "part" in the clichés of their art, he exclaims, getting more and more confused, "I don't know what to say to you. Already I begin to hear my own words ring false, as if they had another sound."

Pirandello invites us to examine the texture of his drama exactly as the cubist invites us to examine the contrasting textures in his painting, the very invitation raising doubt about holding the mirror up to nature. The most "natural" scene in the rehearsal comes when two of the characters, Madame Pace and the Step-Daughter, begin to speak so quietly and casually that the actors—who are trying to learn the "parts"—object it's impossible to play the scene that way. The director agrees: "Acting is our business here. Truth up to a certain point, but no farther." Pirandello thus parodies Cézanne's approach to art: "I have not tried to reproduce nature," Cézanne said: "I have represented it." The manager wishes a single, simple illusion of reality. The Father points out that any such illusion makes drama only "a kind of game." Naturally the actors think it no game: "We are serious actors," they protest; they are artists. In desperation the Father then asks, "I should like to request you to abandon this game of art which you are accustomed to play here with your actors, and to ask you seriously once again: who are you?" The director, badly upset by this remark, resents having his identity questioned by a mere dramatic character: "A man who calls himself a character comes and asks me who I am." By the Father's reply, Pirandello hints that represented forms may be more real than actualities: "A character, sir, may always ask a man who he is. Because a character has really a life of his own. . . ." The reality may be an appearance; as the Father says, "You must not count overmuch on your reality as you feel it today, since, like that of yesterday, it may prove an illusion for you tomorrow." Gide would agree, and T. S. Eliot, who writes

> You are not the same people who left that station
> Or who will arrive at any terminus. . . .
>
> *("Dry Salvages")*

Pirandello is only characteristic of the many others in modern theatre who have tried to break through the boundaries between the stage and life; and besides, the problem became a traditional one anyhow after Hamlet's advice to the players. This does not, however, make it less contemporary.

With Pirandello it was almost obsessive, and coincided with the cubist analysis of illusion and reality. *Each In His Own Way* (1923) returns to the dramatic illusion "based upon an episode in real life." In this play the audience takes part, for among them are "real" persons whose lives have been dramatized in the "play" going on behind the footlights. These persons, objecting that "the author has taken it from real life," gather in the "lobby" after the first act to attack Pirandello and to break up the performance on the stage, which deals with a love affair between "a certain Moreno Woman" and "Baron Nuti," whose names have been in the newspapers. The directions Pirandello wrote for this interlude show how he was experimenting with multidimensional theatre:

> This scene in the lobby—Spectators coming out of a theatre—will show what was first presented on the stage as life itself to be a fiction of art; and the substance of the comedy will accordingly be pushed back, as it were, into a secondary plane of actuality or reality. . . . The Moreno Woman and Baron Nuti are present in the theatre among the spectators. Their appearance, therefore, suddenly and violently establishes a plane of reality still closer to real life, leaving the spectators who are discussing the fictitious reality of the staged play on a plane midway between. In the interlude at the end of the second act these three planes of reality will come into conflict with one another, as the participants in the drama of real life attack the participants in the comedy, the Spectators, meantime, trying to interfere.

Pirandello "destroys" drama much as the cubists destroyed conventional things. He will not accept as authentic "real" people or the cliché of the theatre any more than the cubist accepts as authentic the "real" object, the cliché of deep perspective, the contour of volumes seen in the light of the studio—or under sunlight either. The object, say Gleizes and Metzinger, has no absolute form; it is only a passage in possible relationships, with many relevances that are never fixed. Except by a blunder we cannot drop the curtain on Pirandello's drama because there is no clear boundary between life and art. Nor can the cubist painter isolate or define his object. He can, however, represent its emergence into reality.

The Later Phase: Towards Myth

by Giovanni Sinicropi

. . . *Diana e la Tuda* (*Diana and Tuda*) comes to the limelight in 1927, posing anew to its author the problem of the relationship between art and life and of the search for their coincidence. This time, form is symbolized by sculpture, whose plasticity must have suggested to Pirandello a more dramatic proximity to the concreteness of living things.

In this play, drama is embodied in the conflicting ideals of Sirio and Giuncano, as expounded in Act I. Sirio thinks that "the task of art" is to arrest life "in a gesture enduring" to eternity, outside which it is nothing at all. To Sirio, life is

> today no longer the one of yesterday, tomorrow no longer the one of today: at every moment another: so many! I make it one: that one (*he points at the statue in the other room*) *forever!*

Giuncano instead thinks that the work of art arresting life in a gesture cannot be, and never is, alive:

> but how could it be alive, if living means dying every minute, changing every minute, and that thing there never dies and never will change! Dead forever there, in an act of life. You're the one that gives it life, if you look at it a moment.

He wants to endue the work of art with life, not just form; therefore he is in search of

> a white-hot paste to pour into all statues to loosen them from their set attitudes;

"The Later Phase: Towards Myth" (original title: "Arte e vita nelle opere di Luigi Pirandello") by Giovanni Sinicropi. From *Italica*, XXXVIII, 4 (December 1961), 265-95. © 1961 by *Italica*. Translated by Glauco Cambon. Reprinted by permission of the author and of *Italica* (A.A.T.I.). The pages used here are a part of the article.

to give them "movement along with form"; in short, he would like to shape a work that "can take a body by itself . . . as it almost by itself wants itself to be." We know the value of these statements.

In the play's structure, the contrary ideals of Sirio and Giuncano are reflected respectively in Diana and Tuda. It certainly was a stroke of genius to build drama, at the human level, on an indissoluble tie between Tuda and the statue. Diana is the sublime aspect of Tuda, while she is the real aspect of Diana. The two completely represent the temporal and the timeless phase of Pirandellian dialectic, as glimpsed by Borgese. Their unity is willfully achieved by Sirio's demiurgic action in marrying his model so that she may serve only for his statue, the statue being his first and last act of life, after which he would kill himself. Day after day Diana sucks Tuda's life, and when the demiurgic will stops with the end of Sirio's own life, Tuda's life and Diana's form will remain truncated. They will not recognize themselves, because any relation between them will have broken down.

Thus the prevalence of art on life is posited here, more openly than ever, in Platonic terms. Despite his efforts, all that Sirio can do is render to Diana the life gesture he seized from Tuda:

> Oh, I may also pretend I have nothing in my mind—out of sheer cunning. I fight with artists! I pretend I'm talking as if casually; I turn my head a little, without letting them notice it; I bend it; I raise it; I reach a hand out a wee bit; Heavens, they mustn't see it is I, their model, who does the suggesting: no: on the contrary, I have talked nonsense; I have made a gesture, like this: the thought was born in them. And they are so sure of it that they tell me: "Oh, do you know? I'm thinking that . . . this movement . . ." Or else: "Hush; an idea is dawning on me . . ." And I, seriously: "What movement?" or "What did I say?"—for you have to act like that with some. But with some others, no. Not with this one, for instance" (*She refers to Sirio*).

But the fact is, not even Sirio can escape this silent influence. And Tuda will shout it when, in Act III, the unfinished statue appears:

> She didn't have them, once (*she points at the statue*), these eyes were different, they were *her* eyes!—He took them from me and gave them to her: look at her:—And that hand there which touches the side—do you see it?—it was open, once, that hand! Do you see, now? closed, clenched into a fist. They made me clench it like that, to withstand the torture—and the statue, you see, she too—had it open: she had to close it!—I saw her close it!—she couldn't help it! She is no longer what he wanted to make her!—It is I there now, see? I. . . .

Tuda's drama manifests itself as a constant humiliation of her will by Sirio's demiurgic will. She will make one further attempt to restore balance between the part of life she yields to the statue and that other part, more sacred to her, which she would like to offer Sirio as a really living thing. This offer was the only important thing to her. Giuncano in fact, in Act II, points out to her that she needs to live for somebody who is himself alive, otherwise her desire to live would be incomplete. In Act III, that need will elicit one more burning, mad desire from Tuda's flesh: "Take me, take me, take the life that's left to me, and shut me there in your statue!" Sirio's refusal, consistent of course with the logic of his own life, had to provoke revolt in the name of life. Once more, the coincidence of Diana and Tuda had to be shattered by what vainly claimed its own right to life, and both Diana and Tuda had to be annihilated.

Thus the attempt to found the coincidence of art and life on the intimate rapport of imitation miscarries in the end, in the light of Pirandello's aims. And yet, in *Ciascuno a suo modo* (*Each in His Way*) as well as in *Diana e la Tuda,* imitation had been freed of any mechanizing element. In the former play, a web of passions and heated reactions linked life and art in such a way as to place them on the same level; while in *Diana e la Tuda* the contact and struggle between the two terms had been caused by the intervention of the artificer's necessary will. Now, if on the one hand this position constituted a progress beyond any previous formulations, because both terms were thus accepted in their positive reality, it cannot be denied on the other hand that when conflict breaks out between them, life prevails upon art. Conquered, art loses any autonomy and even the possibility of revenging itself on life, while the reverse always happens.

That this pattern could not be overcome in a play like *Diana e la Tuda* is confirmed also by the fact that Pirandello fails to exploit one of the keenest insights scattered through the dialogue. As we saw, Giuncano at one point asserts that the work of art dies with the life it has frozen into one gesture, and adds: "You're the one that gives it life, if you look at it a moment." That insight (openly contradicting the whole play) will have no consequence in this play, but it will be nailed as a main beam to the structure of *Questa sera si recita a soggetto* (*Tonight We Improvise*).

Dr. Hinkfuss, the "Director" of the play-within-the-play in *Tonight We Improvise,* will remember Giuncano's words:

Frightening, isn't it, a statue, in the immobility of its attitude. Frightening indeed, this eternal solitude of changeless forms, outside

time. Every sculptor (I don't know but I suppose) after creating a
statue, if he really thinks he gave it life forever, must wish that it may
turn loose from its attitude, as a living thing, and move, and speak.
It would no longer be a statue; it would become a living person. But
only on one condition, gentlemen, can that be translated into moving
life which art fixed in the immutability of a form; on condition that
this form will regain motion from us, a life various, diverse and momentary: the life each of us will be able to give it.

Shortly before, he had stated that

> if a work of art survives it is only because we can still remove it from
> the fixity of its form; dissolve that form within us into vital motion;
> and life then is something we give it, something different from time
> to time and for each of us; many lives, and not just one; as you can
> infer from the continuous discussions of art, which rise from our refusal
> to believe this: that it is we who give this life; so that the life I give
> cannot ever be like the life another gives.

If theoretically these statements reached a deeper and more heartfelt
subjectivism, along the trajectory from Romantic to twentieth century esthetic ideas, on the other hand they represented for Pirandello
a compromise solution; for he was thereby sacrificing his ideal of an
absolute objective autonomy to be attained by the work of art just
before absolute subjectivism took over. Hinkfuss himself thinks that

> the best thing would be if the work of art could perform itself, not
> through actors but through its very characters, whom a prodigy should
> endow with body and voice.

And after the "Intermission," as soon as they give him a chance to
speak, he will add that

> theater is above all spectacle. Art, yes, but also life. Creation, yes, but
> not durable: only momentary. A prodigy: form in motion! And the
> prodigy, gentlemen, can only be momentary.

This certainly was the ideal in which the Six Characters would have
recognized themselves. And in *Questa sera si recita a soggetto* the
urge to free creation from any mediation makes itself even more
strongly felt. For the spectators' desired participation in the prodigy
of art, as we shall see, results for the first time in that feat of abolish-
ing any discontinuity between stage and pit which Pirandello had
deluded himself he could achieve in previous works. Always pursu-
ing a graphic immediacy in dramatic portrayal, Pirandello here tries
to obtain it in the coincidence of actor and character; yet he only
manages to obliterate the proscenium.

The miracle takes place, just for a moment, during the "Intermission," but it had already been prepared for since the first lines of the play. What gives it a first start is the mentioned dialogue between the floor and Dr. Hinkfuss; and let us notice that this device reflects also another madly ambitious hope of Pirandello's: to organize not just scenic reality, but all of reality on one and the same level. At a following moment, the group of actors appears as a group of spectators occupying a box. Now it is not quite clear if they are still a part of the stage, for they almost cease to appear as characters, yet not so much that we can acknowledge them henceforth as part of the audience only. The coincidence between stage and pit, with the attendant obliteration of the proscenium, happens in a third phase, during the "Intermission" scene of *Tonight We Improvise,* when the group of actors move from box to foyer to mix and perform with the "real" spectators. Here the prodigy takes place: the actors come to find themselves in the focus of the spectators' attention, curiosity, and maliciousness, namely in the same situation in which the Sampognetta family finds itself on stage, in the center of the smalltown "barbarians' " malevolent curiosity. Here they are actors and characters at the same time. The spectators, on the other hand, find themselves, vis-à-vis the actor-characters, in the same situation as the slandering "barbarians" on stage. Thus they are caught up and transposed onto the level of the stage, and willy-nilly they come to be included in the reality of art, they become themselves a part of the feigned action even though they keep their "true" reality all the while. For the presence of spectators in the foyer is necessary to the performance, which otherwise could not take place. As a consequence, for the first time, I think, in the history of theater, the full union of stage and life is achieved, the intervening barrier having totally disappeared.

Meanwhile Dr. Hinkfuss, to emphasize the "truth" of this reality on the stage, has his fun organizing absolutely fictitious and unjustified baroque effects which he himself will destroy shortly after. Pirandello had realized the dream he pursued through *Sei personaggi* (*Six Characters*), *Cappidazzu paga tuttu* (*Cappiddazzu Pays for All*), *Ciascuno a suo modo* (*Each in His Own Way*), and *La Sagra del Signore della Nave* (*Our Lord of the Ship*).

If the prodigy of coincidence between stage and life had happened in the foyer, another one was to follow on the stage: the coincidence of actor and character. This effect, too, was progressively foreshadowed, as can be seen even from the alternation of stage directions underscoring the several passages from actor to character, especially in the technically perfect scene of the make-up. The effect reaches its climax in Rico Verri's piqued line to the Leading Actress: "Very well! Are you happy now?" The line could be uttered either by the character or by the actor, in that very moment, and it was so timely that the stage direction registers the surprise and bafflement of actress-character Mommina. The balance had been attained for a moment.

But a complete coincidence between actor and character cannot take place on stage as long as Dr. Hinkfuss mediates between them. Having to attain the immediate unity of intuition and expression, the first thing to do was to annul the stage director's mediation, which caused expression to remain twice removed from intuition. If it is true that art can have whatever life "each of us" in turn manages to give it, Hinkfuss' mediating presence is twice illegitimate. Therefore the actors rebel, they refuse to "act the puppets" whose strings the stage director pulls. They want to be really free to identify with the characters outside any mediation, because "life such as it is born cannot brook commands."

And then the scene can be born with the spontaneity of life; or better, here is the scene performed as if it were being born in the imagination at that precise moment: the images taking shape one after the other in time and not in space; things rising to the surface as soon as imagination touches them and not an instant before: everything enshrined in a primeval sphere, untouched by space, time and their accidents.

But had the pursued coincidence really taken place? Not entirely, because Hinkfuss had remained all the time behind the wings to regulate light effects and thereby suggest the action. The mediator's presence had been eliminated, but not mediation in itself. And besides, it was the very actors who wanted the "written parts," the mediation without which the miracle of life could never have repeated itself on the stage.

The breakthrough has not been scored yet: final failure besets the effort to progress beyond the inviolable boundary of art and life. Art endlessly reaches out toward life without ever seizing it, for art is perennially enclosed in form, one of the forms life continuously destroys.

Two years after, with *Trovarsi (To Find Oneself)*, 1932, Dr. Hinkfuss' cue brings Pirandello back to that yearning for miracle: perhaps the prodigy can happen—in fact it does happen every day, at every moment, in the actor's personality. Perhaps life and art coincide in the live flesh of the interpreter, in the actress who finds herself again a woman in life, or in the woman who finds herself identical in the art of the actress. This time it's not just an esthetic consolation, but a sincerely human one, for the drama of art versus life pierces Donata Genzi's heart and mind as had already happened in *Diana e la Tuda*. The freedom Donata could enjoy by virtue of her art, while exorcizing the slavery of circumstance and the fear of the unexpected, did also impose solitude as a necessary condition. The phantoms she had to endue with a living form every evening bade her reject whatever was not perfectly organized and expressed, for every word, every gesture should be recognizable as part of a preordained harmony. But this was solitude, this meant living, not even on a mountain, but right in the stratosphere, beyond any atmospheric disturbances.

And at that starry height Elj's call reaches her: "To me, the beautiful is the sudden"; a program which might have come from the lips of a Dannunzian hero if it had been written twenty years before. But Elj is the legitimate child of Leone Gala and Baldovino: he wants to live "at random, with the soul utterly open to a sense of extraordinary wonder," and to seize the aspect of things at the moment they appear with a new plenitude, as if to redeem their "customary aspects which have reduced life, nature, oh my God, to a worn, devalued coin." He stood, that is, on the other side of the fence where Donata was concerned. If we observe their contrasting aspirations at the same time, if we evaluate them in the same light, they are only two different modes of the same way of life. Both Elj and Donata long to free themselves from any commitment. But once they meet and love each other, once a commitment is reached, it becomes impossible for them to keep estranged from life and its appurtenances. At least, Donata believes, in the attained commitment, that she will possibly find herself truer, leave solitude behind, build the final truth of herself also beyond art. So far, the symbol of her existence was the mannequin to be seen in Elj's study, a thing which can take all attitudes without retaining any. Now she wanted to know if it was possible "to have *also* a life." To build herself on the new dimension offered by hope.

Therefore (and the play requires it for its very structure) Donata is the only protagonist of *Trovarsi*; Elj is to her an invitation, the most alluring she has ever had, but still just an invitation to life; yet to it she must needs respond, unless she is to make up her mind finally to remain a mannequin and nothing more. Elj unfortunately fails to understand that with Donata the actress had given herself to him in the bargain: it is his only mistake. For in refusing to accept

the woman in his life after seeing her on the stage as an actress, he
was basically very consistent with himself: the actress indeed was the
very denial of that religion of the sudden to which his faith in life
ultimately amounted. Once again, the timebound and the timeless
face each other irreconcilably.

"The only truth is that one must create onself, create! And only
then can we find ourselves": this might have been the woman's consolation, but it actually was only the actress'. That new space opened
by hope within the four walls of her artistic life had vanished forever. She had to resign herself to the idea that the reality limited by
the stage should suffice to her existence. Conciliation of the sudden
and the eternal had failed. And if those words could have a consola-
tory ring, sealing a work dedicated to Marta Abba, it was because
Pirandello, at the time of writing *Trovarsi,* thought he had found a
shelter from his restlessness and a haven for his hopes: myth.

*Lazzaro (Lazarus), La nuova colonia (The New Colony), La favola
del figlio cambiato (The Fable of the Changeling), I Giganti della
Montagna (The Mountain Giants),* can be said to constitute a haven
which Pirandello's hope, if not his certainty, reaches, because beyond
their final horizon a future still looms. In the attained region of
myth, Pirandello outlines the last act of the conflict between art and
life. . . .

. . . In *I Giganti della Montagna,* symbol speaks clearer warnings
than elsewhere. Donata Genzi, now degraded into the precarious
Countess Ilse, "a born comedienne," has now definitively renounced
life. She carries in herself only the fable of the poet who died for
love of her, who left his work to live by her and in her: "The life I
denied him I had to give to his work." Ilse, too, like Donata Genzi,
refuses to surrender to life, to the fire of love, and she only longs to
identify with "the beauty of that work." She wants to bring it to the
presence of men, to make it live again for a moment under their
eyes night after night, until she will be killed by those very men.
With the revolt of the bestial bloodthirsty serfs of the Giants against
Ilse and her mummers we revert to the dark forces of instinct, to
Serafino Gubbio's tiger.

In such terms, the relationship of art to life is still seen as art's
inability to acquire the graphic strength which Pirandello thought
should be its first requirement for positing itself as actual life. The
creation of the imagination should be as a creation of nature.

Yet in this play Pirandello breaks through to a vista of hope with
the myth of magician Cotrone. Ilse's death could have been avoided
if she and her companions had followed Cotrone's advice, namely,

not to appear before the Giants' serfs but to return to the villa of
the Unlucky Ones, the only place where the fable could be performed, as he had already shown:

> I wanted to show you, Countess, that your fable can live only here;
> but you want to keep bringing it among men, and so be it! Outside,
> however, I have no power to wield in your service except my compan-
> ions, and I place them and myself at your disposal.

The Six Characters likewise had not resisted the tempting ambition
to go out among men; and they had come to a sad end. There is only
one place where they could live: in Cotrone's "arsenal of appari-
tions," in the poet's imagination that is, for he alone believes in
"the reality of phantoms," and has the magic power of evoking them
with the force of thought. . . .

. . . Pirandello's endeavor as man and artist closes thus with the
recognition of the impossibility of bridging the gap between art and
life. The last act of his creation had aimed at crossing that abyss;
and even though he managed to reduce it to a small size, easily cov-
ered at one jump, it could never be filled up. The leap into the irrational area of myth does not have to derive from that a sense of
renunciation, but one of enrichment, of a necessary completion of
the artist's aspirations. If by leaping into the region of myth Pirandello fails to save his esthetics through logic, he does certainly save it
by a renewed faith in art as a human creation; for human creation
is life, even though enclosed in the artist's imagination.

We must say, then, that the last result he achieves is the ineffability of the image. But thanks to that renewed faith in art and life,
such ineffability spares our author a complete defeat and final failure. . . .

Pirandello Between Fiction and Drama

by Ulrich Leo

. . . In . . . *L'uomo, la bestia e la virtù (Man, Beast and Virtue)* we [can see] how the poetical sense of a work of narrative fiction vanished once that work was adapted for the stage, to make room for theatrical animation: the play had not grasped in its essence the short story from which it was derived. In . . . "O di uno o di nessuno" ("Either of One or of No One"), we [can see] that the relevant play, confined as it was to the dramatic genre's only form of speech, i.e., direct discourse, could not do justice to the rich expressive resources of narrative fiction, which include silence, though on the other hand, thanks to the unity of time which is more germane to theater than to a tale the play in question managed to fulfill the structural unity of a given theme much better than the source story had.

Now we shall see . . . how the short story—by going beyond its genre limits with no loss of poetical force—has become something like a nonnarrative prefiguration of the play; indeed, that it *is* already the play, at the potential stage. . . . The story in question is "La signora Frola e il signor Ponza, suo genero" ("Mrs. Frola and her Son-in-Law, Mr. Ponza"), while the play it generated is *Così è (se vi pare) (It Is So, If You Think So)*. We are reminded of the question "Who had it been?" which abruptly opens the short story "O di uno o di nessuno" ("Either of One or of No One"). That question seemed to issue in all likelihood from both male protagonists of the story, though the possibility remained that it was the narrator himself who uttered it. At any rate he was the one that be-

"Pirandello between Fiction and Drama" (original title: "Luigi Pirandello zwischen zwei literarischen Gattungen") by Ulrich Leo. From *Romanistisches Jahrbuch*, XIV, Band (1963), 133-69. © 1963 by Helène Leo and the Editors of the *Romanistisches Jahrbuch* (Hamburg University). Translated by Glauco Cambon. Reprinted by permission of Mrs. Helène Leo and the Editors of the *Romanistisches Jahrbuch*. The pages used here are a part of the original essay, Sections VII-IX, first paragraphs.

gan to tell the story after the short initial paragraph. Instead, in
the case of "La signora Frola" . . . we find ourselves from beginning to end in a speech atmosphere which—with the exception of
few passages to which we shall return—is no longer that of a fictional
narrative in the proper sense of the word: because the narrator, far
from occupying the obvious center, is simply "not there." And while
in a play the playwright not only does not have to, but actually cannot be "present," . . . a fictional narrative without narrator remains to this day, despite all the transformations this genre has gone
through, a contradiction in terms. Let us then consider the literary
form as it shows itself here.

What we see here is no narrative—and no I-narrative either—it is
a *dramatic monologue.* And if we ask who is the monologue's persona, everything seems to refute the possibility of its being the author himself. Obviously the subjective participation expressed by the
monologue—and in direct discourse, not just in free indirect discourse—is too naïve and immediate for that. Besides, this participation involves a group of what could be defined as "masked people,"
i.e., a compact mass of average men and women who confront two
(or rather, three) "unmasked" ones with a curiosity stubborn and
merciless to the point of fanaticism. The "unmasked" ones, on their
part, want nothing but to live their own life outside the so-called
"normal" sphere, yet they cannot do it in the eyes of the "masked"
people (the impersonal, anonymous subject that Heidegger would
label "das Man," as in *Man sagt,* "people say . . ." while Pirandello
here says "Tutti" [All]). The "speaker" of the monologue is obviously a member of this group and seems to endorse unconditionally
their well-known (to him) viewpoints, prejudices, and ways of conduct. Thus how could this speaker be Pirandello, who, rather, always and everywhere takes the side of the "unmasked," of the de-
fenseless and lonely? Pirandello indeed, who in *It Is So, If You
Think So* will introduce Laudisi (the short story has no character
by that name) as a kind of counsel against the busybodies, and pat-
ently on the author's behalf?

But even if we did not know that the short story "Mrs. Frola and
her Son-in-Law" is by Pirandello and that *It Is So, If You Think So*
constitutes its stage version, we could distinguish the speaker of the
monologue, on stylistic grounds, from the author—for the manner
of utterance bears the unmistakable mark of the dramatic farce.
"But really, can you imagine? all of us will go crazy if we don't manage to find out which of the two is crazy, this Mrs. Frola or this Mr.
Ponza, her son-in-law. Things like that happen only at Valdana, un-

lucky town, the magnet of all eccentric strangers!" Thus it begins, and thus it goes on; and thus quite evidently no author speaks (regardless of which author it may be); this is the voice of an anonymous citizen of a backwoods small town, which to him is the hub of world events (". . . Things like that happen *only at Valdana,* . . ."); and he is speaking in the tone of carping criticism familiar to his cronies. Yes, the anonymous persona speaks not only in the context of that nameless collective which Heidegger calls "das Man": he represents it, he himself is the voice of that collective. He even emphasizes himself to the point of literal equivalence with it: ". . . we all here looking into one another's eyes, like lunatics? . . ." Irrefutably, the speaker is himself part of the impersonal group. And to whom does he speak? Not to his own group (as Laudisi will do in the play when he tries to convey to the naïve and fanatical mass his skepticism concerning truth, Pirandello's own skepticism). This speaker evidently has nothing to tell or to teach that his fellow gossips do not already know. Those he addresses, instead, . . . are the readers (one might almost say the listeners). To them—almost as a delegate of the nameless collective—he tells with great excitement whatever eccentricities happen to be afoot in Valdana at the moment.

This, then, is our "first reading impression"—after we have noticed that what we read here is, with regard to genre, no story but a dramatic structure. Yet the "second reading impression" modifies the first, without of course canceling it. By listening more carefully we still find something in the "monologue" that cannot be so unquestionably attributed to a naïve member of the "People say . . ." impersonal group. The speaker at some points seems to be half conscious of what will be the basic thesis of Laudisi in the play: that truth is defined just by its being unknowable. This naturally would never occur to any really harmless member of the "Tutti" busybodies: for they actually live on the certainty that the secret of Signora Frola and Signor Ponza can be clarified if one but delves enough; that one can know whether Signora Ponza is the first or the second wife of her husband; and whether, according to the answer, Signora Frola or Signor Ponza is the crazy one. This is how the "Tutti" think. But the speaker of the monologue has a phrase which in the course of his talking becomes an actual *leitmotiv,* and it expresses something like a first secret doubt on such a naïve certainty: "not to be able to discover . . . where the phantom is, where reality"; "where is reality? where the phantom?" ". . . where the phantom, where reality may be" (the dubitative question is thereby raised to the status of an overall motto). Still another particularly revelatory passage is to be found right at the beginning: "Naturally, in everybody the fateful suspicion rises that, things being so, reality is *worth just as much* as the phantom, and that every reality may very well *be* a phantom, and vice versa." This "suspicion" is already almost Laudisi's doctrine; and if it really came to life in "everybody's" mind, then the anonymous "people say" attitude would lose its impact. In this connection it pays to observe that, while the keyword for the anonymous speaker in the short story is "realtà" (reality) (with its negative counterpart "fantasma" [phantom]), Laudisi's keyword in the play is "verità" (truth) (without an antithetical concept; at each act's end, and often elsewhere too). "Truth" stands cognitively above "reality" and "illusion."

These doubts on the possibility of seizing truth (reality), within our "monologue," do modify for us as readers the first impression of the speaker's persona: he appears now less naïve, more thoughtful and independent, spiritually a bit closer to the author Pirandello. Another stylistic trait modifies the genre form we have called "monologue," in that it brings that form closer to an authentic narrative: the speaker, that is, does *narrate* the antecedents in fragments inserted between his outbursts, instead of just dissolving all the preliminary facts into exclamations, questions, self-objections, addresses to the fictive audience. That he, and not Pirandello, is the narrator may be seen in his initially twice repeated self-admonition to "order": "But no, it is better to relate everything first in an orderly way"; "But let us proceed with order." (In a formally opposite way Pirandello himself, without any such transition, had begun to narrate from the second paragraph of the short story "Either of One or of No One.") When the speaker narrates coherently, then, he himself interrupts his own impressionist speech, whose center is the reaction of "Valdana" to the events described—but not so much the events themselves; he remembers ever anew that his fictive "listeners" (the readers) must be initiated to what he and his familiars already know. Such narrative pieces are to be found all over, shading always into the reflections of the curious people (especially of the ladies), so that it is never easy to distinguish the objectively narrated facts from the subjective reactions to such narration, whether retold or directly uttered by the speaker himself: another proof that we are dealing with one speaker and one and the same monologue. But the very fact of narration does bring the persona closer to the figure of the author (Pirandello), who in a "normal" short story would have been himself the narrator; on the other hand it distances the persona from the undifferentiated crowd, which is generally present in the monologue only insofar as the persona speaks of it ("le *signore*" [the ladies]; "tutti" [all]; "Valdana"). In the context of these narrative fragments there actually occur the speeches of Mrs. Frola and of Mr. Ponza in the guise of free indirect discourse (on the cue of their visits as reported by the speaker, visits which then are directly enacted in the play). Even a bit of dialogue (between Mrs. Frola and her supposed daughter) is rendered in the form of direct discourse; and there is also a direct discourse by Mrs. Frola. But always from the lips of the monologue's persona, not of the author.

*   *   *

Who, then, utters the monologue? My answer will surprise those who know (as I myself said before) that a character called Laudisi appears only in the play and not in the story. However, I answer the question: the speaker of the "monologue" is neither one of the "masked" people, nor Pirandello: it is rather Laudisi and no one else. Of course not the same Laudisi who in the play will act as mouthpiece of the author against the nameless collective, but his embryonic and still unnamed predecessor in the "short story." I figure for myself the process (which perhaps even Pirandello the author did not consciously realize—we explicators must serve some purpose after all!) somewhat as follows. The cue to the project came —as is known—from a tragic *fait divers*: the destruction of a small town in the Marsica region of Abruzzi by an earthquake in 1915. In the face of this reality the whole idea developed. Pirandello shows, without introducing them directly as he will later do in the play, the ladies and gentlemen of the small, imaginary town of Valdana in their excitement about the consequences of that event for their town. He does this in perspective, through the words of one of them. This person, while speaking as one of them, starts having his spiritual doubts: since an individual by himself is apter to think things over than a crowd. While he intermittently and fragmentarily recounts antecedents and story proper in his monologue, he gets (as if behind his own back) a broader view of the facts narrated by him than is possible to the thoughtless crowd of busybodies for whom he speaks, and who on their part can only see the fleeting moment. Thus the phase of reflection has penetrated the naïveté that can only experience what is momentary; and it has done this—since it's a matter of investigating reality—in the guise of methodic skepticism, even though in its first dawning. The speaker has, unawares, already distanced himself a bit from his impersonal crowd; and this means that the short story already contains, in a nutshell, the "Laudisi" of the play to come. Comparable in this way to the later

Laudisi, the speaker already stands a little disengaged from the nameless collective for which he nevertheless speaks; and this with regard to the writer as well as to the reader. (This of course by no means implies that Pirandello had developed his philosophy right then for the first time. I am describing a literary process, not an ideological one.) The speaker of the "short story" is "a Laudisi *avant la lettre.*" Let us not forget that the wholly developed Laudisi, the skeptic of the play, is also a member of the "crowd": for he is familiar, related, bound to the group of the "masked people" (the busybodies). He is no "unmasked" one, because he knows how to defend himself. He is, besides, no recent arrival, no "Ingénu," "Micromégas," or "Candide": he is from "Valdana" like the others; to that extent he constitutes a legitimate literary descendant of the "short story's" anonymous speaker, who on his part spiritually somewhat prefigures him.

A close examination of the text confirms this from language and style. The expression through which the speaker of the "monologue" finally reveals himself as part of the "Tutti" (". . . *a guardarci tutti negli occhi . . . ,*") recurs almost unchanged on the lips of the play's Laudisi: "*Vi guardate tutti negli occhi? . . .*" (You all look into one another's eyes?). Yet a basic difference is there. The anonymous speaker said "*guardarci,*" to look into one another's eyes (meaning *ours),* because he considered himself part of the "Tutti"; Laudisi says "*vi* guardate," *you* look into one another's eyes, because he consciously excludes himself from the "Tutti." That speaker of the short story, then, has been organically reshaped into the Laudisi of the play. The latter will be hopelessly split from his erstwhile "peers" by his basically antithetic way of feeling and thinking, while his forerunner in the "short story," despite his spiritual "temptations," does remain a member of the crowd to the very end of the monologue.

If my explication is viable, then "Laudisi"—the singular polemical character of the dramatic piece *It Is So, If You Think So,* and certainly in his own right one of Pirandello's liveliest creations—is already latently, potentially there in the pseudo-short-story "Mrs. Frola and her Son-in-Law." The same is now true of almost everything that will otherwise go into the three acts of the play. Since the "short story"—as is by now clear—really is dramatic in nature, we can safely call it a one-acter which prepared the matter of the later three-acter by allusion rather than actual execution. This holds even though Pirandello included the work in question among his "short stories"; and it would not be the only case of its kind.

The play is already potentially present in the "short story." It is not a case of the play's having misunderstood the short story and robbed it of its existential sense; nor is it a case of the short story (which here already has dramatic quality and works mainly with direct discourse) being utterly different from the play in the matter of expression. Some tender nuances do of course get lost in the dramatic elaboration: ". . . she concludes with a sigh which on her lips takes the shape of a sweet, utterly sad smile." This is given in the short story by the speaker's narrative report, but in the play could only have been salvaged (or buried) in a stage direction, for the actress to *show*. Yet such cases are, as we saw, exceptions, because both elaborations of the subject belong to the same expressive sphere, the dramatic one. They effectively relate to each other as a sketch does to a fuller rendering of the same subject.

With such assumptions let us note again the motifs, scenes and acts that are at best hinted at in the "monologue," but constitute structural elements of the play. First of all (to say it once again), the collective "Tutti," who populate the play, are present in the "monologue" only through the mouth of the speaker. The earthquake, natural cause of the whole story, is mentioned only once in the "monologue," and only as "a grave mishap," while in the play it becomes the object of the "people say" group's discussions, and what's more, documents are sought in the devastated small town with a view to unveiling the "secret"—this being one of the two main motifs of Act III (especially scene 1 and 2 with foreshadowings in Act II, scene 1). The attribution of evidential power to documents, which is holy dogma to the "masked" ones, will be one of Laudisi's arguments against the knowability of "truth." In the "monologue," the documents hardly come up, even by way of allusion. The play on its part needed a "third act," and thus there was a reason to extend the action by introducing motifs which the psychologically oriented model had not used. But, unlike the earlier cases, this time the new motifs grow organically from the central idea by which the model was determined in its turn; they do not obscure, they develop it.

As for the other leading theme of Act III and great climax of the whole piece—the personal appearance of the controversial Mrs. Ponza—the very end of the "monologue" suggests just the possibility of questioning her as a last resort to solve the riddle; but the lady herself does not show up, even in the speaker's narrative. Such is the difference between the genre requirements of a dramatic monologue taking the place of the short story on the one hand, and of a full-fledged theatrical piece on the other, however little aimed at extrinsic effects. Act III, the climax of the play, is mainly missing

from the "monologue," save for a few hints. Even the *prefetto,* a
prominent figure of the "people say" group in Act III of the play,
is only mentioned in the "monologue." And the three great scenes
in which both "unmasked" persons pay visits to their tormentors,
the "Tutti," in an attempt to save something of their secret from
the fury of the busybodies, appear as "scenes" only in the play, effectively offsetting each other (I, 4-6). In the "monologue," as we
earlier saw, these visits have already taken place and appear only
retrospectively in the recollective talk of the speaker, partly in narrative form, partly in free indirect discourse, at times even in reported direct speech; and therefore they are much less sharply
divided into contrasting scenes, for they rather make up phases of
the development, in a general recapitulation of Valdana's "eccentricities."

*   *   *

I have endeavored to define something like a new genre by means
of this "dramatic narrative monologue" disguised as "short story,"
from which later a three-act play was to emerge. That in the end,
however, the author stands behind the speaker (though at quite a
distance); that it is after all Pirandello who makes himself heard
through the mouth of this anonymous and still naïve group spokesman, need not be doubted. It is not only the identity of "reality"
and "phantom" (i.e. the unknowability of "truth"), as sensed by the
"speaker," that betrays the author hiding behind him. The excitement, the perplexity of the speaker as such, who means to report
just the group opinion, indirectly mirror the first shock of the author
at the "tragic *fait divers*" to which he owed his inspiration. Into the
scurrilous petty-bourgeois group language of his "Laudisi before
the fact" the author translates his own first reaction as man and
poet: "What shall I do with this process that reality is throwing at
me?" In this sense (but then quite indirectly) one might call our
pseudo-short-story, in the end, an "author monologue": different in
genre from an I-narrative, different from a journal of the kind published by André Gide and Thomas Mann in connection with the
writing, respectively, of the *Counterfeiters* and of *Dr. Faustus,* different as well from a personal letter. It is in fact a little genre unto
itself. . . . At any rate I must count myself among those who say
Pirandello went astray when he left narrative fiction for the drama
. . . Pirandello's short stories and also his novels comprise a wealth
of poetical gems, while in his plays the search for effect only too
often has overruled the spiritual thoughtfulness and the voice of
poetry. . . .

The Experimental Novelist

by A. L. de Castris

I

The Late Mattia Pascal

In a climate of dejection and philosophical bitterness, of *taedium vitae* and cognitive engagement, there arises *Il fu Mattia Pascal (The Late Mattia Pascal)*, one of Pirandello's most remarkable inventions, which the writer himself later seemed to credit as a windfall of the mind, when, on reprinting it in 1921, he added the postscript on the Scruples of the Imagination (*Avvertenza sugli scrupoli della fantasia*). By emphasizing life's unpredictability and its superior inventiveness (or absurdity) vis-à-vis the imagination, he wanted above all to call attention to the bitter *truth* of that apparently paradoxical fable, to its flavor of real life and its significance as an exemplary experience of man. For this, and it starts actually with *Il fu Mattia Pascal*, is the conscious semantic duplicity of Pirandello, the figuration of a universal meaning (the human condition) in terms of an occasional life story.

From the objectively depicted and realistically colored aspects of life's inexplicability (seen in the grotesque situations and in the crisis of human relationships), there takes progressively shape and focus a new drama of everyman, a humorous epiphany of a diminutive Ulysses: the protagonist. He is an Orestes changed into Hamlet, because of his need to advance to the limelight from a background of masks devoid of objective reality, because of his useless will to see himself live and to measure with his consciousness the infinite solitude surrounding him; he is the witness of a failing dialectic,

"The Experimental Novelist" by Arcangelo Leone de Castris. From *Storia di Pirandello* (Bari, Italy: Laterza, 1962). © 1962 by Casa Editrice Giuseppe Laterza & Figli, Bari (Italy). Translated by Glauco Cambon. Reprinted by permission of Laterza Publishers. The pages reprinted here are a part of chs. II and III.

of inexorable rending in the paper heaven which had protected him and made existence finite and knowable.[1] The grotesque scenery, thus rent asunder by man's revolt, suffers in the moans of its inhabitants, mediocre creatures withered by sorrow and by the solitude the writer himself compassionately saw. And yet this is no longer a central suffering to the impersonal witness, who from the crucial rending isolates a riper object of knowledge, a more inward "argument" of inquiry and portrayal. Pirandello's man, who has acquired the responsibility of a new dimension, i.e., of a consciousness mirroring and dramatizing himself, forced as he is from now on to experience the crisis personally, replaces the choral testimonial of the first Pirandellian "crowd."

The different fictional perspective is rendered by style, by the humorous detachment which renews the narrative's tone and structure. A deep decoloration of the milieu, to purge it of the earlier violent and distorting traits which imbued its figures and outlines with grimness, takes place here, in the new novel, through direct narration. Now consciousness sees itself live and confesses itself, and at the outset claims it wants to reduce the proportions of drama, as befits a perspective shaped by awareness of the petty scope of the human adventure. ("And we often and willingly forget we are infinitesimal atoms . . . and we are capable . . . of grieving over certain things, which . . . should look to us like trifles of little account. Well, thanks to this providential absent-mindedness . . . I shall talk of myself. . . ." Second Foreword to *Il fu Mattia Pascal* in *Tutti i romanzi*.) That is the secret of the amused and carefree, if bitter, tone of the initial chapters, where Mattia's family milieu, an old style interior, eschews the gloomy and sometimes vehement tones of the early manner for the sake of an anecdotal, discursive idiom that reminds us of Boccaccio; and the tone barely deepens

---

[1] "If, at the climactic moment, right when the puppet representing Orestes is about to avenge his father's death on Aegisthus and his mother, the paper heaven of the small theater were to be rent . . . Orestes would be awfully puzzled by that hole in the sky . . . Orestes, in a word, would become Hamlet. The whole difference, my dear Mr. Meis, between ancient and modern tragedy consists of that, believe me: of a hole in the paper heaven. . . . How lucky the puppets are —I sighed—since on their heads the sham heaven keeps unsundered! . . . And they can bravely wait and take a fancy to their own comedy and love and esteem themselves, without ever suffering from vertigo, since for their stature and actions that sky is a suitable roof." (*Il fu Mattia Pascal,* in *Tutti i romanzi,* pp. 383-84). The motif is not isolated. It appears in an article dating from Pirandello's youth and in a poem published in 1907, "Richiesta d'un tendone" ("Request for a Big Tent"), now in the verse collection, *Fuori chiave.*

into accents of sorrowful memory when the death of his mother
and little daughter starts in the hero the suffering awareness of the
"immobility of (his) condition."

Thus, in the petty-bourgeois milieu of a Roman boarding house,
that sense of an elusive something, of a life worn out in an ambiguous silence, stylistically signals the occasional nature of situations and persons vis-à-vis the subtle, inward and atomistic process
of consciousness. In these creatures, cryptic in their several ways
and as if brushed by an ancient, imperceptible folly; in Papiano,
Anselmo, Adriana, and the singer, all expressions of a corruption
and a misery rather stifled in the soul than cried out: something
like a bloodless humanity is celebrated, a tortuous shyness which
ideally fits them to deal with a shadow like Adriano Meis. This is
the "feeling of contrast," which, objectified here for the first time
in an independent character, prevents the violent dissociation of
polemical irony and heartfelt compassion, for it is a feeling of contrast committed to extracting from all situations a "universal sense."
And it makes for a nimble discursive tone, for a more rounded and
light, almost serene syntax: a language of "lived" thought, of
"thought" life—the language of an experience which is becoming,
after Leopardi's fashion, a lucid and desperate consciousness.

The consciousness of living is, then, the new dimension in which
Mattia Pascal moves. Life is an absurd prison of vain, provisional
forms whose result for humanity is oppressive and alienating; society
rivets man to a false individuation that warps his wishes and will,
thereby breaking up his unity of consciousness into a deceitful multiplicity. He therefore rebels, escapes, refuses conventions and the
artifice of a hated mask. He starts on his redemptive journey, seeking
truer individuations, such as freedom, authentic love, justice, honor;
and he finally does enjoy a sense of boundless availability, of having
returned to a pure consciousness unfettered by any conditions:

> Having sharply cut off in myself any memory of previous life and
> firmly resolved to begin a new life from that point, I was pervaded
> and lifted up by something like a fresh, childlike joy; I felt my con-
> sciousness restored to the transparence of a new virginity, and my
> spirit watchful and ready to use everything for the construction of my
> new self. Meanwhile my soul surged in the joy of that new freedom. I
> had never seen men and things in this way; the air between them
> and me had suddenly cleared up; and the new relations to be estab-
> lished between them and myself appeared easy and light, for from
> now on I should need to ask precious little of them for my own inner
> pleasure. O delightful lightness of the soul; serene, unspeakable rap-
> ture!

But it is a short-lived rapture: for true love is rapport, justice is confrontation after all, *consciousness* is the others in us. The most tragic
disappointment thwarts that quest of new selfhood, a definitive impossibility of individuation disillusions that pure will to choose:
every experience leads man back to the necessity of a continuous
bargaining for compromise outside which liberty becomes hopelessly
arbitrary in the absence of foundations. A more irreducible chaos
swallows man in his effort to escape from the chaos of men. And he
can only retrace his footsteps, don one by one again the discarded
garments of the old masquerade, and try to recompose the fragments of his former shape. Provisional and false as it was, it yet
turned out to be the only one possible, the only one in which life
could consist and measure itself (". . . outside the law and outside
those particulars, whether joyful or sad, by virtue of which we are
just so, . . . it is not possible to live.").

Far from resolving the character's adventure in an accepted
"triumph of the demands of State bureaucracy," as Croce said,[2]
Mattia Pascal's resigned conclusion actually constitutes the immediate premise to the final drama of Pirandellian man. For the
failure of Mattia Pascal's anarchic attempt includes not merely the
provisional escape of man from the prison of conventional forms,
from mystifying society, in search of a genuineness of selfhood that
will make him free and master of himself.[3] It includes also, and
above all, the discovery of the tragic necessity for that oppressive
form and inhuman prison. Beyond Mattia's humorous return, beyond his sulking reinsertion in the dark, alienating machinery of
social pacts, it is actually his brief experience as disengaged man, as
life's "foreigner" that strikingly foreshadows the real drama of
Pirandello's great creatures.

The rebellion against false masks, which seems to constitute the
polemic of the first Pirandellian "crowd," leads that crowd, through
its representative Mattia Pascal, to a far more devastating experience, the risk of total annihilation. The climax of this experience
coincides with the psychological moment when, entirely possessed
by the transparent joy of an absolute freedom in the awareness of

---

[2] B. Croce, "Luigi Pirandello," *Letteratura della nuova Italia*, VI, Bari, third
ed. (1950), 357.

[3] Up to this point, in fact, the drama of Mattia Pascal, if not always with much
clarity, has been glimpsed and described by the best critics of Pirandello, like
Di Pietro and Janner. Their arguments are well resumed by G. Pullini in a recent essay in *Cinquant'anni di teatro in Italia* (Bologna, 1960), p. 69.

unconditional life, the hero begins to sense the need to fabricate a new feeling of life, and thus to pretend, to invent a new form for himself: the bewilderment of free consciousness reveals the necessity of finding an *ubi consistam,* a set of lines and traits reconnecting him to reality. The human and social symbols in which his desires and vital needs find their focal expression—love, honor, marriage, justice—manifest the ingrained tendency of life to take an institutional shape. Everything eludes him, everything is impossible and unthinkable: a fearsome loneliness looms in the consciousness of fractured man, who drifts toward disintegration in the formless flux of experience.

To escape is, then, impossible, to live is impossible except in the false relationships, in the relativity of social chaos; outside this there is nothingness, beyond the thousand faces one keeps meeting in the pursuit of social intercourse there is no such thing as the "one," the individual *per se,* but nobody. Revolt against corrupt society engenders the discovery of man's native inconsistency; from the idealistic (or pseudo-idealistic) destruction of reality one passes to the relativistic fracturing of the self. Thus, the Pirandellian hero's return to life is tinged with a far deeper bitterness and takes on the meaning of a fully recognized infamous doom. Since all escapes involve a leap in the amorphous dark, he discovers the impossibility of any escape, but lack of philosophical strength in the very act of that discovery inevitably aggravates his original "pain of form" to the point where it becomes existential anguish. Pirandello's positivism and skepticism prevent that forcible reacceptance of the world from evolving into a constructive quest for being in the existent, for the eternal "why" in history's development. But that intellectual failure itself amounts to the condition of his poetry.

II
Notebooks of Serafino Gubbio, Cameraman

The deepest energies in Pirandello's expressive quest . . . seem to tend towards the experience of theater. Now, of this dramatic "projection" there is a specimen which brings us at one stroke the most explicit and organic tension of all motifs so far examined, and that is *Quaderni di Serafino Gubbio operatore (Notebooks of Serafino Gubbio, Cameraman)*, formerly titled *Si gira (Shoot!)*, a novel dating from 1914-15. It is another of Pirandello's works which critics have generally neglected,[4] perhaps because they have considered superfluous that further summing up of well-known Pirandellian themes to which the novel seems to be reducible at a first reading.

Fictionally, I think, *Serafino Gubbio, Cameraman* constitutes Pirandello's most interesting and technically original experiment, for here the use of the diary form as an instrument of objectivity enables the protagonist to identify with the writer and makes the scattered contents of experience portrayable in a unified story. Historical continuity and narrative unity do not lie in the vicissitudes and actions of the characters, but exclusively in the experiencing consciousness, the reasoning diary-like structure which projects symbols and meanings onto those fragmentary events.[5] The perspective of Serafino Gubbio coincides with Pirandello's consciousness: a consciousness engaged in reconstructing into an idiomatic or theatrical unity and continuity what psychologically and narratively is no longer to be reconstructed.

That is why, while Pirandello's other novels are valid as examples of his ideology (apart from their poetical results), *Serafino Gubbio, Cameraman* has value especially as a document of his poetics, as a very eloquent testimonial, in an artistically rich context, of Pirandello's natural yet laboring transition to theatrical experience. The encompassing limits of this inner history, which provides the novel with its unitary structure and continuity, must in fact be sought in an area of purely sentimental and autobiographical import rather than in its technical significance. A trajectory of human sympathy is outlined there, in a progressive stressing of nuances, from relative pity to absolute compassion, from sorrowful commentary to the "inanimate silence" (*silenzio di cosa*); skipping the specific passages and anticipating the conclusions of my critical survey, I would say the overall movement is from a human to a "divine" feeling, from "narrative" pity to the tragic poet's high and invisible pity.

Pirandello's modern insight shows in his ability to make a valid

[4] It is not neglected by the two most exhaustive critics of Pirandello, i.e., Janner and Di Pietro. The former, however, ignores this quality of "poetics" that I consider fundamental, and the latter refers only cursorily to the theatrical significance of Gubbio's impassability.

[5] Here lies the real difference between *Si gira* and *Il fu Mattia Pascal*, though the latter novel, by adopting first person narrative, would seem to rest on the same compositional technique. In *Il fu Mattia Pascal*, the hero is led to experience in his own person a disintegrating course from illusory social escape to the discovery of his doom: exile. *Si gira* is instead an objectively discontinuous story, not of a revelation process but of a disintegration already experienced and accepted.

myth of the imperturbable detachment which Serafino Gubbio pursues throughout the novel, by symbolizing such spiritual state in the unhuman impassiveness of the movie camera. At first Gubbio is upset by the paradoxical cruelty of this symbol of modern civilization; later he wishes to become worthy of it and attain a watching human insensitiveness which will suit the grotesque proportions of contemporary life; finally he knows that its apparent "inanimate silence" harbors the deepest meaning of his compassion. Facing up to the open and irreversible condemnation of man, this novel is exactly the graph of Pirandellian poetics, whose evolution it exhibits from an attitude of participation in the drama of his creatures to an attitude of pure contemplation.

A crisis of compassion, then. This crisis is set forth, to begin with, in terms of a concrete psychological situation with obvious motivations and historical circumstances. The initial meaning of the myth of the "machine" is polemical and negative, rife with the ironic and satirical tensions which reveal Pirandello to be the most mature awareness, in Italy as a whole, of the crisis of the bourgeoisie and of modern society's corruption. The first sections of the great diary contain, in fact, in the guise of a Chaplinesque figuration, a vibrant indictment of the frightful moral void into which modern civilization risks falling, since by the monstrous proliferation of "leviathan," by the inhuman, voracious growth of industrial mass standards, it confines within ever smaller boundaries, to the verge of insignificance, the ethical values of its history:

> Man who once, a poet, deified his own feelings to worship them, now has thrown feelings away altogether as a useless and even harmful burden, and having become wise and industrious, he has set out to manufacture his new godheads with iron and steel and to be their bondsman and slave.
>
> Long live the machine that mechanizes life! . . . The machine is made, and in order to act, to move, it needs to swallow our soul, to devour our life. And how do you think our soul and life are to be returned by the machines in endless mass production? Here they are: by bits and mouthfuls, all molded in the same style, stupid and exact, so that if you heap them one upon the other you can make a pyramid reaching to the stars. Stars? Well, not really, gentlemen. Don't you believe it. Not even to the height of a telegraph pole. A gust topples them and rolls them over, and makes such an awful cumbersome mess of them, no longer inside but outside, that—My God, do you see how many boxes and cans, small and big and medium? Here are the productions of our soul, the tin cans of our life!

This polemic continues through the novel, giving rise to delightful little scenes where the bitterness of protest engenders a free figurative rhythm to encompass, for example, descriptions of the poor extras and chaotic interiors, or incomprehensible dialogues, or the tiger of "Cosmograph," whose death will be the only real thing in the midst of the general make-believe. Nor should we forget the scene of the hansom, and that of the mad violinist who finally knows happiness in playing for the tiger. The protest often becomes poetry when it focuses on the torn limbs of the human victim, the poor men disfigured by the absurdly frantic tempo of mechanization, by the thirst for money, worldliness and luxury, for they are caught in the centrifugal whirl of that alienating process, the civilization of the movies.[6] Man is the unknowing victim of his own violent inhumanity; for the dizzy mechanism produced by his ambition has reduced him to the non-life of inconsequential gestures, of progress without consciousness. The automatism of his moral life threatens to involve him in a total conflagration, salutary and regenerating though it may be:

I look at women in the streets, how they dress, how they walk, what hats they wear; I look at men, at the airs they have or give themselves; I listen to their talk, their purposes; and at times it seems so impossible to me to believe in the reality of what I see and hear that, since I cannot really believe they are all joking, I wonder if this roaring, dizzy mechanism of life, which daily rises in complication and speed, may have reduced mankind to such madness that it will soon erupt to upset and destroy everything. After all, it would be so much the better. Only for one reason, mind me: so we can start from scratch once and for all.[7]

[6] The protest, let us note, is not against the new instrument of expression, but against the civilization which distorts it to suit is own purposes; and also, more particularly, against the naturalistic aberration naïvely propounded by the first esthetical theories of the cinema. Pirandello never harbored any prejudices against film art as such. Besides the many screen versions of his works, authorized by him, and besides his film scenario, *Sogno (ma forse no)*, his article "Se il film parlante abolirà il teatro" is sufficient evidence. This article, written in 1929 and now included in his volume of essays, denies that the talking movies will kill the theater, and acutely shows that film as such will die out if it does not cease to "copy" literature; for it has its own language in the movement of images, and it should leave narrative to the novel and drama to the theater, to "immerse itself" completely in the "pure music" of sounds closely allied to the "pure vision" of its images.

[7] Remember the similar image of cosmic destruction which concludes Svevo's novel, *La coscienza di Zeno*. Actually Pirandello's position is comparable in many ways to Svevo's, the other great Italian spokesman of Decadentism.

But the others do not know. Serafino Gubbio is the awareness of this progressive inanition of man, of his inevitably self-destructive destiny.[8] And yet he sees his own destiny in the others: while he humanly resists the fatal assimilation that the machine imposes on him, he slowly sinks in the abyss of impassiveness, of insensitive objectivity, as life persuades him of the uselessness of both compassion and conscience. In the face of men's littleness and only relative reality, of their inability to live up to the feelings which for a moment seem to stir them from emotional atrophy, in the face of a life which has, by now, abjectly sunk into servility towards the mechanical tyrant by itself created, the only thing left is to "disabuse oneself" and "shoot pictures," i.e., to portray one's own absence. Shutting oneself in one's own silence seems to be not so much an outlet or act of vengeance as the only possible program; what else can one do but adjust to the absurd mechanism to which one is doomed by the necessity of life?

What can we do about it? Here I am. I serve my little machine, my movie camera, for I operate it so it can eat. But soul is of no use to me. My hand is of use; that is, it serves the camera. As for the soul and life, it is you, gentlemen, who must feed it to the little machine I operate. . . I don't deny it: the appearance is light and lively. One goes, one flies. And the wind of the race causes a watchful, smiling, keen anxiety, carries all thoughts away. Onward! Onward, so that one may have no time to sense the weight of sadness, the abjection of shame, which remain inside, deep down. Outside, it's a continuous flashing, a ceaseless glitter: everything dashes by and disappears. . . . The heart's throb is not heard, nor is the pulsing of arteries. Woe if it were! But this whir, this perpetual ticking is heard, oh yes, and it says how unnatural all the whirling fury is, all the flashing and vanishing of images; and how underneath there is a mechanism which seems to pursue it in headlong shrillness. . . . Nothing, nothing any more in this ceaseless parade of phantoms should lure and detain us. The only thing to do is, moment by moment to seize this swift passage

[8] "One day a gentleman who had come to pry around asked me: 'Excuse me, haven't they found a way yet to make the handle turn by itself?' . . . I smiled and replied 'Eventually perhaps, they will, sir. Actually, the foremost requirement in my profession is impassibility in the face of the action unfolding before the camera. In this regard, a mechanism would be certainly apter and preferable to a man. But the most serious difficulty right now is this: to find a mechanism that can regulate motion according to the action being shot. For I, dear sir, do not always turn the handle in the same way. . . . But I do not doubt that in time . . . they will manage to eliminate me. The little machine . . . will turn by itself. But what man will do then, once all the machines turn by themselves, still remains to be seen, my dear sir.' "

of aspects and cases, and go on with it, until the whirring shall stop for each of us.

But the protest against modern man's reduction to amorphous mass is only the initial moment, and the figurative occasion, of Serafino Gubbio's consciousness. On a much deeper level we get the meaning of his renunciation of feeling and of the mechanical impassibility he thinks he is experiencing. The fact is that this novel conclusively summarizes Pirandello's ideological history to document an attitude by now ripe for the theatrical experience. It is the moment when the writer consciously sums up, so as to project them into a symbolic story, the essential phases of his philosophy, and thereby clarifies the meanings and inner tensions of his previous experiences. From the polemical recording of a historical world's collapse, his meditation has extracted the perennial, existential sense of the human condition. Now, from the universal compassion engendered by the conquest of what Leopardi would call the "horrible truth," there rises this significant need to "disappear": the will to objectify the drama in independent creatures, in absolute symbols.

That is the value of Serafino Gubbio's "seeing," a definitive clairvoyance by means of which, turning the handle of his little camera, he fixes in extreme symbols the spectacle of life—a spectacle of chaos and perdition, where the mechanically irrational quality of events and human acts seems to result from an ancient institutional doom. Haggard persons, stiffened into a mask of habit-formed serenity or fixed in the features of sorrow, all of them prey to relativity and arbitrariness and anxiously clinging to the fragments of their lives; sweet unknowing creatures, vowed to anguish and solitude; incommunicable gestures, disconnected thoughts, convulsed feelings, paradoxical jealousies, sudden escapes into memory, embittered returns. In the chaos of a fatuous, mechanized world, the world of cinema, of profligacy and easy money, the mystified world of industrial civilization, a further chaos looms: the by now irremediable disintegration of personality driven into the abyss of relativity. In the figure of Miss Nestoroff, the sphinx-like star with an anguishing past, the sweet tiger replete with countless "relative" lovers, that world takes on a human face. Her restlessness in the indifference of her adventures, her inability to "find herself" while doggedly living her several roles to the point of an absurd empathy, express the tragedy of man, who pursues his own sundered selves, and vainly implores "the others" to help him stop his race towards disintegration.

This "seeing" of the cameraman, and the very objects of his visual recording, are the source of the novel's structure and style. The novel, in fact, is built on two different dimensions: on the inorganic, fragmentary time of the external story, and on the unified tissue of Serafino Gubbio's sentimental story, who comments on the former for the last time, and from the nausea of that moment invokes an absolute "disappearance." The mechanical bent of his point of view makes for the jumpy portrayal, and the story takes shape in a disconnected sequence of photographs, descriptive flashes, synthetic figurations. It is a conscious procedure, which lines up in an inorganic succession scenic openings, captions, theatrical and motion picture elements, scenarios, close-ups, often evincing that taste for what goes on behind the scenes which will make itself felt in Pirandello's future work. It pursues the fragmentary reality of characters and situations, in a mixed rhythm of memories and anxieties, of evasions and vivid mechanical illusions. But it registers above all the meaning of Gubbio's perspective, his evolution from polemical statements to instinctive sympathies, and from the disgust of these in turn to the frightful "stony" deliverance of consciousness, which is superbly envisaged in the objective rhythm, so violently and purposely scenographic, of the last sequence:

And I started turning the handle, keeping my eyes on the background tree trunks from which already the head of the beast popped in low, as if stretched to spy in ambush; I saw that head slowly withdraw, the two forepaws stay firm, close, and the hindpaws gradually gather in silence and the back arch up for the leap. My hand impassibly obeyed the measure I imposed on the movement, quicker, slower, very slow, as if my will had descended, firm, lucid and inflexible, into the wrist, and from here ruled alone, leaving my brain free to think, my heart free to feel; so that the hand kept obeying even when I terrified saw Nuti aim his gun away from the beast to point it slowly where shortly before the foliage had slightly parted and shoot, and the tiger immediately leap on him and mingle with him, under my eyes, in a horrible tangle. Louder than the rending shrieks of all the actors outside the cage who instinctively rushed towards Miss Nestoroff felled by the shot, louder than Carlo Ferro's yells, I heard here in the cage the beast's dull snarling and the dreadful gasping of the man as its fangs and claws ripped his throat and chest open; I heard, I kept hearing over that snarl and gasp the continuous ticking of the camera, whose handle my hand still kept turning by itself; and I expected the beast now to lunge for me, after striking the other one down; and the instants of that waiting seemed eternal and for eternity I seemed to be scanning them by turning, still turning the handle, unable to stop, when finally an arm came in between the bars to shoot a revolver point blank into an ear of the tiger over the already lacerated Nuti; and I was pulled back, wrenched away from the cage with the camera handle so tightly clenched in my fist that at first they couldn't wrest it from me. I did not moan, I did not yell: my voice had been extinguished by terror in my throat, forever.

Here the monstrous process is accomplished. The terrifying reality of man, that incongrous phenomenalism of his shreds of life, becomes the object of an absolute portrayal, of a timeless testimonial. And consciousness, brought to that extreme threshold by the gradual revelation of a wholesale failure of civilization—of which contemporary history represents the last act, in the sharpening of an irreversible process—becomes a silent, frightening clairvoyance.

> Enough now. I want to remain like this. Time is this; life is this; and in the meaning I give my profession, I want to go on like this— alone, silent and impassible—to operate my movie camera.
> Is the scene ready?
> —Watch out, we shoot it. . . .

Serafino Gubbio's impassibility represents the definitive conquest of Pirandellian compassion, the terminal goal of a biographical itinerary which is entirely defined and resolved in the sphere of pity. The cognitive impulse, instinctively at work in the young writer's first, amazed glance, has aroused a need for understanding and clarity; but he who has understood life cannot prescribe for it, he can only refine his instruments of solace until he experiences them to the highest degree, in an utterly disinterested participation. Pirandello removes himself forever from the scene of his creatures, from the explanation of their drama. But this silent detachment, which burns up all human involvements to resolve his whole feeling of life in pure contemplation, is the last and greatest condition of his art:

> If you knew how I feel, at certain times, *my inanimate silence!* And I am pleased with the mystery this silence communicates to whoever can sense it. I wish I'd never speak; I would welcome all things and all men in this silence of mine, all tears and smiles; not to echo that smile myself; for I should not know how: but so that all people could find in me, not just for their sorrows but even more for their joys, a tender compassion to make them brothers at least for a moment.

Pirandello's Drama of Revolt

by Robert Brustein

In 1933, three years before his death, Luigi Pirandello completed an autobiographical play entitled *When One Is Somebody* (*Quando si è qualcuno*). The unnamed hero of the work, whose speeches are preceded only by three asterisks, is an aging writer of great prominence who finds himself imprisoned in a role defined by his public: "I must not move from a certain concept, every detail of which they have decided upon. There I am motionless, forever!" Chafing against the restrictions of his fame, he takes on a "mask of youth," escaping into temporary freedom by writing lyrics under the pseudonym of a young, unknown poet. For a while, the subterfuge is successful: the new poet is hailed as a "living voice." But the ruse is finally discovered, and the hero must return to his unpleasant public duties—being stared at, lionized, and applauded by uncomprehending admirers. Urged by a sympathetic friend to commit some spontaneous, even outrageous act in order to prove that he is still alive, the hero finds he cannot budge. Only when one is nobody, he learns, can one exist in time; when one is somebody, one is petrified, immobile, dead. In the midst of making a commemorative speech on his fiftieth birthday, he begins to turn into a statue of himself, while his spoken words are engraved on the façade of a house behind him.

The play is flawed by traces of vanity and self-pity, but its final image is a stunning consummation of Pirandello's views about the individual's relationship to his life, and the artist's relationship to his art—two subjects which are really the same subject, and which continue to obsess him throughout his career. Pirandello knows that he is alive and changing, but, against his will, he has hardened into the stiff postures of the stereotyped public man, while his words, though formed in the mind of a living being, are etched in marble as soon as they are uttered. To accept a definition—to become a *somebody*—is to be frozen in time, just as art, the defined world of the artist, rigidifies in its prison of form. The typical Pirandellian drama is a drama of frustration which has at its core an irreconcilable conflict between time and timelessness or life and form; and whether the author is reflecting on human identity or (his other major subject) the identity of art, the terms of the conflict remain essentially the same.

Typical in this sense, *When One Is Somebody* is unusual in another: Pirandello very rarely wrote autobiographical plays. Yet, he is one of the most subjective dramatists in the modern theatre, and certainly the most self-conscious. Pirandello is a peculiarity of the theatre of revolt—an imperious messianic artist who writes compassionate existential plays. In him, the Romantic ego is strong, though usually sublimated. When the mood strikes him, he can be as personally vain and pompous as his hated rival D'Annunzio: "The only thing I have been able to do," he writes to Marta Abba, "is to think beautiful and lofty things." About an inferior quasi-religious drama, *Lazarus,* he boasts that it "would put the modern conscience at peace on the religious question," and about the unfinished *Mountain Giants,* he crows: "The triumph of the imagination! The triumph of poetry, and at the same time the tragedy of poetry forced to exist in the midst of the brutal, modern world." [1]

Pirandello, furthermore, often complains about being misunderstood and unappreciated, though he was heaped with honors in his lifetime. When *Lazarus* is unfavorably reviewed, he declares that Italy will "have to live down the shame of having misunderstood" his plays "and of having treated me unjustly." Deciding to open *Tonight We Improvise* in Germany, he remarks, "I have become a stranger to my own country and . . . I shall therefore have to win another home for my art." But when the opening is the occasion of a riot: "Everywhere I am pursued by hatred." Finally, he takes refuge in a bitter, self-pitying misanthropy: "Mankind does not deserve anything, stubborn as it is in its constantly growing stupidity, in its brutal quarrelsomeness. Time is against me; mankind adverse." In the mouth of Ibsen, such sentiments could be noble and courageous; in the mouth of Pirandello, they sound merely egotistical.

But it is rare when such personal egotism informs his work. As a

---

[1] To remarks like these, one is tempted to reply with Nietzsche's admonitory words: "Life is hard to bear: but do not affect to be so delicate!"

dramatist, Pirandello is a stern, uncompromising ironist, but his plays are full of pity for the fate of suffering mankind. It is true that the only playwright mentioned in Pirandello's theatre is Pirandello himself (his name is occasionally on the tongues of his characters). But the references are always ironic, and he always resists the temptation to glorify himself, like D'Annunzio, through the agency of superhuman heroes. Pirandello's messianic impulse, on the other hand, is channeled into a personal philosophical vision. If not present as a character, the author is always present as a hovering reflective intelligence—commenting, expostulating, conceptualizing. In this, he reminds us of Shaw, and he certainly fits Shaw's definition of the "artist-philosopher." Pirandello, in fact, provides his own definition of the type in the preface to *Six Characters in Search of an Author*. There he distinguishes between what he calls "historical writers," those who "narrate a particular affair, lively or sad, simply for the pleasure of narrating it," and what he calls "philosophical writers," those who "feel a more profound spiritual need on whose account they admit only figures, affairs, landscapes which have been soaked, so to speak, in a particular sense of life and acquire from it a universal value." He adds, "I have the misfortune to belong to these last."

Pirandello's philosophy, however, is quite different from Shaw's, since it is pessimistic in the extreme, and based on the conviction that the problems of life are insoluble. Because of this conviction, Pirandello sees no possibility of salvation through social or community life. In fact, he is vigorously opposed to all forms of social engineering, and extremely contemptuous of Utopian ideals and idealists (he satirizes them, rather clumsily, in *The New Colony*). Pirandello, furthermore, considers the social use of art to be a betrayal of art: "One must choose between the objectives of art and those of propaganda," he says in a speech before the Italian Academy. "When art becomes the instrument of definite action and of practical utility, it is condemned and sacrificed." This would seem to put Pirandello at opposite poles from Shaw; but in one sense, they are very much alike. Both create plays in which plot and character are largely subordinate to theme; and both lean toward tendentious argumentation in enunciating their ideas. Indeed, Pirandello's weakness for ideas lays him open to the charge that his plays are too cerebral. This charge he does not deny, but he denies that cerebral plays have to be undramatic: "One of the novelties I have given to the modern drama," he declares, with characteristic bravado, "consists in converting the intellect into passion." After Ibsen and (if we define "passion"

loosely) Shaw, this is hardly a novelty. But Pirandello is certainly the
first to convert *abstract thought* into passion—to formulate an ex-
pository philosophy in theatrical terms.

It must be conceded, however, that these terms are not always
very satisfactory. Pirandello is exceedingly interested in the *idea* of
form, but rather indifferent to form itself. One tends to think of him
as an experimental dramatist, but only his theatre trilogy can be
called a formal breakthrough. The rest of his forty-four plays are
relatively conventional in their use of dramatic materials. As a
twentieth century Italian dramatist, Pirandello had three possible
traditions to tap: the *verismo* of Giovanni Verga, the rhetorical Romanticism of D'Annunzio, and the bourgeois drama of the French
boulevard. Though Pirandello tried to dissociate himself from
Verga's Naturalism and D'Annunzio's bombast, both influenced his
work; but the greatest influence on his dramatic writing is that of
the French *pièce bien faite*. After writing a series of Sicilian folk
plays which have a peasant earthiness reminiscent of Synge and
Lorca, Pirandello devotes himself largely to dramas of the urban
middle class. And unlike most of the dramatists in the theatre of
revolt, who manage to transform mundane reality into poetic images
through symbolic action, character, or atmosphere, Pirandello—
despite occasional assaults on the fourth wall—generally keeps us
confined amidst the ugly paraphernalia of the cluttered drawing
room. Pirandello is not an artist who really develops; as an Italian
critic observed, his drama is a single play in a hundred acts.[2] Not
until the end of his life, when it is already too late, does he begin to
explore the possibilities of poetic myths, in flawed works like *Lazarus,
The New Colony,* and *The Mountain Giants.*

As for his dramatic structure, it is extremely conventional, when
not downright haphazard. Almost all of his plays are crammed into
three acts, "whether they fit or not." Whenever the action flags,
Pirandello contrives a new entrance or a new revelation; and each
curtain comes down on a not always credible crisis. In the act of
converting intellect into passion, Pirandello often tears the passion
to tatters. His plots are bursting with operatic feelings and melodramatic climaxes in an exaggerated Sicilian vein. Hyperbolic ex-

---

[2] Pirandello is very much aware of such strictures, and signals his awareness
through his plays. In his theatre trilogy, for example, the characters comment
frequently on the author's limitations, particularly his obscurity and his thematic
single-mindedness. As a spectator in *Each in His Own Way* remarks about Pirandello: "Why is he always harping on this illusion and reality string?"

pressions of grief, rage, and jealousy alternate with murders, suicides, and mortal accidents; wronged wives, maddened husbands, and bestial lovers foment adultery, incest, illegitimacy, plots, and duels. At times, his monologues turn into arias, and would be more appropriate set to Verdi's music.

The characters, furthermore, seem to lose psychological depth as they gain philosophical eloquence—occasionally, their identity is wholly swallowed up in the author's ideas. Pirandello is even more loquacious than Shaw, and has, therefore, less resistance to the *raisonneur*. Shaw is able to preserve aesthetic distance from a character like John Tanner, but Laudisi in *It Is So! (If You Think So)* and Diego Cinci in *Each in His Own Way* are hardly detached from their author at all. Shaw's drama is a drama of ideas, in which the ideas change from play to play, and the author can support two positions at the same time. Pirandello's drama is a drama of ideas based on a single underlying concept, consistent throughout his career and enjoying the author's wholehearted endorsement. Still, the basic Pirandellian concept is itself dialectical, and subject to endless combinations and permutations. The terms of the dialectic may not change, but the author's point of attack alternates from play to play, from thesis to antithesis, depending on the situation being considered.

The basic Pirandellian concept is borrowed from Bergson, and, briefly stated, it is this. Life (or reality or time) is fluid, mobile, evanescent, and indeterminate. It lies beyond the reach of reason, and is reflected only through spontaneous action, or instinct. Yet man, endowed with reason, cannot live instinctually like the beasts, nor can he accept an existence which constantly changes. In consequence, he uses reason to fix life through ordering definitions. Since life is indefinable, such concepts are illusions. Man is occasionally aware of the illusionary nature of his concepts; but to be human is to desire form; anything formless fills man with dread and uncertainty. "Humankind cannot bear very much reality"—T. S. Eliot's perception in *Burnt Norton* (and *Murder in the Cathedral*) is the spine of Pirandello's philosophy.

The way humankind evades reality is by stopping time, for, as Eliot goes on to say, "To be conscious is not to be in time." Through the exercise of consciousness, or reason, man temporarily achieves the timeless. Existence is chaotic, irrational, in flux; man essentializes for the sake of order and form. To quote Eliot once more, "Except for the point, the still point, there would be no dance, and there is only the dance." For Pirandello's characters, too, there is only the dance, and so each one labors to find his still point in the turning world.

The drama Pirandello distills from this concept is usually described through reference to the face and the mask—a conflict he borrowed from the *teatro del grottesco.* The authors who constitute the grotesque movement—Chiarelli, Martini, Antonelli—use this conflict as the basis for bizarre situations, presented in a ludicrous way. The face represents the suffering individual in all his complexity; the mask reflects external forms and social laws. The individual yields to instinct, but he is also ruled by the demands of a rigid code, and the conflict pulls him in opposite directions. This seems like a modern version of the Heroic conflict of love and honor, except that, in the *teatro del grottesco,* the central character tries to accommodate both demands at the same time. He is, as a result, not heroic but absurd—and the effect of the play is neither tragic nor comic but grotesque. In Luigi Chiarelli's *The Mask and the Face* (*La maschera ed il volto,* 1916), for example, a passionate Italian announces in public that he will kill his wife if she is unfaithful to him. When he finds her in the arms of another, he is reluctant to exact vengeance, so he exiles her, pretends she has been killed, and goes to trial for her murder. The mask of honor and the face of love have both been preserved. But in order to achieve this, the Italian has had to turn actor, playing his role to the limits of his endurance.

Pirandello takes over this antinomy intact, and proceeds to work manifold variations on it, both social and existential. For in his work, the mask of appearances is shaped both by the self and others. The others constitute the social world, a world which owes its existence to the false assumption that its members adhere to narrow definitions. Man, like life, may be unknowable, and the human soul, like time, may be in constant flight, but society demands certainty, and tries to imprison man in its fictitious concepts. To Pirandello, all social institutions and systems of thought—religion, law, government, science, morality, philosophy, sociology, even language itself— are means by which society creates masks, trying to catch the elusive face of man and fix it with a classification. "Basically," writes Pirandello, "I have constantly attempted to show that nothing offends life so much as reducing it to a hollow concept." Concepts are the death of spontaneity, he explains in his essay, *L'Umorismo* (1908), and reason is inadequate before the mysterious quality of existence. The human mystery remains beyond human comprehension; and those who would pluck it out will come away baffled and in tears.

On the other hand, the mind of man, being stuffed with concepts, has no defense against these social definitions. Because he is uncertain of his identity, he accepts the identity given him by others— sometimes willingly, like the heroine of *As You Desire Me,* sometimes reluctantly, like the hero of *When One Is Somebody.* Looking for the elusive self, he sees it reflected in the eyes of others, and takes the reflection for the original. This acceptance of a superimposed identity is one side of Pirandello's *teatro dello specchio* (theatre of the looking glass)—aptly named, since the image of the mirror occurs in almost every one of his plays. Laudisi, for example, examining his image in a glass, asks: "What are you for other people? What are you in their eyes? An image, dear sir, just an image in the glass! They're all carrying just such a phantom around inside themselves, and here they are racking their brains about the phantoms in other people. . . ." Knowledge, facts, opinions, all are phantasms, and even conscience is "nothing but other people inside you." As Diego Cinci puts it, in *Each in His Own Way:* "We have of each other reciprocally, and each has of himself, knowledge of some small, insignificant certainty of today, which is not the certainty it was yesterday, and will not be the certainty of tomorrow." In this sliding world, the human personality dissolves and changes, and like the hero of Pirandello's novel, *The Late Mattia Pascal,* who awoke one morning holding on to this one positive fact, the only thing you can be certain of is your name.

These are the social implications of Pirandello's treatment of masks. The author—always identifying with the suffering individual in opposition to the collective mind—is in revolt against the social world, and all its theoretical, conceptual, institutional extensions. As he said in an interview with Dominico Vittorini: "Society is necessarily formal, and in this sense I am antisocial, but only in the sense that I am opposed to social hypocrisies and conventions. My art teaches each individual to accept his lot with candor and humility, and with full consciousness of the imperfections that are inherent in it." The stoical sound of this qualification, however, suggests that Pirandello's social revolt has existential roots. Indeed it has because, in Pirandello's view, the adoption of the mask is the inevitable consequence of being human. If the mask is sometimes imposed on the face by the external world, it is more often the construct of internal demands. Hamlet says, "I know not seems"—but Pirandello's characters know almost nothing else.

For whether they know it or not, they are all devoted to appearances, as a defense against the agony of the changing personality.

"Continually I hide my face from myself," says a character in *Each in His Own Way*, "so ashamed am I at seeing myself change." The shame is increased by time, for old age etches change, irremediably, on the human features. "Age," observes a character in *Diana and Tuda*, "which is time reduced to human dimensions—time when it is painful—and we are made of flesh." Or, as the aging writer in *When One Is Somebody* complains, "You don't know what an atrocious thing happens to an old man, to see himself all of a sudden in a mirror, when the sorrow of seeing himself is greater than the astonishment of no longer remembering. You don't know the obscene shame of feeling a young and hotblooded heart within an old body." The body is form, but form which changes under the hungry eye of the cormorant, time. To stop time, to achieve stasis, to locate the still point, Pirandello's characters put on their masks, hoping to hide their shameful faces by playing a role.

This is what Pirandello means by *costruirsi*, building yourself up. Man begins as nothing definite, and becomes a *costruzione*, creating himself according to predetermined patterns or roles. Thus, he plays family roles (husband, wife, father, mother), religious roles (saint, blasphemer, priest, atheist), psychological roles (madman, neurotic, normal man), and social roles (mayor, citizen, socialist, revolutionary). No matter how well these roles are played, however, none of them reveals the face of the actor. They are disguises, designed to give purpose and form to a meaningless existence—masks in an infinite comedy of illusion. The true self is revealed only in a moment of blind instinct, which has the power to break down all codes and concepts.[3] But even then, the self is on the point of changing. Thus, Pirandello refuses to idealize the personality in the manner of the messianic rebels; for him, personality remains a fictional construct. Instead, he concentrates on the disintegration of personality in a scene of bondage and frustration—existential revolt in the ironic mode. Pirandellian man has freedom, but his freedom is unbearable; it beckons him toward the waste and void. Though he sometimes plunges into reality through spontaneous, instinctual action, he more often takes refuge from reality in a beneficial illusion. "The greater

[3] Since Pirandello believed so firmly in the power of the sexual instinct, he was compared—by an adoring disciple, Domenico Vittorini—to his rival D'Annunzio. Pirandello's reply is instructive: "No, no. D'Annunzio is immoral in order to proclaim the glory of instinct. I present this individual case to add another proof of the tragedy of being human. D'Annunzio is exultant over evil; I grieve over it." Or, in the terminology of revolt, D'Annunzio is messianic, Pirandello is existential.

the struggle for life," as Pirandello phrases it in *L'Umorismo*, "the greater the need for mutual deceit."

The histrionic implications of this are tremendous—the Pirandellian hero is an actor, a character in disguise. But Pirandello broadens these implications even further. For if his hero is an actor, he is also a critic who cruelly judges his own performance. "Yes I laugh sometimes," say Leone Gala in *The Rules of the Game*, "as I watch myself playing this self-imposed role. . . ." In Elizabethan drama, the disguised character is anxious to protect his disguise from others; in Pirandello, he is also anxious to protect it from himself. Yet, reason, which created the mask, exposes its illusionary nature. In the *teatro dello specchio*, the reflecting mirror is not only the eye of the world but the inner eye as well:

> When a man lives [writes Pirandello], he lives and does not see himself. Well, put a mirror before him and make him see himself in the act of living. Either he is astonished at his own appearance, or else he turns away his eyes so as not to see himself, or else in disgust he spits at his image, or, again, clenches his fist to break it. In a word, there arises a crisis, and that crisis is my theatre.

In another place, he adds: "If we present ourselves to others as artificial constructions in relation to what we really are, it is logical that upon looking at ourselves in a mirror we see our falseness reflected there, made galling and unbearable by its fixity." It is for this reason that a character like Baldovino, in *The Pleasures of Honesty*, experiences "an unspeakable nausea for the self that I am compelled to build up and display in the relations I must assume with my fellow men." If Pirandello's characters want to be fixed, they also want to move.

The conflict between appearance and reality, or Art and Nature, has been a traditional subject of Western literature since its beginnings, with Anglo-Saxon writers generally supporting reality and Latin writers generally supporting appearances. The blunt, plainspoken man, who will not hide his true feelings, is a crucial figure in a certain strain of English drama and satire, while French, Spanish, and Italian literature is often more tolerant of the courteous man, who knows how to moderate his temper and disguise his desires. When the Italian Iago goes into disguise, he assumes the appearance of a gruff, honest soldier; when Molière's "misanthrope" enters English drama, he becomes Wycherly's "plaindealer." In Pirandello's drama, on the other hand, the conflict between Art and Nature is translated into a conflict between life and form, while appearances become illusions; but with him, the conflict becomes a real dialectic. Pirandello evokes sympathy for the man who tries to hide from reality and sympathy for the man who tries to plunge back into it. Life and form—reality and illusion—are opposed, but they are the twin poles of human existence.

Pirandello is similarly ambivalent about the faculty of reason. His philosophy, founded as it is on the belief that real knowledge is unattainable, is profoundly anti-intellectual; yet, it is through the intellect that he reaches his conclusions. Such paradoxes proliferate in Pirandello's drama. Reason is both man's consolation and his curse; it creates a false identity which it can also destroy; it applies the masks to the face, and then rips them off. Under the cold eye of reason, the human ego expands and contracts; the *costruzione* is erected, and then demolished. The disguised character in Pirandello is a creature of appearances, whose intellect has created his illusion, but he also has the capacity, through the agency of intellect, to penetrate to a deeper reality. He escapes from life into form, and from form into life. Or, put into the metaphor of the theatre, the improvising actor struts and frets his hour on the stage before the ruthless critic sends him back to his dressing-room mirror, weeping over the inauthenticity of his performance.

This probably sounds impossibly abstruse, an exercise in epistemology rather than drama, but the wonder is the number of effective situations Pirandello is able to create out of such reflections. For Pirandello's concept always takes the form of conflict, and conflict remains the heart of his drama. These conflicts take an internal and external form, depending on which aspect of Pirandello's revolt is in the ascendant. As an existential rebel, Pirandello explores the roles men play in order to escape from life—revolt turns inward against the elusiveness of human existence. As a social rebel, he attacks the busybodies, gossips, and scandalmongers who think they can understand the unknowable mystery of man—revolt turns outwards against the intruding social world. The two levels of Pirandello's revolt generally run parallel in each of his plays; and, as a result, his drama has a "spatial design," in Eric Bentley's words, which consists of "a center of suffering within a periphery of busybodies—the pattern of the Sicilian village."

Extending this description a little further, let us call those in the outer circe *alazōnes* (imposters or buffoons) and those in the center *eirones* (self-deprecators)—terms by which I mean to suggest the affinities of Pirandello's characters with the stock masks of Aristophanic comedy and the *commedia dell'arte*.[4] In traditional comedy, as Northrop Frye tells us, the *alazōn* is typified as "the *miles gloriosus* and the learned crank or obsessed philosopher." In Pirandello's drama, the *alazōn* is an agent of organized society, and is usually identified with one of its institutions—science, bureaucracy, or the state. He is sometimes a doctor, sometimes a petty official, sometimes a magistrate, sometimes a policeman—always a pretender, whose pretense lies in thinking himself a wise man when he is really a fool. The *eiron*, on the other hand, is a suffering individual who has hidden some private secret under a mask of appearances. Sometimes, he is unaware he is wearing a mask, in which case he is merely a pathetic sufferer—a *pharmakos*, or scapegoat. More often, he is a man of superior wisdom, because, like Socrates (the original *eiron*), he *knows* he knows nothing. Hounded and tormented by his persecutors, the buffoonish *alazōnes*, he replies with the dry mock: ironic laughter is his only weapon. As Diego Cinci puts it, in *Each in His Own Way*: "I laugh because I have reasoned my heart dry. . . . I laugh in my own way, and my ridicule falls upon myself sooner than on anyone else!" He is thus ironic in the original Greek sense of *dissimulation*—of ignorance purposely affected.

The clash between the two groups occurs when the *alazōnes* try to peel off the masks of the *eirones*—an action which has both tragic and comic consequences. On the one hand, this impertinent invasion of another's privacy may be dangerous, since the *eiron*'s illusion is necessary to his life; on the other, the attempt to discover another's secret self is ludicrously impossible, since the face beneath the mask cannot be known. The comic action, then, proceeds along the social level of the play where the *alazōnes* are frustrated in their curiosity, their state changing from knowledge to ignorance, from smug complacency to stupefied bafflement. The tragic action proceeds along the existential level of the play where the *eirones* are dragged under a painfully blinding spotlight which causes them terrible discomfort and suffering. As for the author, his literary endeavors identify him as an *alazōn*, since by writing about the *eirones*, he is meddling in their private affairs.[5] But his tone is that of an *eiron*, since, in his

---

[4] F. L. Cornford was the first to apply these terms to Aristophanes in his book *The Origins of Attic Comedy*; Northrop Frye, in *The Anatomy of Criticism*, applies them to literature as a whole. Pirandello, who was familiar with the stock masks of traditional comedy, uses them, I think, in a much more conscious way than other Western writers.

[5] Pirandello suggests this role for himself in *Each in His Own Way*—a *commedia a chiave*, or comedy with a key. This play, which is based on living per-

sympathetic identification with the sufferers, he expresses ironic contempt for the social busybodies.

One of the most famous, if not the most artful, of the plays in this mode is *It Is So!* *(If You Think So)*—*Cosí è (se vi pare)*—which Pirandello wrote in 1917. Here the leader of the *alazōnes* is Commendatore Agazzi, a small-town bureaucrat, who is supported in his buffoonery by members of his and another family, by the Prefect, and by the Police Commissioner. The sufferers are their neighbors: Signor Ponza, his wife, and his mother-in-law, Signora Frola. The unusual behavior of this family has been arousing curiosity. Why is Signora Frola never permitted to visit with her own daughter? The neighbors are particularly incensed, because they have also been refused admittance to Ponza's house, even though Ponza is Agazzi's subordinate.

As the play proceeds, and Ponza and Signora Frola are cross-examined about their behavior, the mystery thickens. Ponza maintains that he has barred his mother-in-law from his door in order to protect her peace of mind. According to his testimony, her daughter has died in an earthquake and Ponza had married a second time; but when Signora Frola became deranged and refused to believe these facts, Ponza humored her by letting her think her daughter was still alive. Signora Frola, on the other hand, maintains that it is Ponza who is mad. He has convinced himself that his first wife is dead and, to humor him, she let him marry her daughter twice. To compound the confusion, each witness is aware of the other's version of the events, but compassionately labors to preserve the other's illusion.

Meanwhile the Agazzi family and their allies are busy trying to get to the bottom of things. Representing themselves as "pilgrims athirst for truth," they are really "a pack of gossips"—prying into secrets, ferreting out facts, forcing painful confrontations. Only Agazzi's brother-in-law, Lamberto Laudisi, disapproves of this meddling in the lives of others. The Ponza family is a *pharmakos* group—passive, victimized, unaware—so Laudisi becomes their spokesman; he is the *eiron* of the play, and it is on his derisive laughter that each curtain falls. To Laudisi, the truth is something perpetually out of reach, while reality is a movable feast which each man samples from his own table. As the buffoons proceed with their interrogations and in-

---

sonages, is interrupted in the middle by some of the figures being represented on the stage; and it is rumored that they have slapped Pirandello's face in the lobby. "It's a disgrace," one of them cries. "Two people pilloried in public! The private affairs of two people exposed to public ridicule!" In this *roman à clef,* therefore, Pirandello clearly assigns himself the function of the meddling *alazōn.*

vestigations, turning up documents and official papers, yet continuing to be baffled, Laudisi affirms that facts contribute nothing to the matter, since they leave things just as ambiguous as before. "Oh, I grant you," he concedes, "if you could get a death certificate or a marriage certificate or something of the kind, you might be able to satisfy that stupid curiosity of yours. Unfortunately, you can't get it. And the result is that you are in the extraordinary fix of having before you, on the one hand, a world of fancy, and on the other, a world of reality, and you, for the life of you, are not able to distinguish one from the other."

Finally, the only person who can explain the mystery—Signora Ponza—is brought in to testify. She is "dressed in deep mourning . . . her face concealed with a thick, black impenetrable veil." The veil is her mask—but the veil remains down, the mask continues to conceal the face. For Signora Ponza thereupon announces that she is the daughter of Signora Frola, and also the second wife of Signor Ponza. She has become a construction, built up by the demands of others: "I am she whom you believe me to be"—and in herself, "I am nothing." Externally imposed, the mask changes according to the eye of the beholder, while the face remains an imponderable mystery.

As Eric Bentley observes, there is nothing in the play to suggest that there is not a correct version of the story. Rather, the play is a protest against the "scandalmonger, the prying reporter, and the amateur psychoanalyst—and we might add, the sob sister, the candid cameraman, and the Congressional investigator—those who recklessly probe the secrets of others. In *It Is So!*, these secrets can only be protected through concealment. "There is a misfortune here, as you see, which must stay hidden," remarks Signora Ponza, "otherwise, the remedy which our compassion has found cannot avail." Professor Bentley concludes from this that Pirandello *does* believe in the existence of objective truth. This may be—but he will show again and again, in later plays, how this truth cannot be grasped by the inquiring mind, since it is in a continual state of flux and varies with each individual. This existential complaint is only suggested in *It Is So!*, then buried under a barrage of social satire. Instead of developing the deeper implications of his philosophy, Pirandello exercises the animus of his social revolt; and the tragedy which threatens is averted at the end. Their right to privacy affirmed, their secret still hidden from the gossips and the busybodies, the *pharmakoi* depart into darkness, while the *alazōnes* stand lost in amazement, whipped by the savage laughter of the *eiron*.

It Is So! (If You Think So) is a fairly conventional exercise in the mode of the grotesque. As an expression of social revolt, it has its power and relevance, but the split between the *pharmakoi* and the *eiron*—between the sufferers and their spokesman—shows that Pirandello has not yet perfected his structure. Furthermore, the prominence of Laudisi, the *raisonneur,* suggests that, at this early point, Pirandello is less interested in dramatizing his themes than in stating them flatly. In *Henry IV* (*Enrico IV,* 1922), however, Pirandello dispenses with the *raisonneur* entirely, embodying his ideas in a brilliant theatrical metaphor, and concentrating not so much on the social world of the dumbfounded buffoons as on the existential world of the chief sufferer. And now this world is wonderfully rich and varied. The central character of the play is both *pharmakos* and *eiron,* both a living person and an articulate personification, both the mechanism of the action and the source of the ideas. In Henry's character, Pirandello's reflections on the conflict between life and form, on the elusiveness of identity, and on man's revolt against time, achieve their consummation in a powerfully eerie manner. Henry is the culmination of Pirandello's concept of the mask and the face, as well as embodying Pirandello's notions (developed more elaborately in his theatre plays) about the timeless world of art. In trying to fix his changing life in significant form, Henry emerges as Actor, Artist, and Madman, and, besides this, possesses an extraordinary intellect, reflecting on all three.

The structure of the play, a structure that is to become basic to Pirandello's work, consists of an "historical" story within a "philosophical" framework. The historical line is this: Henry IV (as he is called throughout the play) is an Italian nobleman on whom life has played a cruel trick. Twenty years before, indulging his taste for playacting, he had appeared in a pageant, costumed as the medieval Holy Roman Emperor who had been excommunicated by Gregory VII and forced to walk barefoot to Canossa to do penance. His horse had stumbled—pricked from behind, as we later learn, by his rival, Tito Belcredi—and Henry had fallen, hitting his head on a rock. Henry awoke with the delusion that he actually was Henry IV; the pageant had become his reality. "I shall never forget that scene," recalls his former mistress, Donna Matilda, "all our masked faces hideous and gazing at him, at that terrible mask of his face, which was no longer a mask, but madness, madness personified! The mask had usurped the face; the actor had turned madman, losing all distance from his role. When this delirium persisted, Henry's nephew, Charles di Nolli, hired men to play his retainers and counsellors. For the next twenty years, they performed their supporting roles in a drama which Henry, the chief actor, had unwittingly substituted for his life.

For only twelve of those twenty years, however, was Henry really mad; after that, his consciousness returned. But he regained his sanity with the terrible realization that he had been cheated of his youth. He had slept away his life in a long dream, and now he had awakened, gray inside and out, about to "arrive, hungry as a wolf, at a banquet which had already been cleared away." His hunger persisting, unappeased, he determined to revenge himself on time by refusing to return to time. He would play his role again, maintain his mask, and live his madness "with the most lucid consciousness." This consciousness is likened to a mirror which he always keeps before him, invisible to everybody else. The actor had turned madman; now the madman would turn actor, in revolt against existence itself.

Henry managed to escape from time by entering history, which is frozen time. He followed the outlines of a plot already written, foreordained, predetermined, seeking—like Yeats in "Sailing to Byzantium"—a corridor into the world of eternity. Yeats's answer to the agonizing flux of life is to contemplate a golden bird upon a golden bough, in a legendary country where time is suspended; Henry finds consolation for his melancholy and despair by constructing himself into a historical figure, fixed and immutable. By remaining Henry IV at the age of twenty-six, "everything determined, everything settled," Henry never suffers the horrors of age. He is held as firmly in an eternal moment as that youthful portrait of himself in costume, which hangs in the throne room beside a portrait of the young Donna Matilda. And now, as he enacts a masquerade, yet remains outside the masquerade—possessing the weird clarity of his lucid madness—Henry moves through life with the supreme confidence of one who knows what came before—and what comes after. Chance, accident, happenstance, the tricks of time, afflict him no more. Freely suspending his freedom of action, he has moved from time into timelessness, into that still point where the dance proceeds.

Henry's narrative is woven skillfully in the play, and its threads are unraveled through the plucking and pulling of another group of Pirandellian busybodies. Playing the *alazōnes* to Henry's *eiron* are a number of interested parties who have come to observe this "madman" in the hope of curing him: Donna Matilda, his old mistress; Tito Belcredi, her present lover; Charles di Nolli, Henry's nephew; Frida, Matilda's beautiful daughter; and an alienist named Doctor Dionysius Genoni. These characters are subjected to Henry's, and Pirandello's, scorn, but the alienist is a special object of satire. A "learned crank" with total confidence in his curative powers, Genoni is a jargon-ridden quack—a caricature of a professional man—*il dottore* from the *commedia dell'arte*. To him, Henry is merely a case —a conceptual object rather than a complex human being. But, as always in Pirandello, this kind of labeling becomes an insult to the human soul: "Words, words which anyone can interpret in his own manner!" cries Henry. "That's the way public opinion is formed! And it's a bad look out for a man who finds himself labeled one day with one of these words which everyone repeats: for example 'madman,' or 'imbecile.' "

Having so labeled Henry, Genoni suggests that he and the others enter his madness for the purpose of observing him more closely. Since Henry "pays more attention to the dress than to the person," they put on period costumes, assuming a madness of clothes. Each pretends to be some figure in the life of the historical Henry: a Benedictine monk (Belcredi), the Abbot of Cluny (Genoni), and the Duchess Adelaide, mother of Henry's Queen (Matilda). During the audience which follows, Matilda and Belcredi suspect that Henry has recognized them; and indeed he has; but he continues to play his role to perfection. "Madness has made a superb actor of him," Di Nolli has observed, but none of them is aware how brilliant Henry's performance actually is. For Henry is not only playing Henry IV; he is also playing the elderly Henry IV playing the young Henry of the portrait, from which he begs to be freed. His hair dyed, his cheeks rouged, Henry enacts a masquerade within a masquerade. The masks proliferate in defense against the changing shape of life:

> A woman wants to be a man . . . an old man would be young again [says Henry to his visitors]. . . . We're all fixed in good faith in a certain concept of ourselves. However, Monsignor, while you keep your self in order, holding on with both hands to your holy habit, there slips down from your sleeves, there peels off from you like . . . like a serpent . . . something you don't notice: life, Monsignor! Has it never happened to you, my Lady, to find a different self in yourself? Have you always been the same?

Shifting skillfully from one self to another, speaking ambiguously about real and imagined conspiracies, Henry confuses the interlopers, and turns the mirror back on them: "Buffoons, buffoons!" he spits, contemptuously. "One can play any tune on them!" For while the *alazōnes* are observing the *eiron*, the *eiron* is observing the *alazōnes,* and with a much more highly trained eye. "And you," he says to his valets, "are amazed that I tear off their ridiculous masks now, just as if it wasn't I who made them mask themselves to satisfy this taste of mine for playing the madman!" The *eiron's* superiority is clearly established. The *alazōnes* are acting out Henry's masquerade, lacking the wit to create their own; and Henry's advantage over them is his knowledge that life itself is mad, that the so-called sane live their madness "without knowing it or seeing it." Thus Pirandello reverses accepted notions of sanity and madness with a paradox taken from the heart of his philosophy. To live in a world where nothing is stable and man grows old is lunacy itself, while Henry's "conscious madness" is the highest form of wisdom: "This is my life!" cries Henry. "Quite a different thing from your life! Your life, the life in which you have grown old. . . ."

When the *alazōnes* attempt to bring Henry back into their world from his refuge in history, their meddling, as usual, issues in painful consequences. The Doctor, comparing Henry to a watch that has stopped at a certain hour, prepares to get the mechanism going again through a "violent trick." He will dress up Frida, who bears an uncanny resemblance to her mother as a young woman, in the costume of the portrait, and place her moving, speaking figure in the frame. Belcredi warns that the shock of pulling Henry across an abyss of eight hundred years might prove so strong that "you'll have to pick him up in pieces with a basket!" But Genoni, his implacable confidence unruffled, proceeds with his dangerous plan.

At the beginning of the last act, the throne room has been darkened, and the actors are in place: the living figures of Frida and Charles di Nolli have been substituted for the portraits of Matilda and Henry. When Henry enters the room, and Frida calls to him softly in the darkness, the shock is so great that Henry almost faints. The alienist thinks himself vindicated, since Henry is "cured." But Henry quickly reveals that he has been "cured" for eight years, and that this "violent trick" was a foolish and reckless blunder: "Do you know, Doctor, that for a moment you ran the risk of making me mad again? By God, to make the portraits speak. . . ." Henry, meditating a terrible revenge, tells his visitors about his decision to play the madman in order to abdicate from life, "that continuous, everlasting masquerade, of which we are the involuntary puppets, when, without knowing it, we mask ourselves with that which we appear to be. . . ."

But life draws him back again, against his will, in the form of uncontrollable instinct. In Frida, he finds his old love, Matilda, still young and fresh. Time has destroyed, but time, too, has miraculously

resurrected what it destroyed. His passion returning, he finds all the
treacheries and betrayals of the last twenty years have vanished in an
instant. "Oh miracle of miracles! Prodigy of prodigies! The dream
alive in you! More than alive in you! It was an image that wavered
there and they've made you come to life!" Matilda is old and de-
cayed, but Frida is the realization of the timeless dream. Losing control of himself for the first time, Henry goes to take Frida in his
arms, "laughing like a madman." The violent trick proves violent
indeed, and the conclusion is melodramatic. Belcredi intervenes,
shouting that Henry is not mad, and Henry runs him through the
body with a sword. When the *alazōnes* flee in panic, and Belcredi
expires off stage, Henry is left alone with his retainers to meditate
on the "life of the masquerade which has driven him to crime."
Forced back into the role of madman by this act, he is locked in it
now. The mask has obliterated the face. The mantle of Henry IV
has become a shirt of Nessus. Drawing his Valets around him for
protection, he realizes that history has become his prison, and he is
now lost for all eternity in its cunning passages: "here we are . . .
together . . . for ever!"

Henry IV is unquestionably Pirandello's masterpiece, a complex
artwork in which the themes arise naturally from the action—neither discursive nor superfluous, yet, at the same time, eloquently and
coherently stated. In the figure of Henry, moreover, Pirandello has
found his perfect *eiron-pharmakos,* one who acts and suffers, murders and creates, and one who can enunciate the author's ideas about
the need for privacy from interfering busybodies, the vanity of learning, and the way man takes refuge from a harsh reality in beneficial
illusions. In Henry, too, Pirandello has dramatized the dreadful
loneliness of human beings, encased in shells of steel, never able to
know or communicate with another. Pirandello's Henry, like
Brecht's Shlink in *In the Jungle of Cities,* watches the hungry gener-
ations stare coldly into each other's eyes:

> I would never wish you to think, as I have done [he tells his retainers],
> on this horrible thing which really drives one mad; that if you were be-
> side another and looking into his eyes—as I one day looked into some-
> body's eyes—you might as well be a beggar before a door never to be
> opened to you; for he who does enter there will never be you, but
> someone unknown to you, within his different and impenetrable
> world. . . .

This "misery which is not only his, but everybody's," as the author
describes it in a stage direction, is Pirandello's finest expression of

his rage against existence, the source both of his philosophy and his drama. And in *Henry IV*, Pirandello has finally converted intellect into genuine passion, making his existential rebellion the occasion for a rewarding and absorbing play.

Henry IV is also significant for the hints it throws out about Pirandello's view of art—views which form the basis for another important group of his plays. For while Henry suggests certain characteristics of the actor and the artist, a good many of Pirandello's characters actually *are* actors and artists, reflecting self-consciously on the implications of their roles. Pirandello's attention is fixed not on the act but rather on the *process* of the act, as analyzed by the one who commits it. In his more conventional plays, Pirandello imagines men watching themselves live. In his more experimental drama, Pirandello imagines performers watching themselves perform and artists watching themselves create—the mirror remains the central prop of his theatre. Actually, Pirandello's views of art are an extension of his concept of the face and the mask. When man becomes a *costruzione,* placing a mask over his changing features, he stands in the same relationship to his new identity as the artist does to his art—for art is the artist's *costruzione,* the form he imposes on chaotic life. The construction, in each case, is built up by the human demand for order.

In each case, too, Pirandello's attitudes towards the product are split. Like the mask, the work of art is both a limiting and a liberating creation. Art is superior to life, because it has purpose, meaning, and organization—the illusion is deeper than the reality. But art is inferior to life because it can never capture the transitory, formless quality of existence. The work of art is thus a beneficial illusion, an ordered fiction—more harmonious than life, yet still a lie. When Pirandello finds the temporal world unbearable, he takes refuge in the timeless world of art; but when he finds the fixity of art unbearable, he longs to break out into spontaneous life. The author, in consequence, alternates between aestheticism and realism, between nostalgia for permanence and desire for change; and this peculiar ambivalence is never resolved in his work.[6] But Pirandello continues to build his drama not on the affirmation of concepts but rather on the

---

[6] Pirandello's frantic desire for form may account for his attraction to Fascism (he had his Nobel prize melted down for use in Mussolini's Abyssinian campaign!). Like all authoritarian ideologies, Fascism represents a rigid order, providing certainty and definition. Still, considering Pirandello's accompanying desire for flux, and his distaste for propagandistic art, I cannot believe his political position was very serious.

conflict between them—"the inherent tragic conflict," as he phrases it in the preface to *Six Characters,* "between life (which is always moving and changing) and form (which fixes it, immutable)."

Here we can clearly see the existential consequences of Pirandello's sublimated messianic revolt. For the conflict between life and form is really a conflict between life and death. Pirandello's demand for form is literally a death wish, since, as he tells us, whatever is fixed in form is really dead; like his philosophy, his art is a negation of life. On the other hand, his discontent with art stems from an affirmation of life, since he wants to capture the elusive quality of existence. Only one artist was ever able to create living things, and that was God; and "God alone," as he says in *Lazarus,* "can recall the dead to life." The messianic impulse in Pirandello makes him long to be a god, and create a work of art that lives; but the existential recoil fills him with despair over the impossibility of divine creation.

Thus, the agony of the artist in Pirandello's drama is that, for all his ingenuity, he cannot really create life—to make an artistic form is to deaden and kill. In *Diana and Tuda,* for example, the older sculptor, Giuncano, has destroyed all his statues because, as he grew old and changed, they remained perpetually the same. He urges his younger colleague, Sirio Dossi, to undertake a statue of his young and marvelously beautiful model, Tuda, "the way she is now! When she's quivering with life, in perpetual change from moment to moment!" But Sirio argues that art is not the same as life. He is transforming Tuda, a nobody, into *somebody,* a statue—"*that one there. . . . That's the function of art.*" But the melancholy Giuncano feels compelled to add, "And of death too! Death will make statues of both of us when we lie stiff and cold in our beds or in the ground." Death, indeed, makes a statue of the aging writer in *When One Is Somebody,* who is petrified before our eyes, his words hardening into marble—the artwork, like the "somebody," is a thing of stone.

When Pirandello's messianism is the ascendant, however, he argues the opposite point—that the artist's work is superior to God's, because art, unlike man, is immortal: "All that lives, by the fact of living, has a form and by the same token must die—except the work of art which lives forever in so far as it *is* form." Pirandello is playing with semantics, since he has already identified the rigidity of form with the rigidity of death; but he is trying to apostrophize his function, and claim a sanctity for artists. In a more modest mood, however, he will simply suggest that artists are superior to ordinary people because they understand themselves better; they, too, are *eirones.* In *Trovarsi* (*To Find Oneself*), for example, another kind of artist—this time an actress—looking for her essential personality, discovers it lies in her art. An actress *lives* before her mirror, and accepts the various reflections which are thrown back. In the theatrical masks that she wears before an audience her true identity is found: "It is true only that one must create oneself, create! And only then does one find oneself." In short, the artist is superior because he *knows* he uses masks. And the very act of creation—like Henry's recreation of history—becomes a lofty, noble act of rebellion.

The contradictions multiply, and so do the Pirandellian paradoxes; only the basic conflict remains constant. Life and form are irretrievably at odds, and man suffers from his failure to reconcile them. Pirandello's desire to reconcile them explains, I think, his attraction to the theatre, because of all the literary forms, only theatrical art combines the spontaneous and accidental with the ordered and predetermined. In the interplay between actors, audience, and script, life and form merge. The living nature of theatrical art is further exemplified by its immediacy. The novel, with its "he says" and "she says"—speeches already spoken—is a tale of past time; the drama takes place in the present, with nothing separating the speaker from the speech. If anything written is fixed and dead, and literary characters are like the figures in Yeats's *Purgatory*—doomed to eternal repetition of their torments[7]—then anything staged is subject to accident, whim, and change, the actor insuring that it will always be new.

In Pirandello's view, in fact, dramatic characters are not alive at all until they have been bodied forth by actors; the action waits to burst into life, and passion to receive its cue. "We want to live," says the Father to the actors in *Six Characters*, "only for a moment . . . in you." Because the actor is only impersonating the character (*i.e.*, wearing his mask), the theatre performance cannot help but travesty the author's written conception; and much of the comedy in *Six Characters* is based on the disparity between the reality of Pirandello's six and the artificiality of the performers. Still, if the actor dis-

---

[7] Pirandello observes, in the preface to *Six Characters*, how literary characters are forced to repeat their actions forever, always as if for the first time: "Hence, always, as we open the book, we shall find Francesca alive and confessing to Dante her sweet sin, and if we turn to the passage a hundred thousand times in succession, a hundred thousand times in succession Francesca will speak her words, never repeating them mechanically, but saying them with such living passion that Dante every time will turn faint." In Yeats's play, the dead live out their purgatory by continually reenacting their fates, though conscious now of the consequences of their deeds.

torts his role, he is nevertheless essential to it—only he can make it live. This passion for life in art explains Pirandello's fondness for the idea of improvisation. In contrast with the author's writing, the actor's improvisation is vital, immediate, and spontaneous. And theatre, theoretically, reaches its ideal consummation when it springs, unprepared, from the imagination of the performer.

Thus, in *Tonight We Improvise,* the director, Hinkfuss, is pleased to announce that he has eliminated the author entirely: "In the theatre, the work of the writer no longer exists." Borrowing from Pirandello only a brief and sketchy scenario, his actors will improvise their parts in the tradition of the *commedia dell'arte,* substituting for the old stock masks the masks of their own creation. Hinkfuss, a three-foot tyrant with a huge head of hair, is a caricature of the overbearing Reinhardtian *regisseur;* but he also functions as a Pirandellian *raisonneur* in outlining the author's theories. Repeating Pirandello's obsessive conviction that "a finished work of art is fixed forever in immutable form," and that, on the other hand, "life must both move and be still," Hinkfuss goes on to declare that "only on this condition, Ladies and Gentlemen, can that which art has fixed in the immutability of form be brought to life, and turn, and move —on the condition that this form have again its movement from us who are alive." And this essentializes the difference between the theatre and all other forms of literary creation: "Art it is indeed—but life as well, Creation it is indeed—but not enduring creation. A thing of the moment. A miracle. A statue that moves."

On the basis of this theory, the living actors proceed to improvise a drama, pulling in and out of character, commenting on their roles, expressing dissatisfaction with the director ("No one directs life")— until finally they are caught up entirely in their parts and play them to an unexpected conclusion. In the theatre, anything can happen, and the pattern of art is disturbed by the accidents of life. Thus, in *Each in His Own Way,* the play is not even completed, because among the spectators are the real-life counterparts of the characters on the stage; and angered by being represented in this *commedia a chiave,* they attack the author and the actors, and bring the curtain down. For Pirandello, plot and character are now totally subordinated to the theatrical process itself, for that process is life itself. The theory is courageous—but Pirandello is not courageous enough to put it into practice. In Pirandello's theatre, the playright still exists. The "improvisations" of the actors are all composed beforehand, and the spectators are planted, their lines written too. Only through the disappearance of the author can the conflict between life and art be resolved, but Pirandello is unable to relinquish control over his work. Still dominated by his messianic obsession to create an organic art—changing from moment to moment, yet still formed by the hand of man—Pirandello refuses to complete his godlike function by withdrawing from the scene.

In his frustration over forming a statue that moves, Giuncano destroyed his art; Pirandello, frustrated but undaunted, continues to create, and the result is his "trilogy of the theatre in the theatre." *Six Characters in Search of an Author (Sei personaggi in cerca d'autore,* 1921), *Each in His Own Way (Ciascuno a suo modo,* 1924), and *Tonight We Improvise (Questa sera si recita a soggetto,* 1930), were all written at different stages of the author's career, but all are unified by a common purpose. Probing the complex relationships between the stage, the work of art, and reality itself, Pirandello attempts, in these plays, to forge out of the old theatrical artifacts a living theatre, destroying the traditional conventions of the stage by crossing the boundaries which separate art from life. In these plays, the illusions of the realistic theatre—where actors pretend to be real people, canvas and lumber pass for actual locations, and forged events are designed to seem real—no longer apply. Now the stage is a stage, actors are actors, and even the audience, formerly silent and half invisible in its willing suspension of disbelief, has been drawn into the action and implicated in the theatrical proceedings. As for the fourth wall, this fiction has been destroyed entirely—nothing separates the spectator from the stage except space, and even this space occasionally evaporates when the actors enter the audience, and the spectators come on stage. Having disintegrated reality in his more conventional plays, Pirandello is now disintegrating stage reality. Having scourged the peeping and prying of the social community, he is now attacking the community's peek-hole pastime, the theatre. For Pirandello, the fourth wall, designed for the entertainment of Peeping Toms, is an avenue that must be blocked.

Pirandello's experimental plays proceed logically from his theory. He had always been dissatisfied with the mere representation of reality on the stage, a function he assigned, with some condescension, to "historical writers." Since reality was a dense and perhaps impenetrable forest, Aristotelian *mimesis,* or imitation, seemed to him futile and presumptuous. How could anyone presume to know, much less to recreate, the unknowable? It was better to be a "philosophical writer," affirming a personal sense of reality and soaking the work of art in a "particular sense of life." This sounds Platonic; and indeed, Pirandello rejects representational art for Platonic reasons. Since reality lies not in material objects but in the Idea, such art can only be *an imitaton of an imitation,* two degrees removed. Pirandello's apprehension of the shadows in the cave, however, is intensely subjective. As he said in an interview with Domenico Vittorini: "in imitating a preceding model, one denies one's own identity and remains of necessity behind the pattern. The best is to affirm one's own sentiments, one's own life." Pirandello's desire to affirm his personal identity, to come out from behind the pattern, is not compatible with his desire to let the pattern create itself in the autonomous shape of life. But he is too subjective, too Romantic, too messianic a writer to relax his control over events and let them happen.

We have already seen how this compels him to write out the improvisations of the actors. For the same reason, Pirandello is unable to dispense with stage illusion, despite his angry attacks on it. The actors in the theatre trilogy are no longer pretending to be characters, but they *are* pretending to be actors—actors created in the imagination of Pirandello. And though the stage is now strictly a stage, it is still, to some extent, an illusionistic stage. In *Six Characters,* for example, the action takes place during a rehearsal in an empty theatre, but the rehearsal is really a performance, the "empty theatre" filled with paying spectators. Actually, whatever spontaneity occurs in these theatre plays is carefully planned by the author. As is often the case in these matters. Pirandello has destroyed one convention—and substituted another.

This convention is borrowed, probably unwittingly, from the Elizabethan theatre, for Pirandello's experimental drama is constructed on the pattern of the play-within-the-play. The inner action is "historical," the outer action, "philosophical," but both are products of the author's imagination. Pirandello was tending toward this structure in his more conventional drama; Henry's masquerade, for example, is a play-within-a-play. But now he tries to create the illusion that the outer action is improvised by actors, directors, and spectators, while only the inner action is an anecdote composed in advance. Pirandello goes further than any of his predecessors in breaking down the barriers between the inner and the outer plays; but he uses the convention for the same purpose as the Elizabethans—for commentary, criticism, and extradramatic remarks. Thus, Pirandello has not destroyed illusions; he has merely multiplied illusions. Contemptuous of imitation, he is unable to do without it. In his experimental drama, theory and practice fail to merge; idea and action fail to cohere. Unlike his companions in the theatre of revolt, Pirandello is never able to decide just to what extent he should enter his own work. Torn between messianic and existential demands, his Romantic ego is split wide open by its own contradictions.

Still, Pirandello's attacks on the deceptions of conventional realism and the narcotized stupor of the passive spectator had a revolutionary influence on the experimental theatre which followed. And if he does not ever solve the problem of life and form, he does open up a totally new side of it in each of his three plays. *Six Characters* examines the conflict between fictional characters and the actors who play their roles; *Each in His Own Way*, the conflict between stage characters and actual characters on whom they are based; and *Tonight We Improvise*, the conflict between actors who want to live their parts and the director who is always interrupting them. In each case, Pirandello preserves the pattern of the play within the play, preserving, besides, his earlier pattern of suffering *eirones* or *pharmakoi* surrounded by meddling *alazōnes*. In *Each in His Own Way*, the relationships are consistent with his past work. The real characters (*pharmakoi*) are mortified by their stage counterparts (*alazōnes*), who, by assuming their masks, are dragging their painful secrets into light.[8] In the accompanying two plays, however, the relationships are reversed—there the suffering characters are *eager* to have their secrets exposed, and the *alazōnes* are an obstacle to this end. Thus, in *Six Characters*, the six (*eirones-pharmakoi*) try to persuade the actors and their manager (*alazōnes*) to publicize their fictional private lives; and in *Tonight We Improvise*, the actors (*eirones*) are finally forced to throw the director (*alazōn*) out of the theatre in order to expose the inner souls of their characters (*pharmakoi*). In the theatre trilogy, the conflict between the *eirones*, *pharmakoi*, and *alazōnes* no longer serves to make a social point, but rather to illustrate the different levels of reality which the stage encloses.

The initial play in the trilogy, *Six Characters in Search of an Author*, is also the most effective, since its intricate structure permits an elaborate system of ideas to coexist with a striking theatricality. Like the other two plays, this famous work is constructed of a "philosophical" outer action around an "historical" inner action, but while the

[8] The pattern of this particular play is extremely complicated, because there are *pharmakoi* in the inner as well as the outer action. In the play-within-the-play, Delia Moreno and Michele Rocca are being probed and analyzed by the other characters, and suffer from it. In the action which takes place in the lobby, Signora Moreno and Baron Nuti—on whom the fictional characters are based —feel that they are being travestied on the stage, and suffer from it. In the ironic conclusion, however, the real characters find themselves behaving towards each other in precisely the same way as their stage counterparts, and are horrified at seeing themselves reflected in an accurate mirror.

total play is unified, the play-within-the-play is incomplete—*Six
Characters* is subtitled "A Comedy in the Making." As Pirandello
informs us in his preface, he had sketched out six members of a family as subjects for a "magnificent novel," but no longer capable of
telling a straightforward "historical" tale in a narrative vein, he decided to abandon them. The six, however, refused to accept their
fate: "Born alive, they wished to live." And now they have appeared
independent of the author's will—some dressed in mourning, all
bathed in an eerie, luminescent light—to a group of actors and their
manager who are rehearsing, in an empty theatre, Pirandello's *Rules
of the Game*. Fragmented and incomplete—part alive in the world
of fiction and part still in the womb of Pirandello's conception—
they seek another author to complete them. And for this purpose,
they offer themselves to the Manager and his cast. What follows is
designed to have the quality of an impromptu performance—a play
without acts or scenes in which intermissions are provided apparently at random, once when the Manager withdraws to confer with
the characters, once when the curtain falls by mistake.

The relationships between the fictional characters and the living
actors become exceedingly complex; and the conflict of the play, as
Francis Fergusson has perceived, proceeds on several planes of discourse. On the one hand, the characters create friction with the theatre people who first disbelieve their story, then find it too squalid
for the stage, and finally travesty it in the act of imitation. On the
other hand, the characters struggle among themselves, for they de-
test each other, and are bound together in mutual hatred. As the
drama of the characters is interrupted by the comedy of the actors,
and the two parallel conflicts begin to grate, the tragi-comic alterna-
tions create an atmosphere of the grotesque. The characters, furthermore, quarrel among themselves over the details of their story. And
the first act is almost entirely taken up with trying to determine the
vague outlines of this "historical" narrative.

For the author has only completed two scenes of the drama: one
in Madame Pace's dress shop, the other in the Father's garden. The
rest, conceived but never written down, is therefore open to interpretation by the characters. In brief, the written scenes are form
(fixed and immutable), while the unwritten background material is
life (fluid and changing). Together, these elements constitute the
"book," both form and life, which are the constituents of the characters themselves, and can only be learned from them. Here, in Pirandello's mind, is a statue that moves; his fictional creations have
developed an existence of their own. Except for the Mother, who is

unaware she is a "character," and the Boy and the Child, both of whom are mute, the characters possess a reflective life beyond the form their author gave them. In typical Pirandellian manner, they both suffer and think about their suffering; they both perform and see themselves performing, as in a mirror. Immobilized in written roles, caught up in an action which is "renewed, alive, and present, always!" they are also cursed with hindsight and, therefore, know exactly what form their purgatory will take.

The most reflective of the six is the Father, who, indeed, acts as Pirandello's philosophical *raisonneur*. It is his function in the first act to narrate "historical" past events—to provide, in other words, the exposition. Reconstructed from the Father's narrative and the Stepdaughter's angry emendations, the story goes like this. The Father had married beneath him—to a humble, ignorant woman by whom he had the Son. Her simplicity attracted him at first, but soon she began to bore him. And when he noticed that his secretary was in love with her and she seemed to respond, he sent them off together —prodded, he says, by the "Demon of Experiment," an urge to transcend ordinary moral conventions. The Father understands that this is only a phrase, a consoling illusion by which he disguised his real motive, and the Stepdaughter has no use for the Father's rationalizing which "uncovers the beast in man and then seeks to save him, excuse him." But whatever the motive, the Father forced the Mother to abandon her two-year-old Son and, deprived of maternal warmth, the Son grew up loveless, supercilious, disdainful.

When the Mother bore to her lover three illegitimate children— the Stepdaughter, the Boy and the Child—the Father began to take an interest in this family, and visited their city to observe the Stepdaughter as a child. Years went by, and the Father lost sight of them; unknown to him, they returned to his city. When her lover died, leaving the Mother destitute, she desperately cast around for work, finally finding a place as a seamstress in Madame's Pace dress shop. Madame Pace, secretly a brothel madam, employed the Mother because of her interest in the Stepdaughter, whom she wished to add to her stable. Without the Mother's knowledge, she succeeded. And when the Father comes to visit the brothel, he is unwittingly introduced to his own Stepdaughter. With a scream, the Mother interrupts their lovemaking "just in time" (according to the Father) or "almost in time" (according to the Stepdaughter); and this is one of the two scenes to be played. The second scene occurs after the Father has brought the Mother's family into his house, against the wishes of his Son. The Mother is agonized by the Son's disdain; the Stepdaughter is contemptuous of the Father's guilt; the Boy is humiliated at becoming an object of charity. These feelings produce a crisis, and the scene is to conclude with "the death of the little girl, the tragedy of the boy, and the flight of the elder daughter." Neither of these scenes, however, is performed in the first act; they are merely outlined; and the act concludes with the Manager determined to turn this story into a play.

The second act is devoted to the scene in Madame Pace's dress shop, which is performed by the characters involved, and then by the actors who take their parts. For the actors, who "play at being serious," the performance is a game, but for the characters, who are in deadly earnest, it is a compulsion: their drama is their lives. Thus, while the Father and the Stepdaughter *want* to play the scene, the one to expunge his guilt and remorse, the other to shame the Father, the Mother adamantly refuses to play it, in order to protect their privacy and hide their disgrace. But none of them really has a choice —the scene is already determined. When the Manager puts together some makeshift scenery, and a seventh character, Madame Pace, materializes, "attracted by the very articles of her trade" and whispering instructions to the Stepdaughter, the Father and the Stepdaughter thereupon proceed to reenact the origin of their shame and torment.

It is this scene which is altered, censored, and parodied by the actors in a manner which reverberates with Pirandello's shrill animus against the stage. The function of the actors, according to the Father, is to lend their shapes "to living beings more alive than those who breathe and wear clothes: being less real perhaps, but truer!" But although these "living beings" cannot breathe without the theatre, the theatre makes them even less real than they are, and much less true. "Truth up to a certain point, but no further," cries the Manager, when confronted with a scene too violent and strong. He is concerned over the sensibilities of the critics and the audience: the limitations of the theatre are those of a society which will not face an unpleasant reality. The vanity of the star performer, the expediency of the designer, the commercial-mindedness of the director, the timidity of the spectator—all throw a vast shadow between the author's intention and the theatre's execution, a shadow which lengthens in the artificiality of the theatrical occasion.

Still, it is not just that the theatre scants its possibilities; in a deeper sense, it is incapable of realizing the author's vision or capturing the feel of reality. Madame Pace's whispers are inaudible, because "these aren't matters which can be shouted at the top of one's voice"—private conversations are none of the spectator's business.

Similarly, the actor is unable to penetrate the secret heart of a character, because it is as elusive as a human being's identity. And dialogue is an added block to understanding:

> But don't you see that the whole trouble lies here. In words, words [cries the Father]. Each one of us has within him a whole world of things, each man of us his own special world. And how can we ever come to an understanding if I put in the words I utter the sense and value of things as I see them; while you who listen to me must inevitably translate them according to the conception of things each one of you has within himself. We think we understand each other, but we never do.

Like Henry IV, each man stands like a beggar before the locked door of others, and words make the lock secure. Both unwilling and unable to overcome this obstacle, the Manager transforms the sordid, semi-incestuous happening in the dress shop into a romantic and sentimental love scene between the Leading Man and the Leading Lady. And it is at this point that the Father understands how the author came to abandon them—in a fit of disgust over the conventional theatre.

Still, if the second act embodies Pirandello's satire on the stage, the third act embodies his conviction that theatrical art is more "real" than life. The Father has already accused the Manager of trying to destroy "in the name of vulgar, commonplace sense of truth, this reality which comes to birth attracted and formed by the magic of the stage itself." Now he proceeds to show how the reality of the characters is not only deeper than that of actors, but also deeper than that of living persons. As the Father tells the skeptical Manager, a character in fiction knows who he is; he possesses a "life of his own"; his world is fixed—and for these reasons, he is "somebody." But a human being—the Manager, for example—"may very well be 'nobody.'"

> Our reality doesn't change! It can't change! It can't be other than what it is, because it is fixed forever. It's terrible. Ours is an immutable reality which should make you shudder when you approach us if you are really conscious of the fact that your reality is a mere transitory and fleeting illusion, taking this form today and that tomorrow, according to your conditions, according to your will, your sentiments, which in turn are controlled by an intellect that shows them to you today in one manner and tomorrow . . . who knows how? . . . Illusions of reality represented in this fatuous comedy of life that never ends. . . .

The arguments are by now familiar and it is difficult not to share some of the Manager's impatience with the Father's perpetual, and rather windy, "philosophizing." But the cerebrations of the character have been carefully motivated, and it is the Father himself who justifies them: "For man never reasons so much or becomes so introspective as when he suffers; since he is anxious to get at the cause of his sufferings, to learn who produced them, and whether it is just or unjust that he should have to bear them." The Father's sufferings have, Hamlet-like, intensified his introspective tendencies, just as the historical line of the play has intensified its philosophical ramifications. The staple of the argument tends towards verbosity, but it opens the play out of the theatre, and into the theatre of existence itself.

Six Characters concludes in a burst of melodrama, which leaves its various paradoxes unresolved. The garden setting has been arranged, after a fashion, and now the less verbal characters must play their parts. The Mother has overcome her reluctance to perform in order to be near her Son, but the Son refuses absolutely to participate. Horrified with shame, and tortured at having to "live in front of a mirror which not only freezes us with the image of ourselves, but throws our likeness back at us with a horrible grimace," he claims to be an "unrealized character" in an unfinished drama and, identifying with the will of the author in this, refuses to play his part. And yet, as before, the play inexorably proceeds. While the Boy watches in horror, the Child falls into the fountain and drowns, whereupon the Boy draws a revolver and shoots himself. According to the scenario, this is the cue for the Stepdaughter to flee, leaving the original family—Father, Mother, Son—united in "mortal desolation," though still strangers to one another.

But the suicide has created pandemonium in the theatre. The Boy is lying lifeless on the ground. Is he really dead, or is the suicide merely pretence? "Reality, sir, reality," insists the Father, as the actors carry the Boy's body off the stage. Bewildered by this crosspatch of apparent realities and real appearances, the Manager can only throw up his hands in disgust, and on this note of dissonance and irresolution, the curtain falls. The ending of the play, however, suggests another reason why Pirandello left the "historical" action unfinished: it is too operatic to be convincing. But by enclosing this action within the frame of the theatre, he has created a probing philosophical drama about the artifice of the stage, the artifice of art, and the artifice of reality in generally suspenseful and exciting rhythms.

Pirandello's most original achievement in his experimental plays, then, is the dramatization of the very act of creation. If he has not made a statue that moves, he has made a statue which is the living signature of the artist, being both his product and his process. The concept of the face and the mask has become the basis for a totally new relationship between the artist and his work. Thus, Pirandello completes that process of Romantic internalizing begun by Ibsen and Strindberg. Ibsen, for all his idealization of personality, still believed in an external reality available to all, and so did Chekhov, Brecht, and Shaw. Strindberg had more doubts about this reality, but believed it could be partially perceived by the inspired poet and seer. For Pirandello, however, objective reality has become virtually inaccessible, and all one can be sure of is the illusion-making faculty of the subjective mind. After Pirandello, no dramatist has been able to write with quite the same certainty as before. In Pirandello's plays, the messianic impulse spends itself, before it even fully develops, in doubts, uncertainties, and confusions.

The playwrights who follow Pirandello are frequently better artists, but none would have been the same without him: Pirandello's influence on the drama of the twentieth century is immeasurable. In his agony over the nature of existence, he anticipates Sartre and Camus; in his insights into the disintegration of personality and the isolation of man, he anticipates Samuel Beckett; in his unremitting war on language, theory, concepts, and the collective mind, he anticipates Eugene Ionesco; in his approach to the conflict of truth and illusion, he anticipates Eugene O'Neill (and later, Harold Pinter and Edward Albee); in his experiments with the theatre, he anticipates a host of experimental dramatists, including Thornton Wilder and Jack Gelber; in his use of the interplay between actors and characters, he anticipates Jean Anouilh; in his view of the tension between public mask and private face, he anticipates Jean Giraudoux; and in his concept of man as a role-playing animal, he anticipates Jean Genet. The extent of even this partial list of influences marks Pirandello as the most seminal dramatist of our time; and it may be that he will ultimately be remembered more as a great theoretician than as a great practitioner. Still, he has left some extraordinary plays, which continue to live with the same urgency as when they were first written. And the melancholy of his existential revolt still sounds its elegiac music. "A man," he wrote about himself, "I have tried to tell something to other men, without any ambition except perhaps that of revenging myself for having been born."

The Technique of the Unseizable

by Auréliu Weiss

Traditional dramatic technique, staging unitary and well characterized types, contented itself (until Pirandello came along) with manipulating its fable so as to release at a given moment the characteristical reaction of the hero's temper. It was the supreme reason for the scenic conflict, since at the theater situations do not interest us for their own sake, but for their impact on the characters' lives.

Such a technique no longer makes sense in Pirandello's theater, because it goes against his fundamental conception. "You make me laugh," says one of his personages. "Where do you find real *characters* in life?" Everything in Pirandello's theater demonstrates that in real life there is no such thing as definite character. Character is fluid, involved in the eternal flowing of things. Perceptions and sensory truths, those basic axioms of our life, only mislead us about the real nature of phenomena because our spiritual retina retains images that no longer exist. All of our judgments are based on these retarded images. Yet under the apparent immobility are fleeting shapes, ceaselessly replaced by others which vanish in turn. It follows that the so called "characteristic" traits are but momentary reactions, due to certain circumstances which change soon after and provoke correspondingly new reactions.

In traditional drama the high point, otherwise called the supreme conflict, will confirm the character such as he has been represented during the previous scenic development by giving him the most intense expression. The reactions aroused by the Pirandellian conflict, on the contrary, free the individual from conformity and render his

"The Technique of the Unseizable" by Auréliu Weiss. From *Le Théâtre de Luigi Pirandello dans le Mouvement Dramatique Contemporain* (Paris: Librairie 73, 1965). © 1964 by Dimitri Weiss. Translated by Glauco Cambon. Reprinted by permission of Dimitri Weiss and Librairie 73.

natural reflexes to him: he is no longer the same, he becomes other.

These realizations, based on the letter and the spirit of the Italian writer's work, pose serious problems for us. How on earth are we to consider the great dramatic works of the past with regard to the new formula advanced by Pirandello? Should all the great poetical creations, from King Lear to Don Quixote, from Alcestis to Don Juan, from Tartuffe to Knock, to mention only a few examples, be regarded as nothing else than deceitful fictions devoid of correspondence to ever moving human reality? Should Lear, Don Quixote, Don Juan, Tartuffe be seen only as types of certain moments of their life, arbitrarily fixed like the isolated images of a suddenly stopped reel of film? Such a conclusion imposes itself if one takes into account the Pirandellian conception summarized in the words of the protagonist of *Six Characters in Search of an Author*: "The drama . . . is entirely here . . . in the awareness I have and each of us has of being 'one' whereas each of us is 'a hundred,' 'a thousand,' in fact 'as many times one' as there are possibilities in him. . . . With this person, he is 'someone,' with that person he is somebody else!"

"And for all that, we do not discard the illusion of our remaining the same for everybody else, of being just one and the same person through everything we do. Nothing instead is falser!"

This is a basic idea in Pirandello's work, resumed and developed with particular emphasis especially in his novel, *Uno, nessuno e centomila.* "This novel," he said to Louis Gillet "will be the key to my whole work." One can therefore easily realize how much he prized the idea that human personality is manifold and changeable.

But then what remains of the "eternal truth" we ascribe to the great figures of drama and fiction, such as the different ages have bequeathed them to us? According to Pirandello's conception they would be only the result of a trick by which life in motion is abruptly cut to give a durable and stable impression of what is actually momentary and transitory. As M. Doisy remarks in his study of Pirandello, "man, in the Italian playwright's work, sees himself confronted with the fictive character of his unity, with the impossibility of ever being fully himself, with the ineluctable corrosion of his illusory personality."

Agreed. But then, why did the Italian playwright say: "After Shakespeare, I do not hesitate to give the first place to Ibsen"? Was this not an avowal of esteem, and indeed admiration? And how could one admire what is simply trick and sham? For we know very well that these two writers have depicted human types whose traits are as characteristic and permanent as any, and on the other hand no connoisseur of Pirandello's work can be unaware of *Hamlet*'s influence on the conception of *Enrico IV*.

Must we not necessarily accept the idea that, whatever the differences of conception between writers, they see themselves bound by the same essential norms as soon as they tackle dramatic creation? [1] The requirements of the theater compel the playwright to summarize life in a few well chosen features. Thus all poetical thought, having to express itself inevitably in writing, becomes the prisoner of words which fix it in a text, isolate it and make it thereby typical.

In his *Essays on the Immediate Data of Consciousness*, Henri Bergson wrote: *"Language not only makes us believe in the invariability of our sensations,* but sometimes will deceive us as to the character of a specific sensation." And he added: "In short, the word with hard and fast outlines, the brutal word storing whatever is stablest and most common and therefore most impersonal in the delicate, fleeting impressions of our individual consciousness. . . . These words, as soon as they are formed, would turn, of course, against the sensation which gave them birth, *and having been invented to testify that sensation is unstable, they would impose their own stability on it."* (p. 98)

Pirandello could not ignore this immobilizing process, and he shows indeed that he has noticed it. "We do not change, *we cannot change,* become other," the Father confides to the Manager in *Six Characters, "we are what we are forever* (it's awful, Sir!) immutably," and in saying this he does not forget to make a distinction between artistic creation and life in these terms: "Your reality, instead, is timebound, an ephemeral illusion. . . ."

[1] Twenty-eight of his forty-four plays are derived from previously published stories. In his work on *Le Théâtre de Pirandello,* J. T. Paolantonacci proceeds to compare minutely the Sicilian author's short stories with the plays inspired by them, and states that "Pirandello the playwright has neither the verve nor the steady pessimism which stand out from beginning to end of his fiction. The resultant distortion affects not just the characters' make-up and the context of facts, but, vastly worse treason, the meaning of the original story . . . he felt the incompatibility of his story personages with the forms of traditional theater. In most of these cases, he has not succeeded in retaining the original traits of these characters as they appeared in the stories. Finally, he saw himself compelled to modify such and such a situation or epilogue to avoid the spectators' disapproval." (pp. 48-49)

However, where it is the reasoner who explains facts and gives them their sense, as in the trilogy of the "play within a play" [*Six Characters in Search of an Author, It Is So (If You Think So),* and *Tonight We Improvise*], the theatrical characters are conformable to the characters of his corresponding short stories.

We can easily understand the difficulties that rise on every side when the decision is taken to stage the continuous fluidity of life. For if one wants to know the face of the ideal human being in the Pirandellian conception, one only has to read the portrait Benjamin Crémieux sketched of it: "The ideal human being is in Pirandello's eyes one who has enough psychological and moral agility to mold every minute of his life into a form, assume full consciousness thereof, and then renounce the form right away, in order to resume contact with life in the following minute. For Pirandello the only truth resides in this psychological actualism!"

We can undoubtedly figure out what that means, but how is one to present such a human being on the stage? It would be rather the function of a perpetual cinema, and nobody can say what would come of that.

Dramatic action does not consist in a perpetual unfolding and does not present all images in their rigorous succession and kinetic connection. It separates and chooses only essentials in an order designed to strengthen and concentrate their effect.

No writer so far has been able to elude these rigorous laws of dramatic creation and performance. Pirandello is no exception.

For in actual fact, what does he manage to show us by really dramatic means, say, in *Six Characters?* Only a moment in the "Father's" life, which, according to his own expression, is nothing but an accidental "entanglement." But in order to make spectators understand that this entanglement represents only that one moment when he is surprised by his stepdaughter in a place and in a situation she should never have known, the author resorts to an exposition of his ideas, syncopated by the needs of dialogue, and each time resumed with renewed insistence.

The moment of "entanglement" is intensely dramatic, but the exposition which precedes and accompanies it and serves to elicit conclusions has nothing properly dramatic; it could have been the object of a simple commentary on the "moment" portrayed. While complying with the specific form and necessities of dramatic art, Pirandello fought back against them, deep down, in the effort to affirm the essence of those ideas which, since they make the human personality fluid, are, by the same token, antidramatic. He was forced to give a form, a consistency, and an end to what, in our deepest conception, has neither definite form, nor consistency, nor other end than death; he had to fix and imprison what is fleeting and contrary to all immobilization, and to limit what ceaselessly transforms itself.

This is the reason he hesitated to write for the theater, and even when he did, did not believe he could succeed. This is also the reason that for a long time he considered the theater an inferior genre— on account of the rigorous limitations it entailed.[2] He did not know, however, his inborn theatrical genius, which supplied him with the means to conquer a number of apparently insurmountable difficulties. Instinctively, in *Six Characters,* he dramatized commentary by opposing it to the Manager and the actors, and thereby created a parallel conflict. But to avoid impairing the necessary unity of action, he brought progressively closer the two levels of this conflict, the scenic and the purely ideological one, until they fused indistinguishably.

The resulting whole is consistent, but the procedure employed is visible. We can see that the essence of the playwright's dramatic thought can only be expressed by means of the direct commentary with which he expounds and explains it. We can also see the difference between fact, the element of plot, i.e., movement, color and life, and the interpretation of fact, the analytic element. The consequence is that while the "moment" has a fully valid and self-sufficient scenic life, the parallel ideological plot can only live for us by entangling with the other and giving the impression that it fuses with it.

A final consequence is that whereas the reasoner might disappear without damage from the pays of Alexandre Dumas *fils* and other playwrights who adopted that device, such a disappearance would be inconceivable in Pirandello. In his plays, this reasoner is the pillar of the ideological plot, whose essential role has been shown above.

[2] "Certainly," he wrote in his book on *humor* (*L'Umorismo,* 1908), "an epic or dramatic poet can represent warring elements in one of his heroes; but he will *compose* from these elements a coherent character in all of his acts. The humorist instead does the contrary: he decomposes the character into its elements and amuses himself to represent it in his inconsistencies. *The humorist does not recognize any hero.*"

"Art," he said shortly before, "like all ideal and illusory constructions tends to fix life. . . . It proceeds by abstraction. Now it seems to the humorist that this is going too far, to simplify nature and make life too reasonable and coherent. . . . But whatever becomes of this coherence the moment we harbor four or five souls struggling with one another? *When our consciousness takes exactly the attitude [that] each of these souls, provisionally ruling, in turn dictates to it?*"

Directing Pirandello Today

by Luigi Squarzina and Gino Rizzo

Gino Rizzo (interviewer): In the fifteen years you have been working for the theatre, what plays have been most significant in your development as a director?

Luigi Squarzina: My development has been more a change from one style to another than a progression of plays. At first, I felt I had to contribute to the reawakening of Italian conscience that was the task of our generation, and engaged in a kind of social realism which I would no longer indulge in. I recognize the validity it had then, but in no way would I identify myself with it now. I moved on to a more historically-minded *mise-en-scène*, and in that key I did my first Pirandello, *It's Only a Joke (Ma non è una cosa seria)*. Pirandello had never been done that way before. Still later, I freed myself of this preoccupation with historical accuracy, in order to regain the stage as stage. The theatre is used by the director as a painter uses his canvas: each creates his reality in the very moment in which he acts.

Rizzo: How did you approach *It's Only a Joke?*

Squarzina: It's Only a Joke was thought to be—and perhaps it is— one of Pirandello's minor plays. I thought that in order to make the play meaningful to us I had to set it right after the First World War. This, I think, helped portray the situation of She—the typical situation of Italian women—in the narrow microcosm of the men returning from the war, and of He, a petty would-be dictator. Without departing from the nostalgic and humorous tone of the play, I wanted to convey the sense of the impending catastrophe of Fascism. Pirandello was the most sensitive seismographer of his age.

"Directing Pirandello Today" (interview) by Luigi Squarzina and Gino Rizzo. From *Tulane Drama Review*, X, 3 (T31, Spring 1966), 76-90. The section entitled "Notes for *Each In His Own Way*" was translated by Joseph Williman. © 1966 by the *Tulane Drama Review*. Reprinted by permission of the Editors of the *Tulane Drama Review*, of Luigi Squarzina, and of Gino Rizzo.

Rizzo: Why did you choose *Each In His Own Way* for your second production?

Squarzina: 1961 was the twenty-fifth anniversary of Pirandello's death. Ivo Chiesa, who was then the sole director of the Repertory Theatre of Genoa (I joined him three years ago), suggested that I do either *Tonight We Improvise* or *Each In His Own Way*. I chose the second, because it had never been done since Pirandello's day, and because I thought I could see in it a great Pirandello—the equal of Joyce, Kafka, and Musil.

Rizzo: Could you elaborate?

Squarzina: In this play, Pirandello integrates his *ars poetica* into his own art and anticipates the treatment of reality on fragmented levels which is the mark of this century's great art. He approaches reality on the basis of its many probable levels—a quantitative, statistical approach. It was time to free Pirandello from the prison of his so-called dialectics. His thought is much more varied. In the two *entr'actes* of this play, particularly, Pirandello presents a truly original vision.

There are stage directions (which I object to most violently in any author) that are equivalent to the speeches of the characters. I treated the stage directions and the speeches interchangeably, and I was then able to present the "audience" in Pirandello's *entr'actes* as particles of a gas in motion. On the one hand, there is the play within the play: the design is clear-cut, almost angular; the scenes are sharply drawn, with entrances, exits, climaxes, and anticlimaxes all well defined. On the other, there are the scenes where the audience appears: these scenes are pulverized, as if they took place in a cyclotron, with a thousand fragments clashing and colliding without constructing anything. What they present is only a wide spectrum of probabilities cancelling each other out.

This remains my way of approaching Pirandello. When I reread my notes for the production of that play, . . . I still think the way to do Pirandello is to present him as one of the first European writers to contribute to the fragmentation of traditional structures.

Rizzo: You said before that the *mise-en-scène* of *It's Only a Joke* was set in post-World-War-One Italy. Did you do the same with *Each In His Own Way*?

Squarzina: I staged the "world premiere" of the play—it was originally given, I believe, in 1925, the only production until mine. There are speeches like, "Pirandello is on the stage," "He's left," "He's run away," etc., which made the "premiere" setting inevitable.

By accentuating the costumes, I was able to contrast a certain reality —the Italian stage of the Twenties and, implicitly, the stage of any theatre, any time and everywhere—with the reactions of an urban audience, a multifarious collectivity, barely kept together by the fact that at that time any audience was almost completely a bourgeois audience. My preoccupation was no longer with historical accuracy *per se,* as it was in *It's Only a Joke,* but with keeping the stage clearly distinct from the audience. I achieved that by an emphasis on the costuming, and, of course, on the style of the acting.

Rizzo: In your production notes you speak of three levels, as in fact Pirandello does. And you also say that in moving from one level to the other two, we witness a recurrent process of identification-alienation-identification.

Squarzina: What's in question here is no longer a style of acting or the costumes, but Pirandello's epistemology. The actor who played, let's say, Diego Cinci, was in fact asked to play three roles: the character Diego Cinci in the play within the play, the actor who played Diego Cinci, and the actor of the Repertory Theatre of Genoa, Alberto Lionello, who presented those two other levels. Thanks to the actor's skill and the dynamics of his relations to the other actors, I was able to show this one piece of reality in its three contradictory facets.

There, too, my aim was to break the dialectic between fiction and reality of Tilgher's formula,[1] which we should not take seriously any more. Pirandello accepted it, who knows why—perhaps because he found it convenient, or because it helped him in making his work clear and understandable to his audience. I think it did him more harm than good.

By moving continuously from identification to alienation and back to identification again, we presented Pirandello's reality as a playing with mirrors, as I think Pirandello really wanted it to be, but never as a Manichean dichotomy of reality—like *a* and *b,* black and white—never.

Rizzo: At the end of the play, how did you bring these three facets of reality together?

Squarzina: Through a general collision between audience and actors. The character who sees himself and his own life portrayed on the

---

[1] In his *Voci del tempo* (Rome: 1921) and *Studi sul teatro contemporaneo* (Rome: 1923), Adriano Tilgher popularized the interpretation of Pirandello's "philosophy" as a dialectic of fiction and reality, of "form"—the rigidity of the mask each of us wears in his contacts with society—and life.

stage is in the same situation which Pirandello had assigned him in the fiction of the play. He falls into a cliché, and in my production I had a photographer fix him with the flash of a camera, just as Pirandello used to say that we become fixed to a single act of ours. But by freezing him into a photograph, I de-emphasized the ideological value of this kind of identification. I was much more interested in the contrast between the actors with their poses—their absolute incomprehension of what they were acting out—and the audience, which confronted them with the thousand problems raised by the performance on stage. Though you still had two portions of reality coming into conflict, the conflict itself was not dialectical but polycentric, centrifugal.

Rizzo: You have already mentioned essential differences between *It's Only a Joke* and *Each In His Own Way*. Would you say that in the second play Pirandello is no longer interested in the portrayal of a given socio-historical reality and its universal significance, but takes as his point of departure a metaphysical inquiry?

Squarzina: Let us use a term you suggested yesterday, referring to Lionel Abel's book *Metatheatre*. More than of metaphysics, we should be speaking of "metatheatre" in this case. The play within the play, which is also called *Each In His Own Way*, has been put there with the express purpose of having it attacked by the audience and by the protagonists, in real life. Pirandello, like other artists in this century, has not so much written a play as given us the materials for a play: they are *objets trouvés,* a collage made up from the fusion of several of his short stories with dialogues of the worst "Pirandellism." The first two scenes are the most extreme Pirandellism Pirandello ever wrote, and the reason he parodied himself was to break through the solidity of traditional structures and insert his own presence in the play. This is action painting or collage. The socio-historical reality which appears here and there in this play is only one of the collage elements.

Rizzo: What about the criticism that has been made of the melodrama in *Each In His Own Way* and *Six Characters?*

Squarzina: I think such criticism is wrong, of course, because the melodrama is like a piece of newspaper next to a patch of color in a collage. The more melodramatic and "in bad taste" the play within the play is, the more clear the meaning of the total play becomes. Pirandello had this kind of courage—for which he was certainly not given credit the first time the play was produced. He was criticized for having written a poor play, and then building on top of it a ponderous structure.

Rizzo: Don't you think that even *Six Characters* is usually seen as the representation of a dichotomy between art and life?

Squarzina: It should be presented as work-in-progress. In the past, one of the notable interpretations of *Six Characters* was that of German expressionism. I think the time has perhaps come to show it as drama that is taking place at the very moment of the performance —each speech is totally unexpected—the structure is abolished, and we are constantly in the presence of a magma.

Rizzo: This would also justify the title, which otherwise remains incomprehensible. At the close of the play, they are still in search of an author. . . .

Squarzina: They haven't found him yet. But it is Pirandello who has found his *Six Characters.*

Rizzo: To go back to *Each In His Own Way,* you said that the structure of the play consists of the changing perspectives among its three different levels: the play within the play, the discussions among the audience in the *entr'actes,* and finally the irruption of those in the audience who identify themselves with the characters on the stage. . . .

Squarzina: Yes, but there is also a fourth level: the presence of the author, made more tangible and unavoidable by the mention of his name. Pirandello is said to be there at the performance from the very opening scenes.

Rizzo: But is it just his name that gives us the sense of his presence? You have said that his presence was even more intrinsic in the Pirandellism of those two scenes of the Old Gentleman with the Thin Young Man, and then of the Two Young Ladies.

Squarzina: Yes, of course. These two scenes seem to be unrelated to the rest of the play, but they are the best kind of introduction. They are one of the most modern things the theatre of this century has to offer. What you have is an author who presents even the negative side of his own poetics; he parodies himself, as if to say, "See, I can look at myself and see what I'm doing; so, please, let's talk about something else." And this cannot fail to cause alarm among his critics.

Rizzo: In such an overt presentation of his poetics, don't you think that Pirandello could be seen as a forerunner of the absurdists?

Squarzina: Certainly. In Pirandello the non-sense word, spoken without being thought out, used merely as a cliché, appears often enough. In *Each In His Own Way,* there are entire sequences that are built on it. The most obvious one comes in the second *entr'acte,* when you don't know if it is the actor who has slapped the leading actress, or the actress who has slapped the author—no, it's the author who has slapped the actress. It's pure theatre of the absurd, or even better— because Pirandello offers it as only one moment in a work of far greater complexity, rather than as the basis for a whole evening at the theatre.

Rizzo: By and large though, wouldn't you say that Pirandello's logical paradox differs from the non-sense of the theatre of the absurd?

Squarzina: Yes, because he was not confronted with a mass society. In Italy, especially, communication was not yet devoid of information. For Pirandello, the problem was still an epistemological one; it had not become social. This can be a limitation, but also a definite advantage. The theatre after Pirandello had to deal with problems posed by a new social context—the problems of individuals who can no longer find words to express their inner selves. In Pirandello, the exchange between two human beings is not condemned by their society, but by their being. And since every one of us is like that, we will never learn the truth—except as we get to know it by living it out without an end.

Rizzo: We've talked of *Each In His Own Way*'s dramatic structure and the significance of the many levels of this play. Now, as a director, how did you realize them in your production?

Squarzina: In the *mise-en-scène* the problem was to show the play within the play as dated, and to distinguish it from the conversation carried on by the audience—which is also somewhat dated, but very real and such that it could happen any time and anywhere. In the part of the play that shows the stage, there is a double theatrical transposition, since what we are seeing there is how the society of a given time revealed itself on its stage. In the part showing the audience, on the other hand, although there is a certain distance between us and the audience of that time, there is no actual screen. When the actors were on stage, I kept in mind what the theatre was in Pirandello's time. Those were the days of the actor-director type of company, and Pirandello was usually produced by fashionable troupes whose repertory was made up primarily of Hungarian comedies and French *pochades*. In my production, the actors who did those scenes had to follow an outmoded and, for a modern audience, inadequate style, while making their drama credible.

Rizzo: How did you manage these two conflicting effects?

Squarzina: By following the charge of irony you always have in Pirandello. This enables you to wink an eye at your audience, telling them that you act that way because you've got some reason to, or asking them to believe you anyway. And in that portion of the play I observed faithfully the traditional structure: the well-made scene, the *scène à faire,* the *coup de scène.* On the other hand, in the *entr'-actes* where the audience appears, I used, and also further developed, all the techniques with which you can divest a word of its meaning —the word as syllable, as a compound of letters, as assonance, as mere sound, as noise, as the clashing of two sounds, as an orchestrated phrase—a treatment very much like that of *"musique concrète,"* including its cacophony, out of which the main themes developed through the conversation of the audience could finally emerge and be heard.

Here I learned how to turn the stage directions into speeches. I said before that I don't like stage directions. I think they reveal better than anything else the limitations of the bourgeois theatre— a kind of paternalism on the part of the author towards his readers and his interpreters. But in *Each In His Own Way* the stage directions lend themselves beautifully to a total integration of the play. There is, for instance, a digression on smoking, the effects of smoking and why people smoke; I turned it into a speech, having one who's smoking say it while the rest of the action continues to merge and dissolve in a constant fluctuation.

Rizzo: Doesn't the handling of the audience pose certain problems in the stage setting?

Squarzina: The setting of the play within the play was painted canvas, which reproduced in good taste the bad taste of the time. The *entr'actes* showed instead a solid architecture, geometrically defined and characterized by a total lack of pictorial elements, as if to contrast its three-dimensionality with the bi-dimensionality of the other.

Rizzo: How did you work the transitions from the stage to the *entr'actes* at the end of each act?

Squarzina: By using the revolving stage, which was seen in motion only at the end. At the end of the first act I had the curtain fall as if it were time for the intermission. I also had the applause and booing recorded as if it were a performance of Pirandello's time, with the typical reactions of his premieres. When the curtain re-opened almost instantly, the setting showed the foyer of the theatre with people talking and arguing as if coming from boxes and galleries. Curtain again, and when it re-opened there was the second act of the play. Curtain closed and re-opened, and then the setting showed the circular corridor along the boxes, with people listening both to the uproar coming from the orchestra and to a brawl that had started on stage. I thought I found the touchstone of my production precisely at this point. I had the mass of spectators rush through the door leading to the stage, occupying it like an army of invaders. The stage was being blasphemed and desecrated—and, therefore, it too was denounced as a part of reality rather than as a temple devoted to some mysterious ritual.

Rizzo: What happened to Pirandello's wish to have the audience of the *entr'actes* mixed and confused with the audience of today's performance, so that one couldn't tell if the man sitting next to him was a spectator or an actor?

Squarzina: That was Pirandello's intention, no doubt about it, but I believe that in this too we can go beyond such a scholastic dichotomy. Our notion of total theatre has changed considerably since Pirandello's time. And again, I have the feeling that Pirandello used it as a device. Both because I wanted to show the audience as the primary level, and the play within the play as secondary, and because I intended to give an integral rendering of Pirandello's text, I decided to discard this element as banal. I sacrificed surprise and that type of emotion, in order to give my audience a reflection of themselves on the stage—they could see their reality in a mirror, so to speak, rather than having it all around them *à la* Stanislavski.

In my production, I didn't start with the first scene of the play within the play. I had it begin with the Intelligent Spectator. The scene showed the audience entering the theatre. Pirandello has it this way too, when he says that this happens on the street leading to the theatre, but he confines it to the stage directions. What I did, instead, was to turn the stage direction into the first speech of the play. The Intelligent Spectator enters. The scene is otherwise still empty; he lights a cigarette and says, turning to the audience: "Look, this play should begin on the street." In a word, I was explicitly stating my reading of Pirandello by saying that he had intended it in a certain way and I was using his intention in order to create theatre on the stage.

Rizzo: I take it that if you were to do *Six Characters* you would de-emphasize the entrance of those six on stage, their relationship to the audience. . . .

Squarzina: Of course. This is not the main problem in a production of *Six Characters.*

Rizzo: I still haven't asked you how you handled those spectators in the audience who identify themselves with the action shown by the play within the play.

Squarzina: I didn't make them act any differently than the rest of the audience, because, like them, they were supposed to represent the people who live in houses, who get up after dinner to go to a theatre. Rather, it was those who played *as actors* who showed at times that they were being watched by an audience. This also was coming from within rather than without. In saying certain things about the characters they portrayed, they would throw glances toward a hypothetical place—a box, or the orchestra—where they imagined the real people they impersonated might be. You had the old problem, the problem raised by Brecht, of the actor who cannot merely live the part he plays, but must also pass judgment on it. Except that I kept it within the bounds of humor, of professional self-consciousness. The actor is not entirely convinced of what he says, and stops being an actor to become part of the audience, of the critics—everyday life watching its own transfiguration on the stage.

Rizzo: You mentioned Brecht. What about Pirandello's impact on the contemporary theatre, both in Italy and elsewhere?

Squarzina: In the case of Brecht, I think his notion of "alienation" is quite different from Pirandello's. Perhaps you could find some points of contact in one of his pre-Marxist plays, like *Man Is Man.* But even there, Brecht's main preoccupation is the debunking of capitalistic, bourgeois attitudes. In Italy, the playwright who learned most from Pirandello was Ugo Betti. His roots must be traced back to Strindberg, but his handling of the dialogue comes from Pirandello. Outside of Italy, the man who has inherited Pirandello's vision of reality is Genet. Genet is even trapped by Pirandello's notion of reality as theatre. In him any relationship is constantly denounced as theatre. Reality is offered as mere hypothesis, to be either denied or affirmed. This is obvious in *The Balcony,* but you find it also in *The Blacks* and *The Screens.* The distinction between the French and the Arabs, like that between blacks and whites, moves away from its social, racial basis towards the metatheatre so typical of Pirandello.

Rizzo: Now an unfair question. Are you sorry you cannot do Genet?

Squarzina: Yes, indeed. But, after all, in Italy we got rid of censorship only three years ago. The recent reawakening of interest in the theatre must be put in relation to the abolition of censorship. Plays like *Galileo* or *The Devil and the Good Lord* could not have been produced before. This kind of play has almost created a new audience. In Italy it is impossible to do *The Deputy,* and in Genoa we cannot now do Genet. I regret it.

Rizzo: The objections raised against *The Deputy* are not the same that are being raised against Genet.

Squarzina: Of course not. As for *The Deputy,* I saw the Paris production, which was not great; and yet at the end one was almost paralyzed by the exposure of those facts that are thrown at you like handfuls of ice. But it is not a good play. In the case of Genet, instead, I feel restricted in not being able to show one of the great dramatists of our time. This for me is much more serious.

Notes for
Each in His Own Way—
LUIGI SQUARZINA

. . . The drama of modern art and its public, Everyman after Hiroshima faced with the debris of Dubuffet, the chromatic tumors of Wols, the burlap canvases, Burri's industrial red-lead on shards of sheet metal, the orchestral blasts of Nono, the "what cannot be said is better left unsaid" of Wittgenstein's anti-philosophy; a drama already dated, if it is true that the leveling-off of taste, the techniques of psycho-control, the establishment of the marketplace in the cultural sphere all threaten to deprive Everyman (and his artist) of any right to tragedy. In this respect *Each In His Own Way* can be presented, today, not at all as a manifesto of Pirandellism, but rather as nothing less than a lyrical consummation without a trace of discursive reasoning, a poetics that is poetry. For someone working in the theatre it has the same value as a page by Mallarmé on poetry would have for a poet. It seems to say that his theatre, indeed all theatre, is a vast *pièce à clef* in which the actor "of the true drama— of life" is the inescapable, feeble Everyman, at first indifferent, then inept at seeing himself "in the mirror," then indignant at the image of himself which the artist offers him, then irritable if an Intelligent Spectator tries to enlighten him as to what is going on, then fascinated, then, finally, ready to accept identity. ("It is true, we must punish each other! Don't you think?")

. . . Pirandello places himself in question, his very vision of things, his very commitment as poet-philosopher. Accused of extreme subjectivism and of barely concealed solipsism, he projected himself onstage most ostensibly; criticized for the predominance in his works of the rational over the poetic, he offers two hours of cruel, bleak sincerity. The first act seems simply a "discussion about drama"; if the audience wants "a little poetry," a critic points out that the discussion is "the drama itself." But the second act will open with a symbolic glittering and clashing of swords. . . .

. . . "The play's the thing/Wherein I'll catch the conscience of the King": the conscience of mass society, the uncrowned king. Not so much a play within a play, both for Pirandello and for us, as a play about a play. "The performance of this play should start on the street": doormen, ushers, even the playbills perform in this codification of nonsense in the guise of a philosophical thriller, written by the man himself, the celebrated dramatist; performed by brilliant and sophisticated actors, the company of Nicodemi; seen and discussed by spectators—those of the early Twenties; dissected by critics on varying esthetic premises; attacked and ultimately accepted by the protagonists in real life of the tabloid item brought onto the stage. . . .

. . . The pivot is Delia Morello, alias "la Moreno," "and everybody knows who she is" as it says by her name in the cast—so the playbill already suggests, "except herself." Delia Morello, a real female *casus belli*, a sado-masochist on the outside, but inwardly a woman in search of her lost innocence, of her share of truth which is at the mercy of the opinions of others, just as "la Moreno" is at the mercy of the artist who could take care of "what she most needs —her spirit." Certainly this is not up to La Vela (alias Giorgio Salvi) but rather up to him, Pirandello, who takes care of it even as far as revealing the relativity of his own opinions (the third act is not performed, "and after—after the third act—"). . . .

. . . Everything is doubled—the character and the actor who plays that role, Pirandello, author of the total play, and Pirandello, author of his own role in the play, the babbled cues from the audience and those spoken onstage. Diego Cinci makes up for his own failing by becoming analyst-prophet-judge of the acts of others and of their intentions: thus even in the play within the play there is a spectator, a critic; the game of mirrors is really endless. It is a dialectic of identification-alienation-identification (to be performed as "absorption-estrangement-absorption"), but an open dialectic, which can be pursued without ever straying afield, thanks to the irony and humorous imposture of the author. . . .

. . . Too stylized, the speeches of the actors in the inner play would perhaps prove unbearable. My device should become clear enough from the melodramatic pattern of the action playing against the flow of dialogue within the audience; from the painted settings (Italian production, 1920-25) playing against the theatre construction; from a kind of frontal and conventional position playing against the coming and going in the lobby. To point out the conscious and subtle irony in Pirandello's own style, his own rhythms, his own manner: take the first two scenes between the Old Gentleman and the Thin Young Man, and between the Two Young Ladies; take the "cerebral acrobatics" of the duel. . . .

. . . The audience. A most difficult problem, terrifying for any director. One must approach it with humility, restraint, with no claims to grandeur: attempt to produce it with a limited number of individuals (about forty), always the same whether in the foyer or in the lobby or in the corridors—like a statistical graph of public opinion, in motion all the while. A treatment not choral, but rather statistical, of the various reactions, a collective entity forever in imperceptible motion like a chemical gas; a serial treatment of cues (the memorable series of "who has slapped whom"). To show a public in search of a ready-made truth without the bother of a moral choice, its leaning toward a form of knowledge which is egoistic rather than altruistic, idle curiosity and small talk rather than thirst for truth; yet without forgetting that even within the audience there is a kind of life which does not stop at discursive reason, whose reaction provides the zones of sentiment—that is, of action and thus of moral responsibility. It is this element in the audience which recognizes itself in the mirror of the play. To represent the spectators who invade the stage and instinctively lower their voices, as if they had come suddenly into a temple: an inverted mysticism, the blood of San Gennaro will not liquefy. . . .

Pirandello and Possibility

by William Herman

". . . But if this cannot be done," the playwright's Last Testament continued, "let my funeral urn be taken to Sicily and walled up in some rough country stone of Girgenti, where I was born." Thus with his peculiar foresight he was able to write into this document the same characteristic alternatives he had once provided in his theatre pieces. The Greek urn containing his ashes was kept in the municipal museum of Agrigento for—who knows why?—twenty-five years, and on the anniversary of his death was taken back to Caos, the estate where he had been born, and there walled up in a big rock resting beneath his favorite pine tree. "Walled up." The Maestro would have been quick to appreciate the irony. For in the damp of current neglect, the fires of his genius have suffered precisely the fate of his ashes.

". . . THEATRE IN THE THEATRE. . . ."

Luce! Luce! Luce!

—*Luigi Pirandello*

When Georges Pitoëff introduced *Sei personaggi in cerca d'autore* (*Six Characters in Search of an Author*) to Parisian audiences in 1923, he introduced Luigi Pirandello to the world.[1] And his masterly

"Pirandello and Possibility" by William Herman. From *Tulane Drama Review*, X, 3 (T31, Spring 1966), 91-111. © 1966 by the *Tulane Drama Review*. Reprinted by permission of the Editors of the *Tulane Drama Review* and of William Herman.

[1] Charles Dullin had actually staged the first Parisian performance of Pirandello on December 20, 1922 at the Théâtre de l'Atelier. It was known in French as *La Volupté de l'honneur* (*Il piacere dell'onestà*). Some months earlier, Dullin had asked the translator, Camille Mallarmé, if she would recommend and acquire in his behalf an Italian play for that season—possibly something of Verga's. Instead she had contacted Pirandello, whose suggestion of *Così è* she overruled. *Sei personaggi* was translated for the Pitoëff's by Benjamin Crémieux, who re-

strategy for staging the entrance of the Six Characters—they were lowered onto a bare stage in an old elevator, an open cage once used to bring on scenery—was not just a dazzling piece of appropriate theatre. In that surpassing moment, Pitoëff said everything in a single rendering: at once it was clear what the title meant. The central aesthetics of the playwright were demonstrated: the same elevator which dropped his ideas down on stage brought also a prophecy of how Pirandello was to be occupied for years to come. These characters, as we learn almost immediately, are *not* in search of an author—despite the title. On the contrary; their author, Pirandello himself, "no longer wished," once having birthed them, "or was no longer able," to put them into context, i.e., in a play, on a stage.[2] Therefore they seek not an author but a sponsor. Who might this be but a Director? (And here the ideas come sparking away from the stage action in dazzling fashion.) But the Director rehearsing *Il giuoco delle parti* in that empty theatre is powerless to sponsor them without the connivance of the audience watching *Sei personaggi*. And if his cast of actors leave, could we then be sure about his sponsorship? It is a question we gladly lay aside, since it is clear in the next light that the question is too narrow.

In the text the entrance of the Six Characters is in one sense a weakly structured, poorly motivated event. The Doorkeeper, hat in hand, comes fumbling up to the Manager (the Director), just when the Six appear at the back of the stage "in a tenuous light." He advises him that some people . . . well, they've asked to see him. The Manager is furious at the intrusion, but is unable to order them out —he briskly asks what they're doing there and what they want, and the play is thus set in motion. This event is the kind of hasty decision that Pirandello often makes; he is so eager to begin a work that he sacrifices a careful structure in behalf of a more burning interest of wider dimensions. In another sense, however, such a weakness is exquisite art. If the Manager had not had his interest engaged by the sight of the Six Characters—in Pitoëff's production, an extraordinarily impelling sight—if he had not been made curious enough to

---

mained Pirandello's French translator till he was killed in the war. It opened a few months later, on April 10, 1923, under the title *Six Personnages en quête d'auteur*, at the Théâtre des Champs Elysées.

[2] Unless otherwise indicated, translations throughout are my own, for reasons which will be made clear below. The texts used in all such cases are from the series, *Biblioteca Moderna Mondadori*, Arnoldo Mondadori, ed. (Milan: various dates); *Sei personaggi* together with *Enrico IV* make up Vol. 27 (XIth edition, 1965).

overlook his annoyance, he might not have made his inquiry, and simply had the unwanted visitors removed. So that the deliberate structuring of the entrance in an illogical or, rather, ambiguous manner, literally forces the director of *Sei personaggi*, as it does not force the Manager of *Il giuoco delle parti*, to think for his life about how he will inaugurate the *play's life* on the stage: if he does not, there will be no play.

Pirandello shows here the same sort of random event that he so frequently has a character merely *describe*. This is the familiar speech about the effects of actuality on a previously fixed form, such as a mood, an inclination, an attitude. Suddenly a flower, a sunset, an opportunity, or any of the myriad aspects of being impinges upon the fixity initially held by the character. And with that his equilibrium is disturbed and a new configuration gives new and unexpected shape to his being, hence to his activity. So it is with the Manager, whose strictly bounded intentions for the immediate future (a rehearsal) are changed by the entrance of these people—*who are not less real for being less true*. But is this not the moment-to-moment essence of theatre? Which art can lay greater claim to fostering multiple identity, resonant action, and the flowering of choices? And of all our public, hence open, celebrations, only theatre—by virtue of its double nature as closed system, too, whose products are retained and distilled again—can be so uniquely useful. Here, it must have seemed to Pirandello, was a grand gathering of liberated possibility; here was an opportunity for tragic contemplation. Thus the surrender of the bland and linear stage illusion must have seemed a small price to pay for the embracing *actuality* of the life-art conflict: even the dullest imagination could see the stakes involved. And I suggest that after the production of *Sei personaggi*, Pirandello addressed himself to the task of making such a theatre by undertaking first to design and then write the two remaining plays in his trilogy of "theatre in the theatre." *Ciascuno a suo modo* (*Each in His Own Way*, 1924), and *Questa sera si recita a soggetto* (*Tonight We Improvise*, 1930).[3]

THE SIN OF ACCOMPLISHMENT
AND FIGURES EXPOSED

To collections of his plays in Italian, the playwright prefixed an overall title, *Maschere Nude*. There is something flagrant in such an emblem, and a sense that its owner is more than a little aware of dis-

---

[3] The dates given are for the years of first Italian production.

playing a sinful flag. *Exposed Figures* is eminently appropriate to his whole intention as an artist; the personages he put on stage in that condition became his hallmark. But he was never quite so successful in exposing himself as he was in tenderly revealing the *Maschere.*

In his essays *L'Umorismo* . . . and *Teatro nuovo e teatro vecchio,* and in the famous *Preface* to *Sei personaggi* Pirandello established the authority by which he could label his plays comedies, and with precision set out the aesthetics of humor to account for their tragic storms. But apart from *L'Umorismo* these essays were late reflections, made after the fact. (In the *Preface* he expounds cogently on a line of dialogue from the play, the Father's assertion that this is a "comedy in the making.") The passage of time had provided him with the opportunity to reflect on and assimilate a world-wide audience response to the play. Thus he was able to explicate the grand design of both first play and whole trilogy. But the actual composition of *Sei personaggi* must have been in late 1920 or early 1921, and it was not until 1924 that the next part of the trilogy was finished. Then six years more elapsed before Pirandello wrote to Marta Abba from Berlin describing the first night of *Questa sera.* A total of, say, eight years to compose three related plays—by an author who is known to have "dashed off" a play (*Liolà*) "in about a week." Obviously, the task he had set himself was a very great struggle.

Now the place occupied by the middle play in the trilogy may not be known to the reader just because it holds that crucial position; but anyone familiar with *Ciascuno a suo modo* knows its sheer quantities at least. So much dialogue, so heavy a tangle of idea and argument—it is staggering. The writing of this play alone, therefore, must have taken considerable strength from its author. Yet these years were the most fertile in his writing career. In 1922 alone, for example—in addition to three considerable short works—he wrote *Enrico IV,* considered by many to be his greatest work;[4] and the play which seems to me (if not in this category) a seminal vantage point from which to view the tripartite vehicle of his great innovations: *Vestire gli ignudi.* (I will not attempt a translation of the title here, since I must make a point of it later.)

[4] My admiration for *Enrico IV* is unqualified. But my agreement with Mr. Bentley's opinion—that it represents a "version of illusion and reality crystallized," implying as it does that a system has come to rest—together with the enormous difficulties of the breathless first act, diminishes my attachment to this play.

Pirandello was in the midst of his struggle to complete his crowning achievement: the trilogy. But during this period—and here I am all surmise—he had also permitted one of his central, tumultuous ideas to come to rest, by the act of writing *Enrico IV*. Until 1922, after the composition of *Sei Personaggi* and *Enrico IV*, he was still teaching school. Leaving his post at the Rome Normal College for Women must have been a bitter reminder of the years he had spent with his wife, whose psychosis had ended in death four years earlier in an asylum. His mind must have been a turmoil of passions, memories, plans, and a good deal of self-recrimination. The Roman Catholic must have been considering his sins. Perhaps he thought especially of the sin of pride in leaving the school to devote himself exclusively to theatre. After all he *had* done great work while he was still thus engaged. Perhaps also he had been turning over in his mind what *might* have been done for Antonietta—though he had surely done everything possible. With all this: the "sin" of *Enrico IV*, together with the guilty knowledge that there was great work ahead and a need to get on with it.

So, as an unmistakable reminder of what was yet to be done in order to complete the design of the trilogy, there was the dramatic "note," *Vestire gli ignudi*. And I suggest for it yet another purpose: a work of mercy to gain plenary indulgence for his sins.

NAKED: THE SELF AND THE THEATRE

> It is surprising how little has been said as yet of Pirandello's art.
> Even against it.
>
> —*Eric Bentley*
> *Naked Masks*

Ludovico Nota is the name of the "old" novelist in the play, the good samaritan who offers so much to the wretched Ersilia Drei. When she accepts his hospitality and enters his rooms, she is sick, penniless, a stranger, a prisoner of the identity she has forged by telling her story to the newspaperman, Alfredo Cantavalle—and before the play is over she will die. But Ludovico Nota, the old novelist, is the dramatist to be, Pirandello himself. Translating his name literally: "I amuse myself with a memorandum." In Latin, moreover, "nota" may be taken figuratively as a stigma, or disgrace. Thus Pirandello is the real penitent in Ludovico Nota's performance of the seven Corporal Works of Mercy.[5] In Roman Catholic theology devotional exercises of this order gain an indulgence remitting all temporal punishment due to sin. In *Vestire gli ignudi* these works are done on stage in symbolic form: feeding the hungry, giving drink to the thirsty, clothing the naked, harboring the stranger, visiting the sick, ministering to prisoners, burying the dead. And when Ersilia staggers in at the end, having taken poison for the second time, it is Ludovico who is first to grasp that there is no remedy, that she has other needs:

> *Ersilia.* It's too late! There's no help . . . for the love of God, shut up. Leave me alone. And you, Mr. Nota . . . and Signora [Onoria, *sic*] . . . it won't be sudden, unfortunately . . . but I hope it will be quick. . . .
> *Ludovico.* I see . . . then what is it, what do you want?
> *Ersilia.* Your bed.
> *Ludovico.* Certainly—this way!

Thus having ministered to the prisoner she was, harboring the stranger she was to remain to the end, and though performing ambiguously the task of *Clothing the Naked,* Nota provides for her burial at last.

There is in this connection a pattern of trinity in *Vestire gli ignudi* that has obvious reference to the Church, and which would not be important did it not also recur throughout the trilogy. Ersilia's last name is Drei (in Italian, *tre* and in English, three).[6] A trinity of males decides the fate of a "fallen woman." Here they are represented by Grotti . . . , Franco Laspiga . . . , and the singular entity composed of two writers: Cantavalle . . . and Ludovico Nota . . . .

There are several trinities in *Sei personaggi*—one for each of its females *venite ad terram*. For the Step-Daughter: the Father, the Manager, and her own father; for the Mother: the Father, the Man-

---

[5] F. L. Cross, ed., *The Oxford Dictionary of the Christian Church* (London: Oxford, 1958), p. 345. See in the same work the entries "Indulgence," "Plenary Indulgence," and "Spiritual Works of Mercy." The first two provide the basis of theological notions expressed; the last is of some interest in that these may be seen as a silent "plan of action" in doing the trilogy—indeed of his whole canon; but the subject is too large to include here.

[6] Pirandello was a student of philology and received his Ph.D. at Bonn. This note is not to buttress my contention that he had in mind the German word, but to suggest in general that among his skills was a certain linguistic bravura.

ager, the Son. Even the Child has the Father, the Manager, and the Son (who is at once responsible for her death, and the one who discovers her corpse). The ordinal form in Italian is *terzo; Questa sera* was adapted from Pirandello's story, *Terzetto,* or triplet. In that play, Mommina's fate is in the hands of Rico Verri, Dr. Hinkfuss, and her alleged lover, whom Rico identifies as Pomarici but who is a shadow lover, the one hovering over the Italian national psyche since the Renaissance and who might as well be Rico-The-Leading-Man. This same pattern emerges later in *Ciascuno a suo modo.* Delia Moreno, who is the model for Delia Morello, has a visual representative of the trinity in her mysterious Three Male Escorts. They are shown removing her from the theatre, restraining her, ultimately denying her libidinous attraction toward Baron Nuti. The onstage counterpart of Il Barone is Michele Rocca who together with the antagonistic friends, Salvio and Doro, constitutes the trinity of fate for Delia Morello.

Now it is not especially rare to find an author, in describing a character in his own age range, or someone who shares his profession, setting down his own physical attributes and thereby gaining a vicarious pleasure. In Pirandello's plays, however, it is striking to note how often there appears the typical description, "a novelist, perhaps fifty years of age . . ." and the frequency has not gone unnoticed.[7] But when he does this in describing Ludovico Nota—as he had in describing the Father, as he would later in the trilogy with so many *actual* references to himself—his purpose is not at all to draw a series of self-portraits or "autobiography . . . presented to posterity"; it is true that "all artists have an obsessive central experience," but Pirandello's was not of the self *per se:* he was, in fact, secretive about himself.[8]

Pirandello's presence on the stage serves the crucial purpose of insuring that his audience knows the stage for what it is: a stage. Putting himself there created a metaphor whose purpose was to draw the spectator's attention to the platform under his feet. Destruction of the spectator's "belief" in the verisimilitude of stage event was the great innovation of the trilogy; it is the over-riding aesthetic of all

[7] See especially Lander MacClintock, *The Age of Pirandello* (Bloomington: Indiana University Press, 1951), pp. 220ff.

[8] A great many monographs on Pirandello in Italian, especially biographies, have this idea expressed in their titles; here are two: *L'uomo segreto (The Secret Man)* [F. V. Nardelli, 2nd ed., Milano, 1937], and *Il segreto di Luigi Pirandello (The Secret of . . .)* [Pietro Mignosi, Milano, 1937].

three plays. And how he accomplished it in *Clothing the Naked* might best be seen by first looking at this table:[9]

Description of characters:
> [A few samples of character description will be enough; the rest are equally mangled by the translators.]

Pirandello	Livingston	Murray
Personaggi	*Dramatis Personae*	*Characters*
Franco Laspiga, *già tenente di vascello*	. . . ensign in the Italian navy.	[Mr. Murray is more tight-lipped than the original; he says nothing other than to list names, thus omitting even the few details Pirandello *might* have wished to lead before starting.]
Il vecchio romanziere	. . . *a novelist.*	
Ludovico Nota		
Il Console Grotti	. . . *Italian consul of Smyrna.*	

The time:

A Roma—Oggi.	*The scene is laid in Rome in the 20th Century*	Time: *The present*

Setting the scene:

La scena rappresenta lo scrittojo del romanziere Ludovico Nota.	*Study of Ludovico Nota, a novelist.*	*The combination study and living room of the writer, Ludovico Nota.*

Eventually Mr. Murray also has Laspiga in the navy. But Pirandello says only that he is "formerly a ship's lieutenant." In the absence of any indication that the ship was a naval vessel, or anything

---

[9] Pirandello: *To Clothe the Naked and Two Other Plays,* trans. William Murray (New York: E. P. Dutton & Co., 1962), pp. 2-3; Arthur Livingston's translation, *Naked,* appears in William Smith Clark, II, ed., *Chief Patterns of World Drama* (Boston: Houghton Mifflin Company), 1946, pp. 946-1005. Note Mr. Livingston's demotion of Laspiga to "ensign," his addition of "20th century" to Pirandello's "today" and his premature disclosure of Grotti's station. Because of these and even more crucial items of omission and "creativity" I have preferred my own inadequate (but I trust literal) translations.

connoting a passenger liner, one may conclude safely that it was a merchantman. Then—for the purposes of the play, which call for Laspiga to be invested with prestige—a reading could be tolerated making him the executive officer, first mate of a merchant vessel. Such would tally with Ersilia's reference to his uniform in the last speech of the play: an officer in the merchant marine would doubtless wear something impressive. Yet as erroneous as this single instance of mistranslation is, it would be tolerable if it did not signal worse.

For Pirandello refers to "the old novelist," and in the *first words* describing the scene he writes, "the setting represents the writing-desk of the old novelist, Ludovico Nota." The "old" novelist is the new playwright, and the setting—his two furnished rooms—represents the desk on which he will write the drama before our eyes. And this process is yet another reference made by the title. For when Ersilia sets foot into—or, rather, onto—his writing-desk, she is a cipher, a piece of raw stuff for Nota to fix into a formal dramatic aspect. In a sense he fails to do this, and the cause of his failure is the past, the life that is Ersilia's clothing and which will not be denied *its* opportunity to make a drama of its own. In this, she resembles the Six Characters (those fully developed ones, the Father, the Step-Daughter, etc.) whose lives cannot be regulated but clamor for attention and fate. In the opposite way, Ludovico *is* the agent responsible for the denouement; for he and he alone is in a position to deny her contact with Franco and Grotti, and they—in forcing her to experience again the pain of past events—force the ultimate conclusion. Ersilia is stripped bare by the re-enactment with Grotti and Franco of a past we have already begun to sense in the first act. And it is Ludovico who writes into the play the entrances of Grotti and Franco onto the stage of his apartment. Life impinging on art is not a new idea; but it is at the heart of Pirandello's theatre. The life in art and the life in the self are inextricably bound together. Pirandello brings both on stage, in barest condition.

SIMULTANEITY

> The first act . . . of all artists . . . is
> to change the function of objects . . .
> —*André Malraux,*
> *The Voices of Si-*
> *lence*

It may be argued that unless a program note contained the author's scene description, the audience would be unaware that the setting is Nota's writing-desk. But the first scene of the play—from the time Ersilia enters until the end of Nota's bitter little skirmish with Mrs. Onoria—is studded with oblique references to the stage as stage—while several other levels of enactment go on.

At the rise, the harsh clamor of life in the streets is heard coming in through the double windows of the room. And when she enters, Ersilia is immediately distracted and drawn by these sounds. Nota enters and observes this at once. "Here I am!" he says, "Come and sit . . . sit down"; then, racing to close the windows, as if a moment's more intrusion by the hurly-burly life sounds of real life will ruin his commencing dramatic fiction, "My God, these windows are really a curse!" The landlady, Mrs. Onoria, is now discovered to have been in the bedroom changing the sheets on Nota's bed, according to his instructions. And a bitter squabble begins because Ersilia is sitting in a "gentleman's" room. The gist of Mrs. Onoria's complaint is that she runs a respectable house, and she won't have him filling it with women.

Now this is a strange complaint to be taken literally; in accordance with his instructions, she is changing the sheets: she has begun with a compliance that belies her present stance. In addition, one would think she would be armed with more specific details if she wished to press this complaint effectively. The clash is too brief to be taken literally, too full of innuendo suggesting the real source of their conflict. Pirandello is dramatizing once again the opposition of life to art in this encounter: Mrs. Onoria is all of the earth; and her ears are too closely attuned to the ceaseless flow of life outside to be able to accept the artist. Nota is bringing another subject, not life, onto his stage. That is the real difficulty. If banality had walked in with him, *va bene!* Life's a thing to cry about; not its encounter with drama. In the second act—by which time she has seen "real" events reduce the situation to her level—she is quite on the side of Ersilia and Nota. As indeed she is before the first act is over. And to press the point further, the opening of the third act finds her at the windows carrying on in a heated effort to get at the "facts." So that it might be necessary to wait for reflection—until the scene is over—before the scene makes it pointedly clear: the stage is, nevertheless, a stage. Listen to the writing imagery that piles up within a few minutes of Mrs. Onoria's departure:

Ludovico, to Ersilia. . . . As soon as we get here: this lovely scene!

[*As Ersilia apologizes for it.*]

Ludovico. No. It's a year now since I started to fight that witch: A legacy—I don't know—from the nightmare of all this dirt . . . [*writer's paraphernalia, books, manuscripts, etc.*]

[*But he's told the landlady he will leave. He tells* Ersilia *he has the new place; she can pick out some furnishings, and:*]

Ludovico. . . . and you can shape your nest with your own hands.

[*The "old" novelist, versus the new playwright.*]

[*He explains his need to make fresh beginnings, and goes on:*]

Ludovico. But I'm very pleased to have had the inspiration to write to you. . . .

The theatre will henceforth be the site of his writing-desk.

The "nightmare" would be Pirandello's enormous output of fiction; and it alone is enough to have made him a great writer. The short stories are superb, in a realistic vein that is a tribute to his Sicilian master, Giovanni Verga. The fiction was a recent discovery of no less a literary sensibility than Professor Irving Howe, who distinguished them from the plays this way:

> In the plays, where character is replaced by role and identity by personification, the burdens of a middle-class life cease to be a subject to be portrayed and become a springboard for an imaginative leap beyond the limits of verisimilitude.[10]

It is not too far-fetched, in returning to that crucial scene once more, to suggest two other roles for Mrs. Onoria. The first would be Mrs. Antonietta Portulano Pirandello, whose loveliness in the photograph appearing in Gaspare Giudice's recent biography belies her tormented existence.[11] The other is the archetype of actual landladies in whose rooming-houses Pirandello spent time when Antonietta, gripped even harder than usual by her fantasies of her husband's betrayals and sexual excesses, took the children and ran back to Sicily. Infidelity, in marriage or outside it, is the mass of raw dramatic stuff that runs through his plays, and indeed those of his predecessors in nineteenth century Italian drama.[12]

[10] Irving Howe, "Some Words for a Master," *The New Republic*, Vol. 141, No. 13 (September 28, 1959), p. 23.

[11] Illustration facing p. 169, *Pirandello, Volume quinto della collezione, La Vita sociale della nuova Italia* (Torina: UTET, 1963). It is surprising to see even his most astute critics attack the woman with such unanimity. Pirandello might have avoided her paranoid accusations—but all things being equal he *chose not to*. Mrs. Pirandello died in an asylum in 1918.

[12] For a view of the stiflingly narrow focus of this theatre see Domenico Vittorini, *The Drama of Luigi Pirandello* (Philadelphia: University of Pennsylvania

For its breadth of humanism Jacob Burckhardt's view of Italy and Italians was perhaps the grandest. His portrait of the national character is essentially ascribed to the distinction of a native individualism. It is informed, Burckhardt explains, by uncommon powers of morality and imagination.

> And where the imagination has exercised the most powerful and despotic influence on morals is in the illicit intercourse of the two sexes.
> . . . What seems characteristic of Italy at this time, is that here marriage and its rights were more often and more deliberately trampled underfoot than elsewhere.[13]

Thus it is clear that Pirandello's "endless harping on the same string" is not imputed to his marital circumstances alone. Still the pall of the one idea—infidelity—hung low in the air of the playwright's daily existence.

And one marvels at the opportunities he created in all the plays to dramatize this singular theme—at once so private and so public. One of the so-called "Sicilian" plays, *Il berretto a sonagli* (1917), has a denouement very close to what might have been at the time it was written his own fantasy of wish-fulfillment. Ciampa, an old storekeeper (whom Pirandello identifies as keeping a pen over his right ear), cooperates to maintain stability between four people in a community where outrage is easy to enlist: himself, his wife, Fiorica, with whom his wife is having an affair, and Fiorica's outraged wife, Donna Beatrice. This he accomplished by conceiving the inspiration of having the wife of the man who is cuckolding *him* sent to an asy-

---

Press, 1935), Lander MacClintock, *The Age of Pirandello* (Bloomington: Indiana University Press, 1951), and Thomas Bishop, *Pirandello and the French Theatre* (New York: NYU Press, 1960). See also J. H. Whitfield, *A Short History of Italian Literature* (London: Cassell, 1960) and Ernest Hatch Wilkins, *A History of Italian Literature* (Cambridge: Harvard, 1954). Summaries provided in these of works by Pirandello's predecessors such as Verga, Manzoni, Praga, Antona-Traversi, and Giacosa will make this evident at once. As will the play that students of literary influences agree was a touchstone for his work, Luigi Chiarelli's *La Maschera e il volto* (*The Mask and the Face*). A man too cowardly to carry out the threat that he would kill his wife were she to be unfaithful sends her abroad instead, since he cannot bear to have that cowardice revealed. Whereupon his prestige grows enormously and he finds himself surrounded by admiring women! Out of a nearby river, you see, a body has been fished, badly decomposed, obviously a woman. And it had been assumed that it was the wife. But she returns from abroad with predictable results. The play is more Ibsenite than Pirandellian, but is couched in terms that would doubtless have stirred his imagination enormously.

[13] *The Civilization of the Renaissance in Italy* (Modern Library Edition), p. 327. But Burckhardt attributed greatness to its character as well, understanding wellsprings to be indifferently provident.

lum. Viewing the play as part of its author's fantasy life, it is possible to see that psychic process known as displacement. The equations are: Pirandello-Ciampa and Antonietta-Beatrice. Ciampa, an innocent, and Donna Beatrice, another innocent, are displaced by Pirandello—also an innocent, whose relationship to Ciampa is that both require peace and equilibrium to reign over hostile and unstable situations not of their creation—and Donna Antonietta, an offender, as is Donna Beatrice who also speaks the truth (a matter incidental to her identity with Antonietta).

Variations on this theme can be seen in *Clothing the Naked*. Grotti has betrayed both Ersilia and his wife; Franco has betrayed both his fiancée and Ersilia; and Ersilia has been betrayed by both. When it is recalled that Pirandello's marriage to Antonietta Portulano was arranged by the elder Pirandello for his son, who knew the bride-to-be only slightly, we can also mark the perfunctory relations enjoyed by Franco-Ersilia, Grotti-Ersilia, and Nota-Ersilia—all of whose involvements were in no way restrained by the short acquaintances each pair had enjoyed before the floods came. Such a lack of familiarity prior to the start of a deep entanglement can only send the partners scurrying off in search of places to hide, as if in preparation for the uncertain joys of a new life. One is under no imperative to *use* the hiding place, only to have it comfortably nearby should the intimate stranger become oppressive. Keeping the places ready means visits, and when these become regular one might just as well put them to use. And so it goes. For the life of simultaneous existence cannot distinguish between rehearsal and performance.

THE PATTERN AND MEANING OF PASSION

> To me it was never enough to present a man or a woman and what is special and characteristic about them simply for the pleasure of presenting them; to narrate a particular affair, lively or sad, simply for the pleasure of narrating it; to describe a landscape simply for the pleasure of describing it.
>
> —*Luigi Pirandello,*
> Preface to *Sei personaggi . . .*

Early in *Sei personaggi*, the Father remarks to the Manager, "Oh Sir, you know as well as I do that life is full of an infinity of absurd-

ities, all of them so impudent—they don't even need to *seem* probable; simply because they're *true*. This is the first in the cascade of
trilogy dialogues where the equation of art and madness is expressed;
the remarks had been elicited by the Manager's charge of madness at
the Six; and the very next speech of the Father's is an aesthetic pre-
cept which defines acting as that which reverses life's usual situation.
Actors, he says, are professionally engaged in making things seem
credible in order that they can be accepted as true. But the credible,
the plausible, the probable are shadow areas. The landscape is
treacherous. And, as a leitmotif in *Sei personaggi*, we find yet another
limit. This is the ultimate limitation of the actor, who is split from
the character he is to assume. In short, no physical body may occupy
two spaces at the same time. Light is therefore required, and something of a mirror so the actor may see himself at work making credi-
bility.

For these, a master is the requisite necessity. And, always available
to reinforce his notion of the stage's primacy, Pirandello has placed
the stage director squarely in the center of his own theatre. In the
presences of Dr. Hinkfuss, the Manager, and Ludovico Nota are
seen the classical functions of the stage director: the physical mount-
ing of the work, the rendering of its sequential order and ideologic
disorder, and the lending of a certain competence to the actor, in
order to assist him toward anonymous identity and maximum effect.
They are the lights, they are the mirrors.

It is true that the trilogy design can be apprehended from a great
many vantage points, the best of which is at the level of the stage
platform. But it is useful to stay on stage and trace the pattern of the
master there as the trilogy progresses. First, of course, the Manager
seems to be autocratically in control. But the entrance of the Six,
which the reader will remember as the generative event, is most ambiguously under his control. The Manager starts the play only if we,
the audience, are held by an illusion of sorts. If, that is, we believe
in his "reality." And we are held but lightly that way, if one considers how agreeable he is to one of Pirandello's grandest displays of
skill as *boulevarde dramatiste*. That is, the Manager swallows without blinking the appearance of Madame Pace—the *seventh character*, who steps magically out of a light effect when the physical accou-
trements of her shop have been fabricated on stage.[14] It is true that

---

[14] Pirandello displays himself beautifully in the business of Madame Pace's late
appearance. Boldly he lists the lady in *Personaggi* along with the other Six (and
apparently nobody has *counted* them!); then expects the implicit reason for her
exclusion at their first entrance to hold up, i.e., the Six have dropped on stage

his authority over the Company of Actors is firm; but the play is heavily weighted with the Characters' presences, not theirs. And at the final curtain, after his long involvement, he has really been unaffected by his experience. While Actors and Characters hurry off with the bodies of the children, we hear him bellowing, "Ehhh! What a waste! Hey! Somebody light a flashlight at least—I can't put one foot in front of the other!" If he starts the action, he does not stop it, or experience its effects.

Diego Cinci plays the same role in *Ciascuno* as a marvelously subtle balance of actor, director, and producer. As actor, he dramatizes out of his own past the irresistible nature of biological impulse for Doro's mother. It is a vital piece of monologue, serving to confirm Doro's original defense of Delia Morello; the tortuous track of logic in this piece making such demands throughout. In the second act, he is a master dialectician in arranging so long a stay in what should be the enemy camp: Salvio's house. Were he not so good an actor on that occasion he should not have been permitted to stay around long enough to serve as producer-director. This function is exercised when Rocca arrives. It is Diego's relentless interrogations and insights which call forth the truth from Rocca about his relationship to Morello, which in turn is dramatized in the love scene at the act's end. Having "staged" *this* scene, Diego may accede to the producer's office, for the repetition of the moment by Delia Moreno and Baron Nuti ends the play. Thus Diego exhibits somewhat more power than the Manager. Though he does not initiate the action, he manipulates it; and though unaffected by the action, he is the author of its demise.

It is Dr. Hinkfuss who has been blessed with the full power of command—though he appears at times to have less than his due measure.[15] But even when he is evicted from the theatre by the actors, he winds up in just the position off-stage where he may reassert his lost authority: at the electrician's board, where he directs the

---

because of their passionate needs—and obviously Madame has no such need. But this logic will not work, since a volitional motive for the Child—who comes with the Six—would be hard to find. She is four years old. And to make matters worse, the Father, in shrewdly creating Madame's physical habitat to evoke her physical presence, has forgotten that others should have appeared as well as Madame. Another customer, another girl? It is a striking mark of Pirandello's skill that it hardly matters.

[15] Dr. Piscator and Max Reinhardt, who modelled for the Doctor, are the donors of his bristly authority and temper. The odd name, or a variation of it, belonged to Pirandello's landlord during his residence in Berlin during the winter of 1928-29.

crucial light effects in Act III. Dr. Hinkfuss is enough of a threat to elicit a rarely heard address by Pirandello in his stage directions: "But these miraculous occasions are best left to those capabilities residing in the bizarre imagination of Dr. Hinkfuss." With the same stream of sarcastic derision he continues, placing the blame "not on the author of this story," but on Hinkfuss, for making Rico Verri and his cohorts officers in Air Force white; then suggests that doubtless Dr. Hinkfuss, on this very account, will provide a magnificent effect showing an airfield at night for the edification of those who've remained in their seats during the lobby scenes. Thus only a self-created author of Dr. Hinkfuss' dimension could summon so much —even by design—from Pirandello. In keeping with the upward curve of complexity, we arrive at *Questa sera* for the most commanding of the masters. Hinkfuss starts the action, usurps it with his Act I lectures, and declares it over.

Ludovico Nota is squarely an ancestor of Dr. Hinkfuss, prefiguring by his exercise of authority the shape of the Doctor's. Like the others, Nota is the conductor and the grand orchestrator of the drama that he finds on his hands. But unlike Diego and the Manager, who have found it, both Nota and Dr. Hinkfuss create what they conduct. And Nota, like the good playwright that he is, enjoys the spectacle of the divertissement he is making. Nota is Ersilia's author, but his career as a sponsor is a fatally ineffective one. Just why an author should be a bad sponsor is a question having to do with the nature of authorship. The characteristic kindness attributed to authors is not, I think, altruistic. Rather it smacks of the need to see an alternative, to view a range of choices from which action can be charted, character set firmly on its feet, landscape rendered. A bit of something once caught can be set down and altered, perhaps, moved around to another angle, improved. But until it is, blankness is the white and paralytic condition of the author; and any sort of operation that will elicit the bird from the air is his fair game. And not so strangely at all, the game seeks out the hunter.

To see this we have only to demonstrate which of Nota's attributes Ersilia is most sensitive toward. In Act I, the old novelist tells her that the newspaper story had started his mind to work at once on a fictional concept of Ersilia. And it is so vital to her to be precisely what he'd imagined her to be, that she starts to match her actuality against his construct. And when she elicits from him that she is entirely different from the figure of his imagination, she is distraught enough to wish to leave. Thus it is his imagination that causes her the deepest pain. No matter how kindly its cast, or decent its colors, the mere fact of its power to clothe is intimation that it is privy to the worst secrets concerning her self: that *she* is shopping for clothes. And it is a touching scene indeed that culminates in her speech, just prior to Cantavalle's entrance, which starts her toward nakedness. It indicates firmly the constancy of her need if she is to stay alive:

> *Ersilia* [replying to *Ludovico's* questions about whether she feels she is being cheated out of a life story]. Exactly. Out of its happenings—out of my whole life's experience! You see . . . I didn't *want* any more of living. I suffered *all* the fine desperations . . . So—excuse me if I'm direct—I think it's only right for you to give me at least enough life in your story—which will be a beautiful thing, oh, so beautiful. . . . Like the other novel of yours I once read, wait, what was it called? *The Outcast.* That's right. *The Outcast!*

Ever an economist, Pirandello finds the chance to mention his novel, and by having Nota cast aspersions on it, his name too. It is the pattern of a master. A moment later Nota leaves the room to find out what Cantavalle wants before letting him upstairs to see Ersilia. But he ushers him directly into the room, then finds out. Of course it is far too late, for Cantavalle's revelations in front of the girl have all to do with initiating the downfall she suffers. Ludovico Nota, the sponsor of possible subjects, has once more demonstrated he knows how to stage an effective entrance. It is a mastery shared by Hinkfuss and Diego Cinci, and the means by which it fulfills its designs are surprising.

THE PASSION OF THE MASTER

> *Lie:* . . . Individuals fanatically devoted to truth, like some social reformers and political and scientific theorists—individuals given to system-building—frequently falsify facts out of a sense of altruistic grandiosity: "I am the shepherd, you are the sheep . . ."
>
> —*The Domesday Dictionary,* Louise J. Kaplan, ed.

The plays of Pirandello are dense with word, argument, thesis, aesthetic declaration, and outright lecture. Whether the habit of prolix-

ity is found in other forms of his enormous total output I cannot say.
But the loquaciousness we find in his dialogue is certainly related to
the fertility of his imagination. And the imagination of the artist is
not entirely beyond illumination, as are the ultimate sources of, say,
genius. For example, an instrument of productive imagination can
be thought of as continually discharging its freshly made objects.
This is no occasion for dispensing with the popular mystique of
artistic work, but it should be noted that a genius with a relatively
small life's work to show is nevertheless in such a state of continual
activity. That this fecundity does not always register on the world is
less a matter of its questionable existence than of the problems of
the artist in making a formal organization for the material. When
this latter case obtains, outlets for excess are required. Frequently
they are found, and in rare instances an artist finds one that is perfectly felicitous. In the case of Pirandello, the mind that was predis-
posed to make theatre found a perfect solution: the great hue and
cry raised by passion wherever it goes. The tumultuous histrionics
suited the nature of his overproduction admirably.

Now in the general sense, passion means strong feelings, especially
in the areas of anger, hate, or sexuality. Specifically, passion is used
to connote Christ's torment on the cross. It need hardly be noted
that the word, when it has any currency at all, is a coin tinged with
embarrassment. Where it *has* a place in actual usage, what is usually
meant is "the highest pitch of experience." And one assents to the
definition with the vital qualification that claims be carefully examined. For the passionate nature is less often perceived by the detached observer than claimed for himself by the passionate-natured.
To believe in very many such claims is not at all a sober subscrip-
tion. Some basis for judgment may perhaps be found in Picasso's
remark that "there are no concrete or abstract forms, but only forms
which are more or less convincing lies." So similarly have these men
performed in quantity of imaginative production, that the painter's
words might easily be ascribed to the playwright. The views *sound*
like Pirandello. Lies and counter-truths and more lies; and all of
equal weight? Yes. But then what of passion, Pirandello's least convincing lie? There is reason not to charge it against him entirely.

In *Clothing the Naked*, as representative of the flood of passions,
there is the sordid and empty life of Ersilia, the cliché social standards of Laspiga, and the pitiable whine of Grotti—who signals not
the dark and irresistible pull of evil lust as Ersilia would have us
believe but rather the shoddy urges of the hemmed-in and middle-
aged. And what of Nota? Ersilia evaluates herself, "To serve . . .

to obey . . . to find it possible to be *nothing*. . . ." Is this the object of Nota's passions? One isn't convinced on the strength of such declarations as, "I was offended that you should have thought my only interest in you was to satisfy my writer's curiosity. . . ." It is no fault of Pirandello's if one cares to fall for this prestidigitation. But it is not to be believed. And the tip that gives the hand away is contained in that solo attempt of Nota's to make a pass at Ersilia. It is half-hearted, in retrospect, since it is never really seen to be repeated; and it is so easily and so quickly ended.

The long operatic cast to the last play in the trilogy is the cue for Pirandello's intent in creating the passionate floods. They are diversions, just as are all loud and long demonstrations on the theatrical scale. The storms are comic; they divert the attention away from the absence of characterization. The operas are containers for the full and abundant mental product of Luigi Pirandello, enabling him through opera's unique capacity, to unleash the Sicilian, the sufferer, and *Il trovatore*. But there is no coldness there. And in truth Ersilia *is* the object, after all.

". . . EVERY POSSIBLE CONFLICT . . ."

Luce! Luce! Luce!

—*Luigi Pirandello*

Nota's real interest in her, his passionate cause, is irresistible: it is the fate of Ersilia Drei as an object of artistic production. She has been an enthralling necessity, a ceaselessly changing source of new configurations. Thus it is not her actuality that interests him, only the possibility she carries within herself. And possibility suffers irreversible damage at the hands of actuality. Even if the penitent author of *Clothing the Naked* found it desirable to offer her his bed at the end, a burial under his auspices, Ludovico Nota speaks only once more between the time he makes that offer and Ersilia's death. And a plaintive cry it is: "I'm sure if you would have been able to *think,* Signora! You could have stayed here with *me!*" No intervening stage directions specify what Nota is about while she says her farewells to Grotti and Franco Laspiga, but obviously he is watching—fiercely, casually, drinking it up like milk; and regretting *his* loss in a way that neither of the other men can know. *This* is the way of his passion.

And of Pirandello's. To be absorbed; to have one's feelings rise to

their highest pitch, would require for a sensibility like "the old novelist's" something far beyond the petty story of the governess. Nota's
farewell message reeks with loss. Think of it, he says, you could have
stayed, and I should have had the chance to remake you again and
again and—each time—be engaged with the great multiplicity, with
the multiple tangles of art. To reach out for these, to know the tragic
model of vision required of those who will face the steamy conflicts,
was finally the object of the man through the objects in his art. Having seen the mission, nothing would do but to pursue it. Embracing
conflict, he could embrace a geometry of alternative and choice, of
possibility; he could agree to the task and make the required theatre.
In *Ciascuno,* he was forced to reel through a mountain of irrelevance
to reach his intermissions, the Choral Interludes. And having arrived
—for the sole purpose of bringing together the Actor-Character pair
he had had to split in *Sei personaggi*—he found a moment, the end
of the Second Choral Interlude, just a moment; but the interludes
were not the intermissions he thought he might have had, they were
staged scenes. And so he had another problem, another set of the
possibles with which to make happy contention. He found in *Questa
sera si recita a soggetto* that he could divest the pair of all their differences, if he would invest more heavily in their common opponent,
the manager, Dr. Hinkfuss. Thus the pair are really one in *Questa
sera;* Rico Verri and the Leading Man share precisely in one body
and two identities. Hinkfuss on the other hand has been made into
a fiendishly well-equipped theatrician: the first abstract impressionist of theatre could now gather together real elements (of authentic
impressiveness), such as opera, white uniforms and blue nights, an
old lecher dying and a fat mother alive, and with them work endless
affecting variations. So that the theme one should have thought in-
violate, that you can't play with passion, is actually reversed here in
the pearl of the trilogy: that you *can* play with passion is both its
theme *and* its program. But as Eric Bentley said, there is even more
in him "for younger men to find." Because we are still learning to
become Luigi Pirandello's contemporaries, to understand the voice
that cried out for light.

Chronology of Important Dates

1867   Luigi Pirandello born in Girgenti, Sicily, on June 28. His father, Stefano, was a former soldier under Garibaldi and a rich mining contractor.

1887   Enrolls at Rome University.

1888-95   Studies philology at Bonn University in Germany. Graduates with a doctoral dissertation on the phonetics of his native dialect.

1889   *Mal giocondo (Joyful Pain)*, a collection of poems, published in Palermo.

1891   *Laute und Lautentwickelung der Mundart von Girgenti (Sounds and Phonetic Development of the Dialect of Girgenti)*, Pirandello's dissertation, published in Halle. *Pasqua di Gea (The Easter of Gea Tellus)*, his second collection of verse, published in Milan.

1893   Returning to Rome, Pirandello meets influential writers in the Roman milieu, of whom the novelist Capuana, a fellow Sicilian, will be particularly helpful. Verga also encourages him.

1894   *Amori senza amore (Loves Without Love)*, the first collection of short stories, published in Milan.

1894   Marries Antonietta Portulano, daughter of his father's business partner.

1895   *Elegie Renane (Rhine Elegies)* published in Rome.

1896   *Elegie Romane di W. Goethe* (Goethe's *Rome Elegies* in Pirandello's translation) published in Leghorn.

1901   *L'Esclusa (The Outcast)*, Pirandello's first novel (written in 1893) is serialized by Rome's *La Tribuna;* appears in book form in 1908 in Milan.

1902   *Il turno (The Turn)*, another early novel, published in Catania. More volumes of short stories appear in this and in the following years.

1904   As a consequence of bankruptcy, striking both father and father-in-law, Antonietta Pirandello breaks down mentally. Pirandello obtains a teaching position at the Istituto Femminile di Magistero, a girls' college, in Rome. He will keep it until financial independence comes in the early postwar years from his success as a playwright. *Il fu Mattia Pascal (The Late Mattia Pascal)* is published in Rome and well received at home and abroad.

1908   *L'Umorismo (Humor)*, a literary essay, published in Lanciano.

1911   *Il dovere del medico (The Doctor's Duty)* first performed. *Suo marito* (*Her Husband*), a novel, published in Florence; its main character is based on Pirandello's wife.

1913   *I vecchi e i giovani* (*The Old and The Young*) published in Milan after having been serialized in 1909.

Lumie di Sicilia (*Sicilian Limes*) and *La morsa* (*The Vise*) are performed at the Metastasio Theater in Rome at Nino Martoglio's insistence. The author does not attend.

1915   Italy enters the war against Austria and Germany; Pirandello's two sons are enlisted, Stefano right away, Fausto eventually. Stefano will be gravely ill during captivity.

Angelo Musco, the Sicilian comedian, visits Pirandello to solicit a play.

1916   *Si gira* (*Shoot!*), later renamed *Quaderni di Serafino Gubbio operatore* (*Notebooks of Serafino Gubbio, Cameraman*) is published in Milan after serialization during the previous year. First performance of *Liolà* (originally written in the Girgenti dialect), *Il berretto a sonagli* (*Cap and Bells*), and *Pensaci, Giacomino!* (*Think it Over, Giacomino!*).

1917   *Liolà* published in Rome in its dialect version.

Il piacere dell'onestà (*The Pleasure of Honesty*) and *Così è* (*se vi pare*) (*It Is So, if You Think So*) first performed. *La giara* (*The Jar*) first performed.

1918   First performance of *Il giuoco delle parti* (*Each in his Role*) and *Ma non è una cosa seria* (*It Can't be Serious*). The Treves firm of Milan publishes almost all the extant plays in a four-volume series entitled *Maschere Nude* (*Naked Masks*), and the title will be retained by Pirandello's successive publishers, Bemporad of Florence and Mondadori of Milan.

Antonietta Pirandello is committed to an insane asylum. She will die shortly after.

1919   *Berecche e la guerra* (*Berecche and the War*), short stories, published in Milan. *Il carnevale dei morti* (*The Carnival of the Dead*), short stories, published in Florence. Publication of the play *Ma non è una cosa seria* (*It Can't be Serious*). Publication and performance of *L'innesto* (*The Grafting*). Performance of *L'uomo, la bestia e la virtù* (*Man, Beast and Virtue*) and of *La patente* (*The License*).

1920   Publication of *La patente, Lumie di Sicilia,* and *Il berretto a sonagli*. Performance of *Tutto per bene* (*All for the Best*), *Come prima, meglio di prima* (*As Well as Before, Better than Before*), *La signora Morli, una e due* (*Mrs. Morli, One and Two*).

1921   Publication of *Come prima, meglio di prima* and *Sei personaggi in cerca d'autore* (*Six Characters in Search of an Author*). The performance of *Sei personaggi* in Rome at the

Teatro Valle causes pandemonium, and the author and his daughter Lietta have to be rescued from the crowd. The play is more calmly received in Milan.

1922 Performance of *Six Characters in Search of an Author* in London and in New York. Max Reinhardt acquires the rights for Germany. *Enrico IV (Henry IV)* published and performed. Performance of *L'imbecille (The Imbecile)*.

1923 The company of Georges Pitoëff performs *Six personnages en quête d'auteur* to an enthusiastic Parisian audience. Since December 1922, *Il piacere dell'onestà (The Pleasure of Honesty)* is also performed in Paris. Pirandello comes to Paris to attend the performances and is officially honored by the French Government. Publication of *Vestire gli ignudi (Naked)*. Performance of *L'uomo dal fiore in bocca (The Man with the Flower in His Mouth)*, *La vita che ti diedi (The Life I Gave You)* and *L'altro figlio (The House with the Column)*.

1924 *Ciascuno a suo modo (Each in His Own Way)* published and performed. First American performance of *Henry IV* at the 44th Street Theater of New York. Pirandello visits New York.

1925 *Uno, nessuno e centomila (One, No One and a Hundred Thousand)*, Pirandello's last novel, published in book form after serialization. Performance and publication of *La sagra del Signore della Nave (Our Lord of the Ship)*. Publication of *La Giara (The Jar)*. With the official sponsorship of the Italian Government and the support of a group of friends, Pirandello founds a National Art Theater housed in the Palazzo Odescalchi of Rome. Marta Abba joins the company and soon becomes the mainstay of Pirandello's productions.

With Pirandello as director, the Odescalchi company tours Europe and America. Its leading male actor is Ruggero Ruggeri.

1927 Publication and performance of *Diana e la Tuda (Diana and Tuda)*. First performance of *It Is So, if You Think So* (titled *Right You Are, if You Think You Are* in A. Livingston's translation) at the Guild Theater of New York.

1928 *La nuova colonia (The New Colony)*, a political fable, published and performed.

1929 Pirandello becomes a member of the Accademia d'Italia. Publication and performance of *O di uno o di nessuno (Either of One or of No One)* and *Lazzaro (Lazarus)*.

1930 Publication and performance of *Questa sera si recita a soggetto (Tonight We Improvise)*.

1932 Publication and performance of *Trovarsi (To Find Oneself)*.

1933 Publication and performance of *Quando si è qualcuno (When Someone Is Somebody)*.

1934   Pirandello is awarded the Nobel Prize for literature.
        La favola del figlio cambiato (The Fable of the Changeling) first performed.

1935   Publication and performance of *Non si sa come (One Does Not Know How)*.

1936   Pirandello dies in Rome on December 10.

1937   Publication and performance of *I Giganti della Montagna (The Mountain Giants)*, an anti-totalitarian allegory.

1938   *Novelle per un anno (Stories for a Year)*, the collected short stories (365 in number), published in two volumes by Mondadori of Milan.

1941   *Tutti i romanzi*, the collected novels, published by the same firm.

1948-49 *Maschere Nude (Naked Masks)*, the collected plays, published by the same firm in four volumes.

1939   *Saggi*, the collected essays as edited by Lo Vecchio Musti, published in Milan.

Notes on the Editor and Authors

GLAUCO CAMBON, the editor of this volume, taught in his native Italy before joining the faculty of the University of Michigan (1958) and then of Rutgers University, where he is currently Professor of Romance Languages and Comparative Literature. He is a Fellow of the Indiana School of Letters and has published various translations as well as books and articles on American, Italian, and modern European literature; among these are *La lotta con Proteo* (1963) and *The Inclusive Flame, Studies in American Poetry* (1963). He has written an Introduction to *Eugenio Montale: Selected Poems* (1966).

STARK YOUNG, the native Southerner and adoptive New Yorker who died in 1963 at 82, was one of the liveliest figures in the American cultural scene. After a brief teaching career, he served on the editorial board of *Theatre Arts Monthly* and became drama critic of *The New Republic* from 1921 to 1947, with an interval as drama critic for *The New York Times* during the season 1924-25. Besides five books of studies on the theater, he wrote fiction, verse, and drama, and occasionally directed plays (by Lenormand and O'Neill). He was in touch with many of the prominent dramatists and actors of the age.

ADRIANO TILGHER, an Italian thinker who died in 1941, established himself with *Voci del Tempo* (1921) and *Studi sul teatro contemporaneo* (1923) as a drama critic, pioneering in the field of modern European theater and of Pirandello studies in particular. He wrote extensively on aesthetics and ethics.

FRANCIS FERGUSSON, a graduate of Harvard and Oxford, had further training in the Laboratory Theatre of New York, where he was to be assistant director for two years. He taught at Bennington and directed the Princeton Seminars in Literary Criticism, and has now been for many years on the faculty of Rutgers University as University Professor of Comparative Literature. Besides translations and original poetry, his publications include *The Idea of a Theater, The Human Image in Dramatic Literature,* and two books on Dante, the most recent of which was published by Macmillan in 1966.

THOMAS BISHOP is Professor of Romance Languages at New York University and directs the *Maison Française* in New York. He combines a basic commitment to French literature with an awareness of the wider context of European culture.

WYLIE SYPHER, Head of the English Department at Simmons College, has distinguished himself for his bold attempt to describe the historical variations of Western taste and thought in terms of a unified concept of style which applies to all the arts. This has resulted in books like *Four Stages of*

Renaissance Style, From Rococo to Cubism, and *Loss of the Self in Modern Literature and Art.*

GIOVANNI SINICROPI, a native of Italy, has had both an Italian and a Canadian academic training, earning his Ph.D. at Toronto University. In 1964 he joined the Department of Romance Languages of Rutgers University, where he teaches Italian literature. He has just completed a critical edition of Sercambi's short stories and is at work on an extensive study of Pirandello's style.

ULRICH LEO (1890-1964) was, with Leo Spitzer and Erich Auerbach, one of the foremost German scholars of Romance literature in the *Stilforschung* tradition founded by their teacher Karl Vossler. In the Hitler era he left Germany for Venezuela and eventually Canada, where he taught at Toronto University until his death. Along with many other works on Spanish and Italian literature, he published studies of Fogazzaro's style (1928), of Dante (*Sehen und Wirklichkeit bei Dante,* 1957), of Romulo Gallegos (*Romulo Gallegos, Estudio sobre el arte de novelar,* 1954), of the *Libro de buen Amor* (*Zur dichterischen Originalität des Arciprestre de Hita,* 1958), and a posthumous essay on the problem of stylistic analysis and poetical unity (*Stilforschung und dichterische Einheit,* Munich 1966).

ARCANGELO LEONE DE CASTRIS teaches Italian literature at Bari University, Italy, and has published significant studies of Italo Svevo, Pirandello, and Italian Decadentism. His latest contribution to date is a book on the Romantic novelist, poet, and playwright Alessandro Manzoni.

ROBERT BRUSTEIN, formerly associated with Columbia University, now heads the Drama Department of Yale University, and has made a name as drama critic of *The New Republic* and as author of *The Theatre of Revolt.* His reviews have been published recently in book form under the title *Seasons of Discontent.*

AURÉLIU WEISS (1893-1962) was a French lawyer and jurist of Roumanian extraction, who wrote extensively on Pirandello, Ghelderode, the spirit of tragedy, and the fortune of great drama. Some of his essays have appeared posthumously in such American journals as *Tulane Drama Review* and *Journal of Aesthetics.*

LUIGI SQUARZINA, one of the most active figures to emerge in the Italian theater since World War II, is a well known playwright and director associated with the Teatro Stabile (Municipal Repertory Theater) of Genoa, which, largely owing to his contribution, has risen to national prominence. Among his own plays are such searching pieces as *Tre Quarti di Luna* (*The Three-Quarter Moon*), *La Romagnola* (*The Girl from Romagna*), and *La sua parte di Storia* (*His Share of History*).

GINO RIZZO, the interviewer of Luigi Squarzina in this volume, has now joined the faculty of New York's City College after teaching Italian literature for many years at the University of North Carolina at Chapel Hill, N.C. He has edited and translated a collection of plays by Ugo Betti.

WILLIAM HERMAN is a playwright residing in New York City whose "man OUT LOUD, girl quiet" was recently produced there. He has previously produced "Theatre as Enterprise," also published in the *Tulane Drama Review,* and is currently at work on a book, *Theatre Anthology,* a collection of his plays, film scripts, and criticism, to be published in the Spring by Lancer.

Selective Bibliography

1. Bibliographical Aids and Recent Translations

Lo Vecchio Musti, Manlio, *Bibliografia di Pirandello*. Milan: Arnoldo Mondadori, 1937, 1940, 1952. An up-to-date bibliography is announced by the Pirandello Institute of Rome through its curator, Dr. Alfredo Barbina of Rome University.

Useful bibliographical appendixes are to be found in:

Bàccolo, Luigi, *Pirandello* (see below);
Bentley, Eric, ed., *Naked Masks: Five Plays by Luigi Pirandello*. New York: E. P. Dutton & Co., Inc., 1952;
Bishop, Thomas, *Pirandello and the French Theater* (see above);
Starkie, Walter, *Luigi Pirandello* (see below);
Vittorini, Domenico, *The Drama of Luigi Pirandello* (see below).

In Lo Vecchio Musti's (1940 ed.), Starkie's, and Bentley's books the reader will find listings of available English translations. Several of Pirandello's works remain untranslated to this day. Among the more recent additions, of particular interest is *The Mountain Giants and Other Plays*, translated by Marta Abba (New York: Crown Publishers, Inc.), 1958. Miss Abba, who undertook this work on behalf of the Pirandello Society of New York, has also translated *Diana e La Tuda* for the publisher Samuel French. Other recent additions are:

Keene, Frances, trans., *The Merry-go-round of Love*, and Lily Duplaix, trans., *Selected Stories*. New York: New American Library, Signet T210, 1964;
May, F., ed. and trans., *Short Stories*. New York and London: Oxford University Press, 1965;
Murray, W., trans., *Pirandello's One-Act Plays*. Garden City, N.Y.: Doubleday Anchor, 1964;
Weaver, William, trans., *The Late Mattia Pascal*. Garden City, N.Y.: Doubleday, 1964.

2. Criticism (Complementary to Studies Anthologized)

Bàccolo, Luigi, *Pirandello*. Milan: Bocca, 1938, 1949.
Bentley, Eric, *In Search of Theater*. New York: Knopf, 1953; Vintage Books, 1957.

Borgese, Giuseppe Antonio, "Pirandello," in *Tempo di edificare*. Milan: Treves, 1924.

Chiaromonte, Nicola, "Così è, se vi pare," "Si recita a soggetto," and "Pirandello per tutti" in *La situazione drammatica*. Milan: Bompiani, 1960.

Crémieux, Benjamin, "Pirandello," in *Panorama de la littérature italienne*. Paris: Kra, 1928.

Croce, Benedetto, *La letteratura della nuova Italia*, Vol. III. Bari: Laterza, 1950. This volume contains the articles and reviews Croce published on Pirandello's work in his journal *La Critica*, from the review of *L'umorismo* in the May 20, 1909 issue to the essay in the January 1, 1935 issue.

Di San Secondo, Rosso, "L. Pirandello," *Nuova Antologia*, CLXXXI, 1057 (1916), 390-403.

Gramsci, Antonio, "Il teatro di Pirandello," in *Letteratura e Vita Nazionale*. Turin: Einaudi, 1950.

Janner, Arminio, *Luigi Pirandello*. Florence: La Nuova Italia, 1948, 1960.

MacClintock, Lander, *The Age of Pirandello*. Bloomington: Indiana University Press, 1951.

Mennemeier, Franz Norbert, ed., *Der Dramatiker Pirandello, Zweiundzwanzig Beitraege*. Cologne: Kiepenheuer & Witsch, 1965.

Nardelli, Federico Vittore, *L'uomo segreto, vita e croci di L. P.* Milan: Mondadori, 1932, 1944.

———, *Vita segreta di Pirandello*. Roma: Vito Bianco, 1962.

Puglisi, Filippo, *L'Arte di Luigi Pirandello*. Florence: Casa Editrice G. d'Anna, 1958.

Rauhut, Franz, *Der junge Pirandello, oder das Werden eines existentiellen Geistes*. Munich: Verlag C. H. Beck, 1964.

Salinari, Carlo, *Miti e coscienza del decadentismo italiano*. Milan: Feltrinelli, 1962.

Starkie, Walter, *Luigi Pirandello*. London and Toronto: J. M. Dent & Sons, Ltd., 1926; 3rd ed., Berkeley: University of California Press, 1965.

Vittorini, Domenico, *The Drama of Luigi Pirandello*. Philadelphia: University of Pennsylvania Press, 1935. Now reprinted by Dover Books.